Writing & Speaking FOR BUSINESS

3RD EDITION

WILLIAM H. BAKER

D1601801

BYU ACADEMIC PUBLISHING

BYU ACADEMIC
PUBLISHING

Managing Editor: Kent Minson

Design and Typesetting: Kent Minson

Illustrations: William H. Baker and Jacob Wilson

ISBN: 978-1-61165-005-1
For more information or permission to use material from this text or product contact:
BYU Academic Publishing
3991 WSC
Provo, UT 84602
Tel (801) 422–6231
Fax (801) 422–0070
academicpublishing@byu.edu

To report ideas or text corrections email us at:
textideas@byu.edu

1st Printing

CONTENTS

PREFACE

Before writing this textbook, I taught business communication for over 30 years. During this time, I used several business communication books, but they all seemed inadequate in three important ways: they were too expensive and too long (I wondered why they needed 500 pages to teach how to write concisely), and the content was not presented in a clear, brain-friendly manner. As a result, most of my students sold their books at the end of the semester.

After seeing that no one else was addressing these issues—and with encouragement from colleagues—I decided to tackle the job myself. *Writing & Speaking for Business* is the result. Through three editions I have tried to stick with my original goals—to hold down the cost, restrict the length, and design the content for easy learning, remembering, and applying. The result is that student and faculty comments have been extremely positive, and over 90 percent of students keep the book at the conclusion of each semester.

In one way or another, many wonderful people have assisted with this work. First, I thank my wife, Jeannie, and our family for their patience throughout the long days and nights I have spent on this book. I especially thank Matt and Marianne Baker for their exceptional help with this edition. I also express deep gratitude to the many students and fellow teachers who have given honest and insightful feedback on earlier editions. Further, I appreciate and acknowledge the major contributions of Kent Minson, not only for designing the book, but also for helping to polish the writing and enhance the visuals. He has been a true colleague in every sense of the word. Finally, I appreciate the encouraging and supportive environment of Brigham Young University, which encourages the expansion of both mind and soul in the pursuit of knowledge and wisdom.

My best wishes to all who will take time to learn from these pages.

BILL BAKER

Chapter

1

COMMUNICATING IN BUSINESS

Effective communication skills are critical in business. Across all organizations people exchange millions of texts, emails, telephone calls, letters, proposals, and reports each day. They are involved in countless face-to-face interviews and meetings, hallway conversations, and presentations, and each of these messages is expected to be clear and accurate. People who write and speak well advance more quickly in organizations and, as a result, have higher incomes. People who fail to communicate effectively are usually overlooked for promotion, and often they are terminated or never hired in the first place because of their communication deficiencies.

Because many people have poor communication skills, business and government organizations have to spend millions of dollars each year for communication training. The

Figure 1.1 Effective communication is important at all levels in business organizations.

National Commission on Writing (2004, 18) reports that the annual cost for providing writing training in the private sector could be as high as $3.1 billion. That doesn't include the training provided in the public sector, nor does it include other types of communication training, such as speaking skills. Clearly, these statistics emphasize how important it is for students to develop writing and speaking skills while in school.

This chapter discusses communication at three levels, from the top down. The first is the broad organization level, including management functions and special communication situations. The second level discusses communication in teams and includes tips on collaborative writing and meeting management. The third level is communication at the interpersonal level and covers social skills, trust, networking, and etiquette.

COMMUNICATING IN ORGANIZATIONS

Communication is both a function and a process in organizations. As a function, it exists to move important information upward, downward, and throughout the organization. Like the vascular system that carries oxygen-rich blood throughout the body and returns the blood back to the heart, an effective communication system carries critical messages from management to supervisors and frontline employees and then critical performance reports and feedback to management. The most successful top managers communicate their objectives clearly and get widespread buy-in from employees throughout the organization.

As a process, communication consists of capturing

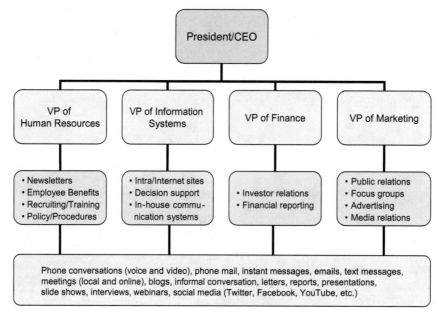

Figure 1.2 Different types of communication are found throughout an organization.

information, composing messages, and sending messages. The receivers of the message repeat the process, sending feedback regarding the original message and giving other appropriate information. The process can involve only one sender and one receiver, such as in an interview or a phone call, or it can involve larger groups of senders and receivers, such as in a meeting.

Figure 1.2 shows a typical organization structure, along with different types of communications utilized by the various parts of the structure.

Management Functions

Managers work to achieve organizational objectives while striving to minimize resource use and maximize results. Minimizing resource use is referred to as being efficient; maximizing results is referred to as being effective. Obviously, achieving effectiveness and efficiency requires delicate balancing and tradeoffs.

Managers are also expected to lead, to inspire people to follow them in accomplishing the organization's goals. Management and leadership are often separated for definition purposes, but the assumption in this book is that managers are also leaders and that leadership is a vital part of management.

Different thinking is required for leadership and management activities. On the one hand, leaders look at the larger picture, interpret current conditions, predict future conditions, and creatively chart a course based on their interpretation. Leaders develop a vision for the organization. They are thinkers and dreamers; they focus on direc-

tion and innovation and develop long-term goals and strategies.

Managers, on the other hand, seek to accomplish the goals of the leaders. Managers focus their thinking on their organizational operations—on processes and sequences, inputs and outputs, feedback reports and system adjustments, predictability and stability, and efficiency. Leading and managing involve extensive communication—reading, writing, interviewing, questioning, holding meetings, explaining, clarifying, delegating, listening, announcing, persuading, and expressing confidence.

The management challenge is to achieve optimum performance and productivity from every resource, especially people. In performing management and leadership functions, managers must find a comfortable balance between tasks (getting the job done) and relationships (maintaining good relationships with people). Managers who are too task oriented have problems with employee morale, while managers who are too relationship oriented fail to get the task accomplished as they should. The most effective managers are those who achieve a good balance between concern for task and concern for people.

Four basic functions of management include planning, organizing, monitoring, and leading. Communication is critical in all of these areas. Suggestions in the following sections will help you effectively carry out these functions.

PLANNING

- Be proactive. Listen and remain aware of what is happening in your organization, in your field, and in society at large, and then take appropriate action to innovate and improve.

- Involve employees appropriately in planning and decision making, particularly when the decision affects them, when buy-in is important, when they have useful knowledge to contribute, or when the experience would be useful for their development.

ORGANIZING

- Identify roles and responsibilities for each position, and make sure they are clearly communicated. Delegate effectively. Explain in detail who will do what, at what performance standard, and by when. Explain also how and when to report back. Then give as much latitude as appropriate while employees work to accomplish the task. Show trust in employees by avoiding the temptation to watch and critique their every move—don't micromanage.

- Provide regular training and development. Foster continuous improvement. Provide ongoing education and training. Encourage and provide for knowledge sharing.

MONITORING

- Identify and communicate all evaluation factors and measurements.

- Regularly document, review, and monitor performance. Remain aware. Show interest in your subordinates' work context. Drop by and visit occasionally at their work sites. Listen to their concerns. Hold regular performance interviews. Discuss their responsibilities, agree on objectives, receive their stewardship reports, and highlight their achievements. Be clear and honest in your feedback. Expect and foster excellence.

- Resolve all performance violations in a timely manner. Strive to solve problems without hurting human relationships or morale.

Figure 1.3 Effective managers involve their subordinates in planning and decision making.

LEADING

- Clarify an organizational mission and vision, and work to achieve employee buy-in. Communicate regularly and often to let employees know what is going on at the management level. Listen to your subordinates to remain aware of what's going on within their groups and throughout the organization. Be honest. Build relationships of trust.

- Provide a supportive environment that fosters growth, productivity, and encouragement. Empower employees to take needed actions within appropriate guidelines. Standardize policies and procedures adequately, without stifling creativity. Socialize adequately, but avoid becoming too informal or casual. Give frequent recognition and positive reinforcement. Praise and celebrate the accomplishments of both individuals and larger groups.

In addition to communicating with people under your direction, you must also communicate effectively with managers who oversee your work. First, clarify your manager's expectations of you. Then deliver results! Second, keep your manager informed about what you are doing. Third, don't talk negatively about your manager. Negative comments might spread through the grapevine and eventually get back to your manager. Fourth, be honest. Give truthful opinions but always be tactful. What you say and how you say it are both important. Fifth, be sensitive to your manager's busy schedule. Be efficient with your communications so the time your manager spends reading your emails, reviewing your work, and answering your questions is minimized. Sixth, give appropriate compliments and expressions of appreciation. Help make your manager look good in public.

Special Communication Situations

As a manager, be prepared to adjust your communications according to the diversity of your employees, including disability challenges and cultural variances.

DISABILITY CHALLENGES

Be sensitive to those who have special communication challenges, such as visual or hearing impairments. The Americans with Disabilities Act (ADA) of 1990 provides legislation to help anyone who has "a physical or mental impairment that substantially limits one or more major life activities" (Department of Justice 2003). The following quotations highlight the critical elements of this legislation regarding communication-related aspects of work.

Title I of the ADA requires employers with 15 or more employees to provide qualified individuals with disabilities an equal opportunity to benefit from the full range of employment-related opportunities available to others. For example, it prohibits discrimination in recruitment, hiring, promotions, training, pay, social activities, and other privileges of employment. It restricts questions that can be asked about an applicant's disability before a job offer is made. . . .

Section 255 and Section 251(a)(2) of the Communications Act of 1934, as amended by the Telecommunications Act of 1996, require manufacturers of telecommunications equipment and providers of telecommunications services to ensure that such equipment and services are accessible to and usable by persons with disabilities, if readily achievable. These amendments ensure that people with disabilities will have access to a broad range of products and services such as telephones, cell phones, pagers, call-waiting, and operator services, that were often inaccessible to many users with disabilities. (Department of Justice 2003)

As you work with individuals qualifying under the ADA, some may need special accommodations in the communication domain. With visually impaired workers, for instance, you may have to use braille. With hearing-impaired workers, you may have to arrange for a "signing" interpreter. Whenever a new person with disabilities is hired, ask about special accommodations that will be needed.

PEOPLE FROM DIFFERENT CULTURES AND LANGUAGES

Doing business with people around the world introduces several differences that influence communication. Important on this list are cultural differences, nonverbal communication differences, and language differences.

Cultural Differences

Cultural variations can be observed in different nationalities, ethnic groups, and geographic regions. When working with an international organization or with people from other countries, consult various resources available on the internet to learn about information such as the following:

Background—land, climate, and history

People—population, language, religion, general attitudes, and dress

Customs and Courtesies—greetings, gestures, visiting, and eating

Lifestyle—family, dating and marriage, diet, recreation, holidays, and commerce

Society—government, economy, transportation, communication, education, and health

Figure 1.4 Communication varies among people from different cultures.

By becoming more culturally aware, you can overcome ethnocentrism and learn to appreciate why people from different cultures behave the way they do. For example, Asians prefer to first establish relationships and then move on to the task. Americans and Europeans move more directly to the task. People from northern and eastern Europe and Asia are more formal in their communication; Americans and southern Europeans are less so. Also, Asians, compared with Americans, are more concerned about their organizational and social rank.

Nonverbal Communication Differences

Nonverbal communication varies significantly from culture to culture. For example, many forms of gesture, posture, and eye contact mean one thing in one culture but something very different in another. For example, children from many Latin American and Asian cultures show respect by avoiding eye contact with an authority figure. In the U.S., this behavior might be interpreted as a sign of disrespect. Further, in areas of the Middle East and South America, people stand very close to each other when talking. Americans like to have more distance between them when they interact.

Many hand and finger gestures used in a U.S. culture are obscene and taboo in other cultures. For instance, giving a "thumbs up" to a person in the U.S. sends a good-luck message. In the Middle East, it's the U.S. equivalent of holding up the middle finger. In the U.S., you can indicate the number two by holding up the first and second fingers, with the knuckles toward the audience. But if you do the same in England, you've just committed a social blunder. Further, making the American OK sign by forming a circle between the index finger and the thumb is taboo in other cultures. Thus, be careful with anything to do with finger gestures. The open palm is internationally safe, however, and should be the preferred form of hand gesture in intercultural settings.

Language Differences

Because of the frequency of international business communications, business professionals need to show greater sensitivity in creating messages that cross national borders and that are read by speakers of English as a second language (ESL). Certain industries have developed specific rules, grammar, and word choice for international communication. The intent of this controlled English is to eliminate ambiguity and confusion caused by words that won't be understood by international audiences. Remember the following guidelines when writing for international audiences.

Words:

- Use simple, concrete words; avoid abstract words and lengthy, compound words.
- Use the active voice, with strong, clear verbs and simple verb tenses.
- Use words consistently (avoid potentially troublesome synonyms).
- Avoid slang, puns, abbreviations, and culturally symbolic language. For instance, a worker from the United States likely will understand what a "wild-goose chase" is, but a person from Brazil will not.

Sentences and Paragraphs:

- Use simple sentence construction.
- Be careful with question marks and ampersands that are used differently in different languages.
- Keep paragraphs short.

Visuals:

- Use international icons, such as those in Figure 1.5, and avoid any symbolisms that mean one thing in one culture and another in another (e.g., the owl represents wisdom in the U.S., but people from China consider it to be a stupid bird).

Figure 1.5 Standardized symbols are useful in communicating with international audiences.

To ensure that people from the culture, language, or country you are writing for can understand your writing, pilot test your work with a person who is representative of that audience. The extra time and expense will help prevent many embarrassing problems.

COMMUNICATING IN TEAMS

In today's organizations, you often work as a member of a work group or team, and effective communication is critical in achieving team success. The following two paragraphs highlight some of the communication differences between effective and ineffective teams.

Communication in Effective Teams. All members participate, not just the vocal minority. Opposing ideas are encouraged and welcomed. Participants show respect by listening carefully to each other. As a result, people are open, honest, and trustful. People avoid gossiping about others. Decisions are finalized when everyone buys in to the solution or at least understands the reasoning and can support the outcome.

Communication in Ineffective Teams. The most assertive, fastest thinking, and loudest members get all the speaking time. Opposing ideas are seen as unwanted conflict. People are disrespectful and interrupt each other. As a result, people are closed, guarded, and distrustful. They also talk secretly about each other. Decisions are finalized by a vocal few or a simple majority vote.

Teams go through various stages in their movement toward team maturity. One of the most well-known theories of team progress includes the stages of forming, storming, norming, and performing (Tuckman 1965). The forming stage occurs when the group is created. The team members are generally polite as they first meet and learn about each other. When they start to move into their work roles, differences in personalities, procedures, and preferences can spawn the storming stage and can generate interpersonal conflict. Teams usually work through this stage to the norming stage by establishing appropriate roles, responsibilities, and procedures to enable effective and efficient team performance. Finally, the fourth stage, performing, is characterized by smooth working processes and the achievement of desired goals.

Two common communication activities of teams are collaborative writing and meetings. The following sections discuss these activities.

Collaborative Writing

One of the great communication challenges for teams arises when collaborative writing is required. Problems can arise involving communication breakdowns, unequal work distribution, missed deadlines, personality conflicts, and formatting confusion. With collaboration, pay attention to the writing process as well as the product you are trying to prepare. The following six guidelines can help improve collaborative-writing projects.

1. *Understand the writing task.* Agree on the goals, con-

straints, deadlines, primary and secondary audiences, expectations, and all relevant aspects of the context.

2. ***Select an effective writing team.*** Make sure each person on the writing team has the needed skills, knowledge, interest, experience, and time necessary to make a worthwhile contribution.

3. ***Create a detailed sketch or outline.*** Be sure all group members contribute to and agree on the final outline. Use the outline-checking procedure from Chapter 2 to test the structural soundness of the outline.

4. ***Develop a style guide*** that addresses the following writing issues.

   - Writing style (e.g., first, second, or third person; imperative or indicative mood)
   - Heading hierarchy (e.g., first-, second-, and third-level headings formats and fonts)
   - Art (e.g., type of bullets for emphasis lists, guidelines for photos, business graphics, and tables)
   - Typography (e.g., Times New Roman, 11 point, normal for the body text, two columns)
   - Spacing (e.g., margins, line spacing)

5. ***Assign tasks skillfully.*** Members of the group can perform one or more of the following important tasks.

   - Writing—requires good composition skills and a good understanding of the content and context of the writing situation.
   - Editing—requires good writing skills and a good understanding of the content and context of the writing situation.
   - Production and design—requires good keyboarding skills and the ability to enhance the visual aspect of messages.

Figure 1.6 Collaborative writing is frequently required in business organizations.

Three obvious options are available for collaborative writing. First, the entire group can sit around a computer and compose the text; however, this approach usually is slow and sometimes frustrating. Second, one person can do all the writing, after which everyone critiques. This approach ensures that a consistent style is applied, but the unequal workload sometimes causes the writer to feel animosity toward the other group members whose workload is much lighter. A third approach is to assign different parts of the document to different group members, according to their interest, knowledge, ability, and time availability.

When members send electronic copies of a document back and forth in a collaborative writing situation, they can insert comments in Microsoft Word with the "track changes" feature, which keeps track of changes that are made by any team member. The main author can then accept or reject those changes in the final version of the paper.

6. ***Establish deadlines and monitor progress.*** Once the project has been launched, you must evaluate progress carefully to ensure that completion dates are met. Project tracking can include both oral and written reports and both informal and formal communications. Informal communication is handled on an as-needed basis usually by email, phone, text messages, or informal meetings. But formal communication must also be built into the process. Periodic meetings, interviews, and written reports work very well. Because some people procrastinate and then work extra hard just before deadlines, establish frequent reporting times. If you have weekly progress meetings each Friday, for example, your team likely will work extra hard on Thursday so they will have good progress to report in Friday's meeting.

Maintain a positive, although realistic, outlook on the project and the team members. Give positive reinforcement and express confidence in each person. Let all team members know you believe in them. As you give positive reinforcement, make sure it is sincere and specific, rather than manipulative and general. People can recognize compliments that aren't really genuine.

To keep track of how all aspects of the project are progressing, consider using project-management tools, such as Gantt charts, PERT charts, or basic project-tracking forms.

A Gantt chart (see Figure 1.7) is a horizontal bar chart that shows (a) projected completion times and (b) actual completion times. Developed in 1917 by Henry L. Gantt, the Gantt chart has been used for decades. Its simplicity and flexibility allow it to be used

Systems Analysis and Design												
Project Phases	Report Date	x	x	x	x	x						
	Weeks	1/01 to 1/07	1/08 to 1/14	1/15 to 1/21	1/22 to 1/28	1/29 to 2/04	2/05 to 2/11	2/12 to 2/18	2/19 to 2/25	2/26 to 3/3	3/4 to 3/10	3/11 to 3/17
Requirements Analysis	Projected	■										
	Actual	▒	▒									
Design	Projected			■	■							
	Actual			▒	▒	▒	80% done					
Coding	Projected					■	■	■				
	Actual											
Testing	Projected							■	■			
	Actual											
Documentation	Projected							■	■	■		
	Actual											
Implementation	Projected									■	■	■
	Actual											

Figure 1.7 Gantt charts are useful for showing project phases and time segments.

with all types of audiences, regardless of their level of sophistication. As Figure 1.7 shows, the various project phases are written as a vertical list down the left side of the chart. Projected completion times and actual completion times are then charted as horizontal bars according to the time elements listed along the top of the chart.

PERT charts are process diagrams and are sometimes preferred over Gantt charts for complex projects because they better reveal project sequences, interrelationships, and critical paths. Like Gantt charts, PERT charts break down projects into small phases, actions, or events. However, PERT charts can show much more information. For each step, the PERT chart can show projected start times; pessimistic, realistic, and optimistic completion durations; sequen-

tially dependent relationships; and critical paths (activity sequences in which there can be no idle, or waiting, time). Figure 1.8 shows a basic PERT chart.

Both Gantt chart and PERT chart software are available for computer applications. The internet can provide additional information about these and other project-control procedures and software systems.

As problems are identified during the evaluation phase of projects, new procedures must be implemented. Various options, such as the following, can help get projects back on track.

- *Modify the goals and objectives.* This action is appropriate when circumstances change or when earlier thinking proves to be faulty. No one can predict the future clearly, and managers must make adjustments when circumstances require it.

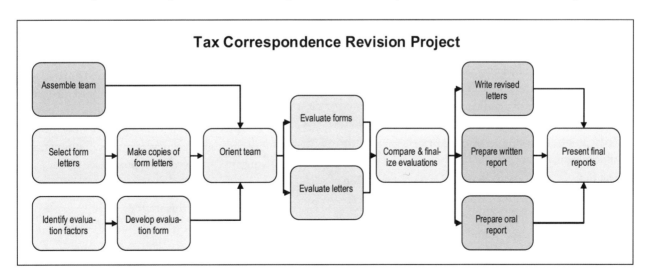

Figure 1.8 PERT charts show the sequence of steps in projects.

- *Change the procedures or methodologies.* Sometimes a method being followed proves to be less effective or efficient than is desired. Thus, a change to a better methodology becomes appropriate.
- *Change work assignments.* Occasionally managers will find it necessary to change work assignments for team members. If one person is struggling to meet deadlines, another person may have to be reassigned to help.
- *Increase resources.* Sometimes managers have to secure more resources, such as more funding or additional members of the team.

Meetings

Meetings are another important part of team communication, but many meetings are ineffective and can be major time wasters. Meetings can fail for many reasons, including the following:

Poor planning before the meeting: Bad meeting time or place, wrong people invited, or unclear purpose or agenda

Poor meeting management: Too much group input, too little group input, or agenda not followed

Poor follow-up after the meeting: Minutes not sent out, assignments not carried out

To have effective meetings, pay attention to details in planning, conducting, and following up after the meeting.

PLAN THE MEETING

The cause of many meeting failures is in the pre-meeting phase. Too many managers go into their meetings unprepared. Here are some guidelines to consider.

1. *Prepare an effective agenda.* Decide specifically what you want the participants to know and do as a result of the meeting. Then prepare a good agenda that accomplishes the objectives. As appropriate, give meeting participants the opportunity to suggest additional items for the agenda, perhaps with an online shared document. Arrange agenda items in an appropriate order. For time-management purposes, you can put the time allotment for each item.

2. *Arrange an appropriate time and place to meet.* Consider people's schedules, energy levels (higher in the morning, lower in mid-afternoon after lunch), and work demands. Also, choose a room that is appropriate for the size of your group and that has appropriate media support. If people are not located in the same office building, consider holding an online meeting, using remote-meeting software such as that from www.gotomeeting.com.

3. *Notify participants.* Announce the meeting as far in advance as appropriate and give all relevant information so attendees will be properly prepared when they arrive. Consider sending an agenda to each participant, and appoint a person to take minutes. If you are holding an online meeting, notify all participants of the exact time, the phone numbers to call, and the online-meeting web address to access.

4. *Prepare appropriate materials and finalize other details.* Pay attention to details. Assemble all essential information, materials, equipment, and food. Managers can often benefit from having printed materials to distribute. In group decision making, for instance, some managers may orally explain the group's task and then allow an unfocused and meandering decision-making process. Instead, they could develop a handout or slide presentation that efficiently explains the material, thus sharpening the manager's own thinking and presenting clearer information for the participants.

CONDUCT THE MEETING

When you conduct a meeting, you must move methodically through the agenda, paying attention to three parallel tracks of activity: task, procedure, and relationship.

The task track focuses on the "what" and "why" aspects of the meeting—the main purpose of the meeting. The following comments are typical of the task track:

- We've seen a 15 percent increase in rejects in this part of the plant.
- What if we merge these two units and have Rob manage them both?
- Our quality-improvement effort seems to be stalling.

The procedure track focuses on the "how." This is where sequence, voting procedures, time management, turn-taking, and other related issues are addressed. Procedural factors may be openly addressed at any point in the meeting, whenever it seems appropriate to talk about how the group should work through a particular matter. Comments like the following are common in the procedure track:

- Let's go around the room and have everyone state their key concerns about this strategy.
- Let's not vote on this today. I think we need some time to think about it.
- Let's first make sure we understand the problem and then get into brainstorming.

The relationship track focuses on the "who" aspects of the meeting. It is where people's feelings are addressed, making sure people are psychologically all right. Conflict is important in the task track, but not in the relationship track. To achieve highest performance, members of the group must interact in a non-abrasive manner. If things go wrong in this track, people get their feelings hurt, get offended, refuse to go along with an idea, or sometimes even actively work against the rest of the group. Typical relationship comments sound like the following:

- Samantha, you have a lot of experience in this area. Could you share your thoughts with us?

- Ben, how are you feeling about the direction we're going?

- Thanks, Terry. That's an insightful comment.

Some remarks might cross two or more tracks, such as, "Ryan, you're always well organized; could you be our time-keeper today?" This comment compliments Rich (relationship track) and implements a time-management element (procedure track) at the same time. Figure 1.10 illustrates these tracks and lists different types of actions that are typical of each track.

Some managers follow a discuss, decide, and delegate format for many agenda items.

a. *Discuss the items.* Establish a climate of openness where everyone feels free to make comments or suggest ideas, even imperfect ideas. Eliminate overly judgmental responses that create defensiveness or insecurity.

b. *Decide.* After the discussion, make a clear and distinct decision. Examples might be to implement a new policy, modify a procedure, or organize a training session.

c. *Delegate appropriately,* such as (a) *who* (b) will do *what* (c) by *when.* Give the assignment clearly, specify who is to work on the task, and explain when they are to

Figure 1.9 Meetings are an important part of team communication.

report back. Record all such assignments in the minutes to ensure appropriate follow-up and reporting.

Do your best to stick with the schedule and stay on time—although don't be so rigid that you damage the quality of the meeting by doing so. When the agenda is completed or time runs out, close the meeting. As you conclude, summarize the results of the meeting, restate assignments given, and thank the attendees for their participation.

FOLLOW UP AFTER THE MEETING

As soon as possible after the meeting, distribute meeting minutes with action items highlighted (e.g., highlight individual members' assignments with a yellow marker). Then follow up on assignments to make sure they are completed.

COMMUNICATING INTERPERSONALLY

Interpersonal communication is the most frequent type of communication activity for most of today's managers and professionals. The ability to interact well is highly correlated to a person's professional success.

THREE MEETING TRACKS		
Task	Define problem Develop implementation strategy Evaluate options Brainstorm Decide
Procedure	Agree on voting procedure State agenda Resequence agenda items Assign speaking sequence Determine closing time
Relationship	Validate a comment Draw out a quiet person Paraphrase a comment Check on a person's feelings

Figure 1.10 Managers must be aware of three parallel meeting tracks.

1. *Interpersonal interaction* (face-to-face), telephone calls, conversations, and meetings constitute the majority of communications. These interactions involve exchanging routine information, solving problems, planning and coordinating, socializing, and monitoring performance.

   Daniel Goleman contrasts the difference between academic intelligence and emotional intelligence. Academic intelligence is important in the college classroom, but even the most academically qualified individuals will have problems on the job without emotional intelligence—the ability to control one's own emotions, to sense the emotions and feelings of others, and to interact effectively with others (1995, 317).

2. *Written communication* is also vitally important. Almost all important matters end up in an email, memo, or report, and all professionals are expected to be able to write well. Errors made in writing damage the writer's credibility and may close the door to future opportunities.

3. *Oral presentations* are given in meetings, in training sessions, and in conferences of societies and associations. Professionals must be able to prepare well-organized presentations and to present their messages in a clear and convincing manner. Visuals are often a part of these presentations, so the ability to create handouts and slide shows is important.

Written communication and oral presentations will be discussed in later chapters. The following sections address several basic interpersonal topics of which you should be aware.

Listening

The goal of conversation is to achieve understanding, not just to talk. But we humans can think much faster than we can talk, so we think of other things while listening—and that distracts from our listening. We're also often more interested in what we want to communicate than what the other person is saying, so we think about what we're going to say next; that also distracts from our listening. Thus, good listening requires discipline and self-restraint.

Three aspects of interaction are important when listening. First, be responsive when you are listening (Figure 1.11). People will speak longer and more completely if the listener demonstrates nonverbal and verbal responsiveness.

- Nonverbal: Orient your body toward the speaker, lean forward to show attentiveness, maintain eye contact with the speaker, take notes, or nod your head to indicate that you understand.

- Verbal: Make comments like "I see," "I understand," "That's a good point," "I see how you feel," "Tell me more," "That is interesting," or "Mmm-hmm."

Second, don't interrupt people before they have finished their message. Doing so is rude and it prevents speakers from giving their complete message. Our natural human tendency is to listen to enough facts to draw a conclusion, and then to focus on our next response. Instead, listen completely and be patient until the person has finished talking.

Third, use a technique called reflective listening (often called *active listening*). After the speaker makes a substantive comment, you paraphrase what you think the speaker is trying to say to you. The reflective paraphrase can address both content (facts and opinions) and feelings (emotions). Examples follow:

> "So you're saying Pat wasn't very receptive to your ideas?" [Response to content.]

> "Let me see if I understand you. You have doubts about whether Brian's plan will actually work unless it addresses Andrea's concerns?" [Response to content.]

> "In other words, you're feeling much more optimistic about the sales projections this month than last month?" [Response to feelings.]

To complete the communication loop, the speaker either affirms that your understanding is correct or gives appropriate clarification. If understanding has been achieved, the communication has succeeded. If not, the speaker can correct the misunderstanding in any of the following ways:

- Restate the information in a different way
- Give an example
- Tell a story or personal experience
- Use a metaphor

Figure 1.11 Good communicators are responsive when they interact with others.

After receiving the new information from the speaker, you can reflect again with something like, "Oh, so you're saying that . . ." When the speaker can say, "Yes, that is what I am saying," you have achieved understanding.

Socialization

Socialization is the process of learning and adopting the behavior of the community in which a person lives. Children usually learn socialization skills at an early age, and throughout life we all have to make minor adjustments in our social skills according to the different contexts and cultures in which we live and work. The unique social behavior of each group in a society determines the culture of that group.

Some people, for unknown reasons, suffer from dissemia, an inability to correctly read and interpret the social messages around them. As a result, they struggle with knowing what is socially appropriate and are often avoided or rejected in society. Your ability to socialize with others is important.

The Personal Attributes Chart in Table 1.1 highlights ten personal attributes that are valued in most organizations. You might wish to score yourself on each to identify where you need some work. Higher ratings (4–6) indicate agreement with a statement; lower ratings (0–2) indicate disagreement with a statement. A neutral rating is 3.

Ratings in the 4–6 range suggest that a person is more emotionally well adjusted. Ratings below 4 suggest a need for improvement. To improve, set long-term goals and establish specific plans for improvement. Check yourself often to ensure that progress is being made. Remember that the most important element in improvement is your own desire to improve.

Trust

Everything that happens within and between organizations is based on some type of relationship, and the more the participants can be trusted, the better the relationship will be. Without trust, organizations would cease to exist. The following descriptions apply to those who merit the highest levels of trust.

1. They are honest and ethical; they always tell the truth, even when the truth is unpopular.
2. They can always be counted on to fulfill their responsibilities and to complete what they say they will do.
3. They do good-quality work.
4. They work for the good of the team or organization, not for their own selfish interests. They are others-oriented, rather than self-oriented.
5. They make sound decisions based on careful thinking.
6. They act appropriately, regardless of the setting. They are guided by principle rather than just by situational factors.
7. They keep their emotions under control. They are mature, rather than immature.
8. They are sensitive to the feelings of others.

People who are trusted, who score high on these eight factors, are chosen to work on important projects, chosen to work on teams, and chosen for promotions. Throughout your career and your life, strive to live so you earn and keep the trust of others. It will give you many opportunities to be a powerful influence for good in your profession, in your community, and in your home.

Table 1.1 Personal Attributes Chart

Agree			Neutral		Disagree		Ten Attributes
6	5	4	3	2	1	0	1. Thoughtful and careful rather than impulsive and impetuous
6	5	4	3	2	1	0	2. Sympathetic and caring rather than calloused and unsympathetic
6	5	4	3	2	1	0	3. Calm and composed rather than anxious and nervous
6	5	4	3	2	1	0	4. Optimistic rather than pessimistic
6	5	4	3	2	1	0	5. Respectful rather than disrespectful
6	5	4	3	2	1	0	6. Open and flexible rather than defensive and closed
6	5	4	3	2	1	0	7. Patient rather than impatient
6	5	4	3	2	1	0	8. Teachable rather than proud and arrogant
6	5	4	3	2	1	0	9. Self-confident and secure rather than insecure and apprehensive
6	5	4	3	2	1	0	10. Honest and forthright rather than devious and hidden

Networking

Networking, or building relationships with other people, is important to your career. A network consists of two elements: people and relationships. People in your network can be within your organization or in different organizations, and your relationships can be based on personal, professional, cultural, religious, political, or other connections.

The value of networks is that they can be called on for information, for influence, or for help, such as requesting assistance in finding new employment. For example, if you have 150 people in your network, you have a rich resource to draw on for assistance, because each of the 150 people in your network probably has an additional 150 people who can be called on to help (see Figure 1.12). However, networks are not just to help you. You are also expected to help others. Thus, approach networking from the standpoint of what you can give, as well as what you can get.

How do you establish a good network? First, consider all events or gatherings as an opportunity to network, whether they be workshops, conferences, community events, church events, or social gatherings. Establish new acquaintances at every event you attend. Don't associate just with people you already know; instead, take advantage of opportunities to meet people you don't know.

Second, work on your conversation skills. Make sure to keep current on local, regional, national, and international issues and events; movies and entertainment; industry issues; and sports so you can engage in the typical kinds of information exchange that are common in social gatherings. Read newspapers or news websites to keep up with current news.

Third, don't be bashful—greet people and then introduce yourself. Tell a bit of information about yourself, such as where you work, what type of work you do, and so forth. Then learn as much as you can about the other person. To get people talking, ask open questions that can't be answered with a simple "yes" or "no." For instance, ask about

where they work, what type of work they do, where they fit in their organization, what their current projects entail, and so forth. Engage in *turn-taking* so you and the other person have a relatively equal amount of time to talk. Learn what you could possibly do for the other person at some time in the future and what the other person could do for you.

Fourth, exchange business cards with others so you will have appropriate contact information. Have a supply handy, located where you can retrieve them easily and quickly. Make sure your cards are complete and accurate, including your name, company, position, phone number, and email. Present your card face up and oriented so the other person can read it. As you take the other person's card, take time to look at it and read it, pronounce the person's name, if unsure, and comment on some positive aspect of their organization. Perhaps write a memory-jogging note on the business card, such as where and when you met the person and any other information you want to remember.

Fifth, when socializing in large groups, don't stay with one person or group too long. At an appropriate time, excuse yourself with a comment like, "Well, it was nice meeting you," and then go visit with another person or group. Look for individuals standing alone or for people in small groups. As you enter a group, just listen for a few minutes to capture the essence of what they're talking about and then join in.

Finally, using appropriate online social media (e.g., Facebook, LinkedIn, MySpace, or Google Plus+), establish a network with business contacts. Enter your own information, including your name, business, position, and other relevant information. Then link with others you know so you can maintain contact and communicate with them from time to time. Use your network for announcing job openings, finding employment, sending updates about your own employment situation, and keeping track of the business activities of others.

Etiquette

Because different cultures have established ways of behaving in social situations, they establish rules of etiquette. Here are a few rules that are appropriate for social behavior in the U.S. culture.

GENERAL

1. Be on time for social gatherings.
2. Be courteous; put the needs of others before your own. Open doors for others. Be respectful to everyone. People like to associate with "nice" people. Kindness produces kindness.

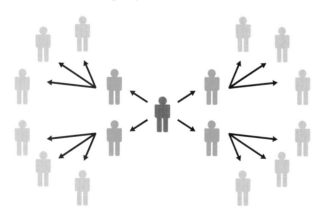

Figure 1.12 The number of people in a social network increases exponentially with each level of contacts.

3. Thank others whenever they do something for you. Write thank-you notes when others have helped you.

4. Avoid phone interruptions in meetings and other social gatherings. Turn off or silence your electronic devices. If you must answer a call, leave the room so others cannot hear your conversation.

5. Avoid using computers and other electronic devices when they will have a negative effect on others (e.g., in a meeting, the image on your computer screen might distract others who can see your screen).

MEETING PEOPLE

1. When you first meet people, listen carefully to their name and then think of a way to remember their name.

2. Shake their hand with appropriate firmness (not too much and not too little).

DRESS AND GROOMING

1. Dress appropriately, never less formally than others. Look sharp, even when the dress is "business casual." Buy mix-and-match clothing for greatest versatility.

2. Avoid excessive jewelry or faddish hair and dress styles that detract from your appearance.

TABLE MANNERS

1. Closely observe what others are doing. Take cues from the leader or host. Wait until your host is seated (or invites you to be seated) before you sit down. A male should help seat his female partner.

2. When you sit down, notice the table setting (see example in Figure 1.13). Use the utensils properly. For multiple utensils, generally use those farthest from the plate and then work inward toward the plate as the meal pro-

gresses. After using a utensil, do not put it back on the table. When cutting meat, hold your utensils correctly, depending on American or Continental style. Place your fork and knife in the five o'clock position on your plate to signal to the waiter that you are finished.

3. If you must leave the table during the meal, place the napkin on the seat of your chair. After the meal, leave the napkin on the table (you don't need to refold the napkin).

4. The server will serve you from your left and remove used plates from your right. In tight quarters, you might be asked to help pass an item to someone sitting at the back of the table. Make sure everyone at your table is taken care of—pass the water pitcher, salt and pepper, dressing, rolls, and other items as needed.

5. In self-serve "buffet" settings, take smaller portions initially. Make sure there is enough food for everyone.

6. Before you eat, wait for the host or guest of honor to begin. In a no-host situation, wait until everyone has been served before you begin. Don't be a fussy eater or complain about the food.

7. Chew with your mouth closed, and don't talk with your mouth full. If you encounter food you cannot swallow, inconspicuously remove it from your mouth the same way it went to your mouth (with a fork or spoon) and place it at the edge of your plate. If others have a problem with food, pretend not to notice.

8. Keep your elbows off the table. Hands or wrists, however, may rest on the edge of the table.

9. In restaurants, remember to leave a tip (the rate varies in different countries). In addition to tipping, always express thanks to the servers.

10. When you leave, push your chair back to the table. A male should pull his female companion's chair from the table so she can stand, and then he should push her chair back to the table as she leaves.

CONVERSATION

1. Remember appropriate turn-taking in conversation. If you see that some people are being overlooked, ask them a question to draw them in.

2. Help keep the conversation going with "5W2H questions" (who, what, where, when, why, how, and how much). At a business dinner, you might ask, "What is your position in your organization?" "How long have you worked there?" "What are your major products?" "Who are your main clients?"

3. Show interest in the comments of others. Eye contact,

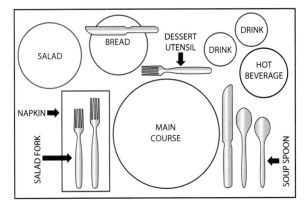

Figure 1.13 Professionals must understand the rules of etiquette related to a formal table setting.

nonverbal acknowledgment, and paraphrasing are all good ways to show you care about what others say and how they feel.

4. Be optimistic and happy. Smile. Avoid negative comments about others. Use humor carefully—avoid comments or jokes that are in poor taste.

CHAPTER SUMMARY

Communication is both a function and a process in organizations. As a function, it exists to move important information upward, downward, and throughout the organization. As a process, communication consists of capturing information, composing messages, and sending messages. Organizations come in various types and sizes, and the communication that occurs in each type can be heavily influenced by the nature of the organization.

As a manager, you employ resources to achieve organizational objectives, minimizing your resource use and maximizing your results. Minimizing resource use is referred to as being efficient; maximizing results is referred to as being effective. You are also expected to lead, to inspire people to follow you in accomplishing your organization's goals. Four basic functions of management include planning, organizing, monitoring, and leading. Communication is critical in all of these areas. In addition to communicating with people under your direction, you must also communicate effectively with managers who oversee your work.

As a manager, be prepared to adjust your communications according to the diversity of your employees, including disability challenges and cultural variances. By becoming more culturally aware, you can overcome ethnocentrism and learn to appreciate why people from different cultures act the way they do.

In today's organizations, you work often as a member of a work group or team. Effective communication is repeatedly cited as a critical element in successful teams. To manage a team, you need good meeting-management and project-management skills. You must also be able to speak well, to listen well, and to participate effectively when collaborative writing is required. Finally, you must be aware of proper etiquette when participating in social settings.

WORKS CITED

Department of Justice. Americans with Disabilities Act, 2003.

Goleman, Daniel. *Emotional Intelligence*. New York. Bantam Books, 1995.

National Commission on Writing for America's Families, Schools, and Colleges. *Writing: A Ticket to Work . . . Or a Ticket Out*. College Entrance Examination Board, September 2004. (Full report is available at http://www.writingcommission.org/prod_downloads/writingcom/writing-ticket-to-work.pdf.)

Tuckman, Bruce W. "Developmental Sequence in Small Groups." *Psychological Bulletin* 63, no. 6 (1965): 384–399.

CHAPTER QUESTIONS

1. List and describe the four basic management functions.
2. Describe the American with Disabilities Act.
3. Why must you be careful when using hand gestures in different cultures?
4. List three guidelines for writing to people for whom English is a second language.
5. Explain three differences between successful and unsuccessful teams.
6. What are the three main ways to write collaboratively?
7. What is a Gantt chart and how is it used?
8. How is a PERT chart different from a Gantt chart?
9. What are the major reasons for meeting failure?
10. What are the three major tracks of activity that occur during meetings?
11. What are the three main elements of delegation during a meeting?
12. What is reflective listening and why is it important?
13. Why is trust so important in organizations?
14. What is networking and why is it important?
15. List what you consider to be important rules of etiquette for cell-phone usage.
16. What is turn-taking and why is it important in conversation?
17. What is the basic usage rule to follow when you have multiple forks or spoons at your place setting?
18. List the four major stages through which teams progress as they move toward team maturity.

CHAPTER ACTIVITIES

1. Write a paragraph describing the effectiveness of the communication in an organization that you have been affiliated with.
2. Your manager has to travel to a different country and has asked you to research that country and write a one-page memo discussing the highlights of what you find. Conduct research on a country of your choice and write the memo.
3. Write ten sentences in which you use a figure of speech

that would likely be misunderstood by someone from a different culture. Then rewrite the sentences, using wording that would be understood. For example, "The bottom line is that we should adopt the new plan" could be changed to, "Our conclusion is that we should adopt the new plan."

4. Interview two or three people who are originally from different countries, and ask them to describe the problems they encountered when they first came to your country. Write a short report about their responses.

5. Practice reflective listening in a conversation with another person. Write a short paper describing the impact of reflective listening on your conversation.

6. Describe a negative experience you have had working in a team setting (may be a sports team or an organizational team). Explain why it was negative and suggest what could have prevented the problem from occurring.

7. Prepare a Gantt chart or a flow chart for some process you have been involved with. This may be a process involving a group or involving just you.

8. Complete the Personal Attributes Chart. In a small group discussion with several of your classmates, tell about one of your highest- and lowest-scoring social attributes. Share an experience in which these attributes were exhibited. Write a paragraph that describes two or three attributes that you want to improve.

9. Go out to dinner with a group of friends and practice good etiquette. Write a short report about your experience.

10. Think of a person you trust. Write a paragraph in which you explain what that person has done to earn your trust.

11. Design a business card for yourself (design guidelines are given in Chapter 11).

PLANNING AND OUTLINING MESSAGES

Writing is a critical skill in business. Most significant organizational activity usually ends up in written form, and the ability to write well affects the degree to which you will be promoted to management positions. Thus, if you don't write well, your career will likely suffer.

For many people, writing is a difficult process. For all people, writing is work, but following a proven process will enhance your ability to write well. The basic writing process explained in this book consists of four major phases (see Table 2.1). Chapter 2 includes five sections: clarify your purposes, analyze the audience, create an outline, evaluate the outline, and develop an effective strategy.

CLARIFY YOUR PURPOSES

As you prepare to write, decide what you want to accomplish. Most messages have three distinct purposes. First, all messages must inform; second, many messages must persuade; and third, all messages should build relationships of trust. Thus, as you plan each message, ask yourself the following three questions:

1. What do I want the audience to know?

   Example: I want the reader to know about my plans to expand my business.

2. What do I want the audience to do?

   Example: I want the reader to lend me $200,000 to expand my business.

3. How do I want the audience to feel?

   Example: I want the reader to feel that I can be trusted and that I am a good credit risk.

Regarding the feeling element, make sure each message contributes to positive, trusting relationships. Never send

Table 2.1. The Four Major Phases of Writing

1. Content	(Chapter 2) Determine the information you want to communicate (use 5W2H questions—who, what, where, when, why, how, and how much) and then develop a strategy.
2. Organization	(Chapter 2) Arrange the information into an appropriate order and structure.
3. Writing	(Chapter 3, 5) Compose and revise the message.
4. Design	(Chapter 4) Apply appropriate formatting and visual design (headings, art/visuals, typography, and spacing).

a message you have written in anger. Rather, take time to cool down and then write a rational message that achieves your purpose and strengthens relationships.

ANALYZE THE AUDIENCE

To create a message that fits the audience, try to understand their unique frame of reference. Empathize with the audience; look at the situation through *their* eyes. Knowing who they are and what they're like, how they feel about the message, and how they feel about you (the messenger) will help.

- *Audience:* Analyze their basic nature, character, personality, professional goals and objectives, and self-perception. A bit of demographic and personal information might be useful as well, including age, educational background, cultural background, hobbies and interests, and values. Also, understand the person's *context;* e.g., position in the organization and competing factors such as time constraints, financial constraints, political and peer pressures, and conflicting or competing messages.

- *Message:* Consider how much they know about the subject matter and how they *feel* about it (positive, neutral, or negative). Determine whether the message will be interesting and useful to them, or whether they might ignore it and toss it aside.

- *Messenger:* Find out how much the audience knows about you and how they feel about you. Determine whether they like you, trust you, and believe you. Understand your organizational, social, and emotional relationship with them.

The emotional state of your audience can impact the effectiveness of your delivery. Use Table 2.2 to help analyze the emotional state of your audience. Note that emotions can be broadly classified as negative, neutral, or positive. Your audience may feel one way about the message but another way about the messenger. Once you've analyzed the emotional state of your audience, tailor your message appropriately. Build on positive emotions and seek to address and resolve negative emotions.

Remember that audiences subconsciously ask the

Table 2.2 Audience Emotional States

Negative	Neutral	Positive
Frustrated	Passive	Interested
Defensive	Complacent	Motivated
Angry	Apathetic	Enthusiastic
Hostile	Aloof	Happy

WIIFM question: "What's in it for me?" Regarding the WIIFM concerns, consider both the cognitive and affective parts of each message. The cognitive focuses on the logical and rational aspects, such as money savings, time savings, or system improvements. The affective focuses on the psychological and emotional aspects (both positive and negative), such as improved self-esteem or damaged social reputation.

Obviously, the audience might be more than one person, perhaps even dozens or hundreds of people. Include the needs and expectations of all these different stakeholders in the audience analysis. In such cases, you won't be able to tailor the message for individuals; you will have to choose an approach that fits the general nature of the audience.

CREATE AN OUTLINE

For a variety of reasons, few people create an outline as a preliminary part of their writing. Some feel that it takes too much time, others don't think it will help their writing, and still others have bad memories of trying to outline when they were in high school. Nevertheless, research consistently shows that outlining improves writing.

Even artists outline as part of their drawing process. The three images in Figure 2.1 illustrate the progression from a preliminary wire frame to a rough sketch to a finished drawing. Use the same basic process in your writing—create an outline, compose the rough draft, and revise and polish to produce the final document.

Figure 2.1 Illustrations by Ward Greenhalgh.

Before beginning your outline, gather relevant information to provide all 5W2H information (who, what, where, when, why, how, and how much). Good information sources include your own thinking, talking and brainstorming with fellow employees, reviewing previous correspondence about the topic, analyzing original data, reading reports, searching the internet, and searching online libraries.

When you're ready to begin outlining, choose between a top-down and a bottom-up approach. Top-down outlining starts with the major ideas (categories) and moves to the details. Bottom-up outlining first lists the details and then uses inductive logic to determine the major ideas (categories). If you know in advance the main segments of the message, use a top-down outlining method. If you don't know what the major segments of your message will be, use a bottom-up approach.

Top-down Outlining

Three effective methods for top-down outlining include the traditional outline, tree structure, and mind map. Traditional outlining is the method most people are familiar with, but mind mapping has become much more popular in recent years. Whereas traditional outlining involves working exclusively with text, mind mapping includes text as well as visual elements (circles and lines).

TRADITIONAL OUTLINE

To create a traditional outline, first list the main categories and then list supporting elements beneath them. Because each additional main category adds complexity and reduces learning and retention, about three to four main categories is ideal.

Word-processing software should have an automatic outlining feature that can help with this process, including the ability to cut and paste lines of text after the original outline draft has been created. Identify the main categories with Roman numerals and supporting elements as shown in the following example:

Title: Why We Need a Training Director
I.   Increase in employees
   A.   First supporting element under I
   B.   Second supporting element under I
II.   Increase in errors
   A.   First supporting element under II
   B.   Second supporting element under II
      1.   First supporting element under B
      2.   Second supporting element under B
         a.   First supporting element under 2
         b.   Second supporting element under 2
III. Overburdened line managers

An advantage of traditional outlining is its familiarity; most people become acquainted with it as they go through the public school system. A disadvantage is that some people find it too rigid and confining. It is also totally textual, and some people prefer to use methods that are more visual in nature, such as mind mapping.

TREE DIAGRAM

A tree diagram is a graphic representation of the information to be included in your message (see Figure 2.2). The structure is much like that of a pedigree chart, with children listed for each set of parents. For the trunk of the tree, write the main idea, such as, "Why we need a new police officer." For the branches (or children) of that trunk, write the main supporting ideas, such as (a) population has increased and (b) crime rate has increased. Add secondary branches to the main branches as needed for more detail.

To create a tree diagram, just construct the information structure like an organizational chart, with the title at the top and the branches extending downward from there. Or you might work from left to right, with the trunk on the left side of your paper and the branches extending to the right. Write the main title halfway down the page on the left side and then work from left to right from there. Leave adequate white space among the various branches to accommodate the addition of new branches.

MIND MAP

Mind mapping is another top-down process. Like the tree structure, a mind map is a graphic representation of the information, somewhat resembling a spiderweb. Write

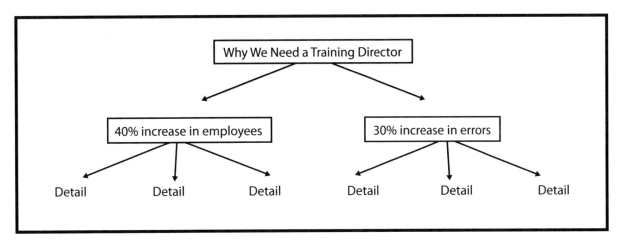

Figure 2.2 A tree structure is like a pedigree chart or an organization chart.

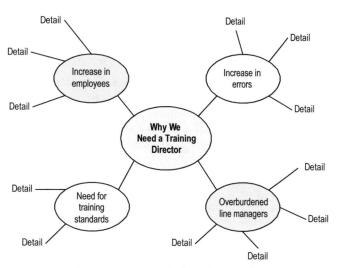

Figure 2.3 Mind mapping is useful for outlining and information mapping.

Free List

Small jobs used to tie up large expensive presses

Cost was high

Delayed critical large jobs

Small-Doc Shop established in 200X to handle jobs too small for big presses

In Small-Doc Shop, results have been bad

Lots of delays, customer complaints

Result has been good for large presses—improved costs and printing time

Problems = poor management, poor job quality, poor job tracking, lots of customer complaints, poor communication with customers, no accountability for press operators re. delayed jobs

Proposal: Hire new mgr, revise job form, and track each job for better accountability

Savings = from replacing old supervisor with younger, improving thru put time, eliminating do-overs

Figure 2.4 Creating a free list is a good way to get started on a writing assignment.

---

the main topic inside a circle in the middle of a page. Then draw lines to connect the main circle to the first level of categories, which may also be inside circles. These first-level categories can be used as the primary headings in the final document. The first-level categories are then further connected with subcategories by additional lines (see Figure 2.3). This process of adding more connecting lines and more details can go on for as many levels as desired.

Many people like the mind map because of its visual nature and its flexibility. It is a top-down process because it begins with the big idea and extends down to smaller ideas, and its flexibility allows for additions in a somewhat random nature as thoughts come to the writer's mind. Further, the circles may be changed to rectangles or other shapes if desired, and visual sketches of objects may be inserted anywhere on the chart. For instance, a mind map for a document that will evaluate four different vendors could include the vendors' logos inside four first-level categories.

Bottom-up Outlining

Bottom-up outlining works just the opposite from top-down outlining. It consists of (a) creating an unorganized list ("free list") of details, (b) categorizing the information, and (c) sequencing the categories. The final result is an outline that can be used as a blueprint for writing the final text.

CREATE A FREE LIST

First, create a free list. A free list is an unstructured listing of information to include in a message. The free list can result from data gathering (e.g., interviews, questionnaires, or database searches) or from brainstorming. When creating a free list, consider your message objectives, as well as

the needs and wants of the audience. Think of the information needed to answer all relevant 5W2H questions: who, what, where, when, why, how, and how much. Be thorough and detailed in your thinking. Figure 2.4 shows a brainstormed list of information related to a problem in a printing operation.

While creating a free list, don't worry about sequence or organization—just add the ideas to the list as they come to your mind. You'll organize them later. For example, examine the order of the information in Figure 2.4. Notice that the sequence in the list is purely random. Further, notice that the creator didn't worry about spelling, capitalizing, or careful writing of the ideas. The main concern was to generate a rough listing of information to include in the message.

CATEGORIZE THE INFORMATION

After constructing a free list, put all the items into categories. Examine all the items and determine commonalities among the various items on the list. As you find two or more closely related items, choose a heading that describes the category of the items and use that heading as the category label. If you are struggling to identify categories, consider again the 5W2H words (who, what, where, when, why, how, and how much). Most of the information we need to share with other people can be classified into one of these seven word categories.

The classification process can be accomplished on the computer screen or on paper. On the computer, make a ver-

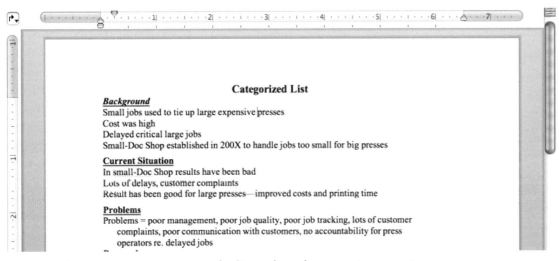

Figure 2.5 On a computer screen, items in a free list are dragged to appropriate categories.

tical list of the categories above the free list as you consider each item on the list. Then drag the items from the list up to the appropriate categories, resulting in the various headings listed vertically, each one followed by the related free-list items, also listed vertically as shown in the Figure 2.5.

For simple outlines, you can use a pen and paper and a three-column approach. On your writing pad, draw two vertical lines to make three columns, as shown in Figure 2.6. In the first column, create your free list. In the second column, determine appropriate categories. (You may want to copy your free list items into the appropriate categories.)

Free List	Categorize	Sequence
Hard working	Work ethic	Interpersonal Skills
People skills	Hard working	Communicator
Communicator	Reliable	Personality
Reliable	Honest	People skills
Personality	Interpersonal Skills	Positive
Worked at Macy's	People skills	Experience
Worked at Wal-Mart	Communicator	Worked at Wal-Mart
Honest	Personality	Worked at Macy's
Positive	Positive	Work ethic
	Experience	Reliable
	Worked at Macy's	Honest
	Worked at Wal-Mart	Hard working

Figure 2.6 A three-column outline can be created with pen and paper.

SEQUENCE THE INFORMATION

After classifying, arrange the information into an appropriate sequence. In the third column in Figure 2.6, both the categories and the subordinate free list items have been sequenced. Notice that the information in the third column is now arranged so that it can be used as an outline.

When deciding on the sequence, think of information

as being either non-chronological or chronological in nature.

Non-chronological information is stationary, unmoving, and somewhat like a photograph. For instance, you might describe three different automobiles you are considering for purchase. Describing static information involves telling about different parts or different attributes of the whole at a certain point in time, not over a period of time. A description of three different automobiles, for example, would probably include their price, reliability, efficiency, and so forth.

To arrange non-chronological information, arrange the information in a category order, quantitative order, spatial order, or comparative order, depending on the information and the needs and expectations of the audience.

- *Category order:* City X is divided into six sections—NE, N, NW, SW, S, and SE.

- *Quantitative order:* City X has eight golf courses, City Y has five golf courses, and City Z has only one.

- *Spatial order:* Six banks are located from north to south along Highway 213.

- *Comparative order* (also known as compare and contrast): Person A has more technical knowledge and leadership experience than Person B and C. Person B possesses the highest educational degree, but that achievement does not place her ahead of Person A. Person C lacks in all three areas of technical knowledge, leadership experience, and education.

Chronological information consists of a series of happenings, somewhat like a movie. It involves different events that happen over a period of time, such as a few minutes, a few days, or even a few years. It is narrative—one thing happening after another. For example, you might describe the increase of traffic through an intersection over a five-year period, during which a neighborhood grows from just a few houses to a few hundred houses.

- *Time-series order:* Intersection X's traffic five years ago was 238 cars per day; now the volume is 307.

- *Problem-solution order:* Crime is up by 15 percent; therefore, we need more officers.

- *Cause-effect order:* If we adopt this plan, we'll be able to reduce crime by 25 percent.

- *Narrative:* The problem started when the delivery was late. Then when the customer discovered a partial delivery, he returned the package and canceled the order. Unfortunately, billing wasn't notified of the cancellation and sent an invoice, which further angered the customer.

No structure or information sequence is right or wrong, but rather is more or less appropriate. Therefore, consider the context of each situation and choose the sequence that seems to be best for the situation.

EVALUATE THE OUTLINE

After you have created your outline, take time to evaluate its structure, especially if the structure is somewhat complex. Use a five-step procedure (Baker 1994) that consists of evaluating each outline cluster, or family. A family is one group of parallel categories, such as I, II, III or A, B, C, D. Each occurrence of a I, A, 1, a, (1), or (a) in an outline signifies the first item in a family. This is a top-down process that starts at the first-level categories and then progresses family by family to the most detailed level of the hierarchy.

The five outline tests are as follows:

1. *Inclusion* (or presence) test: Given the title, heading, or parent of a family, are all appropriate items (children) included? If not, add the missing items or restrict the scope of the title or heading to fit the items that are present. Make sure every family contains at least two children (e.g., A *and* B, 1 *and* 2).

2. *Exclusion* (or absence) test: Given the title or heading of a family, are all inappropriate items excluded? If not, delete the inappropriate items, or expand the title or heading to fit all the items in the family.

3. *Hierarchy* (or horizontal) test: Are the items in the family hierarchically parallel in the correct generation? If not, shift the nonparallel items to the appropriate level (e.g., from the A, B, C level to the 1, 2, 3 level), and make other adjustments necessary to ensure hierarchical parallelism. In most cases you'll find no specific right or wrong hierarchy, because most subject matter can be organized in a variety of ways. Just decide which organization seems most logical in each circumstance.

4. *Sequence* (or vertical) test: Are the items in the appropriate sequence? Determine whether the family is a noun or verb type, and then decide which sequence seems to be most appropriate for each family. Make this decision from the perspective of the audience.

5. *Language* (or wording) test: Are the items in the family grammatically parallel? If not, change the wording to achieve parallelism. Test 5 is important only if the items are used as headings in the final text. If they are not, you may skip this test.

Remember these tests by thinking of *presence* and *absence* (Tests 1 and 2), *horizontal* and *vertical* (Tests 3 and 4), and *wording* (Test 5).

The five tests can be easily understood when applied to a real family, as illustrated in Table 2.3

The following example shows the outline tests being performed on the first family (first-level categories) of the *Results of Management Audit of Administrative Services Division* outline.

Table 2.3   The five outline tests help ensure the structural integrity of outlines.

Test 1: Presence	Test 2: Absence	Test 3. Horizontal	Test 4. Vertical	Test 5: Parallelism	Final
Parents: K. & T. Cox	Parents: K. & T. Cox	Parents: K. & T. Cox	Parents: K. & T. Cox	Parents: K. & T. Cox	Parents: K. & T. Cox
Brooklyn Williams Ethan Anthony Madison Hyer Emily Abbey Sam	Brooklyn Williams Ethan Anthony Madison Hyer Emily Abbey Sam Jasmine	Brooklyn Williams Ethan Anthony Madison Hyer Emily Sam Jasmine	Brooklyn Williams Ethan Anthony Madison Hyer Emily Sam Jasmine	Sam Emily Brooklyn Williams Ethan Anthony Madison Hyer Jasmine	Sam Cox Emily Cox Brooklyn Williams Ethan Anthony Madison Hyer Jasmine Cox
Are all children present? No. Add sibling Jasmine.	Are all non-family members absent? No. Delete Abbey, a neighbor girl.	Are all members siblings? No. Ethan and Anthony are grandchildren.	Are all children in the best sequence? No. Arrange in chronological order by date of birth.	Do all the names have parallel structure? No. List all last names.	The Cox family now passes all tests. The next-generation Williams family now needs to be tested.

Test 1 (Inclusion/Presence Test):

Title: Results of Management Audit of Administrative
Services Division

    I.   Introduction

    II.   Information Services

    III.   Human Resources Department

    IV.   Accounting

    V.   Accounts Payable

    VI.   Accounts Receivable

    VII.   Marketing

    VIII.   Conclusions and Recommendations

Are all units in the Administrative Services Division present? No, the Purchasing Department is missing and needs to be included.

Test 2 (Exclusion/Absence Test):

Title: Results of Management Audit of Administrative
Services Division

    I.   Introduction

    II.   Information Services

    III.   Human Resources Department

    IV.   Accounting

    V.   Accounts Payable

    VI.   Accounts Receivable

    VII.   Marketing

    VIII.   Purchasing

    IX.   Conclusions and Recommendations

Are any units included that are not part of the Administrative Services Division? Yes, Marketing is not part of the Administrative Services Division and should be excluded.

Test 3 (Hierarchy/Horizontal Test):

Title: Results of Management Audit of Administrative
Services Division

    I.   Introduction

    II.   Information Services

    III.   Human Resources Department

    IV.   Accounting

    V.   Accounts Payable

    VI.   Accounts Receivable

    VII.   Purchasing

    VIII.   Conclusions and Recommendations

Are all the items in the family hierarchically parallel (on the proper level)? No, Accounts Payable and Accounts Receivable are divisions of Accounting. Therefore, they should be shifted to the second level as subdivisions A and B under Accounting and later be tested as a separate family.

Test 4 (Sequence/Vertical Test):

Title: Results of Management Audit of Administrative
Services Division

    I.   Introduction

    II.   Information Services

    III.   Human Resources Department

    IV.   Accounting

        A.   Accounts Payable

        B.   Accounts Receivable

    V.   Purchasing

    VI.   Conclusions and Recommendations

Are the items in the most appropriate sequence? This family is a noun-type family; therefore, it will not be arranged in a time sequence. Items I and VI are arranged in the sequence in which we want the reader to encounter them in the report. Items II-V could be arranged by order of size (e.g., largest to smallest) or by severity of management problems identified in the audit (e.g., most to least). However, an alphabetic arrangement seems to be more appropriate.

Test 5 (Language/Wording Test):

Title: Results of Management Audit of Administrative
Services Division

    I.   Introduction

    II.   Accounting

        A.   Accounts Payable

        B.   Accounts Receivable

    III.   Human Resources Department

    IV.   Information Services

    V.   Purchasing

    VI.   Conclusions and Recommendations

Are the items parallel in language? No, items II, III, IV, and V are departments, but only item III includes the word *Department*. Therefore, *Department* should be added to items II, IV, and V.

With all the necessary changes made, family *I-VI* now passes all five tests:

Title: Results of Management Audit of Administrative
    Services Division

    I. Introduction

    II. Accounting Department

        A. Accounts Payable

        B. Accounts Receivable

    III. Human Resources Department

        A. Employment

        B. Benefits

        C. Training and Development

    IV. Information Services Department

        A. Computer Systems

        B. Records Management

    V. Purchasing Department

    VI. Conclusions and Recommendations

After the tests are completed on the first family (the children level), they should be repeated on all remaining subfamilies (the grandchildren level). For this example, you would next complete the outline tests on the three remaining families in the following order: (a) II, A-B; (b) III, A-C; and (c) IV, A-B. If there were additional generations, they would be identified and tested in the same manner. For example, if Employment had two subdivisions, it would be identified as family III, A, 1–2 and would be tested after family III, A-C.

Remember two additional guidelines when working with outlines. First, make sure each subdivision has at least two items: a 1 and 2, or an A and B. Do not have a 1 or an A by itself. Second, limit the number of items in each family to about seven. The average human brain cannot easily process or remember more than about seven items. If you have too many items in a family, reorganize the material by placing the items into fewer categories.

This outline-testing procedure is a comprehensive, yet relatively simple, writing tool. The five tests encompass every type of change you can make in an outline: (1) addition, (2) deletion, (3) horizontal movement, (4) vertical movement, and (5) change of wording. Tests 1 and 2 help ensure that the proper content is included in each family; tests 3 and 4 make sure the items are properly located (horizontally and vertically), and test 5 guarantees proper language parallelism.

Four important benefits come from testing outlines:

1. Tests 1 and 2 address content issues, helping to ensure that all relevant information is included and that all irrelevant information is excluded.

2. Tests 3 and 4 address structural issues, making sure content hierarchy and sequence are orderly.

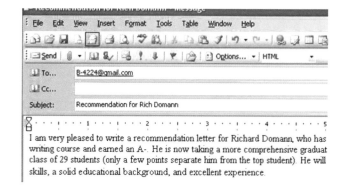

Figure 2.7 Emails are a widely used communication channel because of their convenience.

3. The outline-testing process helps you compose text more efficiently—writing becomes a straight-forward process of expanding the outline, rather than a perplexing process of not knowing what to write next.

4. The final text will be easier to read and comprehend.

DEVELOP AN EFFECTIVE STRATEGY

Once you know the purpose of the message, understand the audience, and determine the message content, you must develop a strategy for presenting the information in an effective way. After all, both *what* you say and *how* you say it are important. Developing the best strategy includes both channel choices and psychological decisions.

Channel Strategy

Messages can be sent via different types of communication channels, such as face-to-face, phone, text messages, email, instant messages, podcasts, paper, or video. Each communication channel can be evaluated on five factors:

Richness: Richer channels are those where multiple message aspects are communicated. Face-to-face communication is the richest channel, because verbal and nonverbal messages are being sent simultaneously. A telephone call contains verbal and audio, but no visual messages. Emails and other text messages are the least rich, because they contain only words and no nonverbal accompaniment.

Convenience: The most convenient channels are those that require the least amount of effort to use. Email, texting, and phone mail can be exchanged asynchronously—senders and receivers do not have to be online at the same time. Email and text messages can also be sent simultaneously to multiple parties.

Speed: This factor refers to the speed of transmission. Mail sent through the U.S. Postal Service is very slow compared to electronic messages that arrive in seconds.

Permanence: The permanence factor refers to whether a record is kept of the message. Paper messages score high here because the paper copy of the message can be stored and retrieved at a later time. A telephone call, on the other hand, leaves no permanent record for later reference.

Cost: This factor is self-explanatory. Equipment, air time, paper, time to compose and read, time to listen, and monthly subscription rates can all enter into the cost of a particular channel.

Many messages are sent over just a single channel, but other situations may call for the use of multiple channels. For instance, you might have a face-to-face interview (high in message richness but low in permanence) and then follow it up with a written document (low in message richness but high in permanence) that creates a record of the interview.

When selecting a communication channel, remember that people are overwhelmed with messages—emails, phone mails, instant messages, text messages, memos, reports, pop-up ads, visits from fellow workers, and endless meetings. Hundreds of messages are received throughout the day. People are so overloaded with incoming messages that some of the messages have to be overlooked. Thus, don't assume that just because you send a written message, the intended reader will read it. If your email message is competing with 45 other emails a person receives in a day, your message might be ignored, lightly skimmed, or even deleted without being read. Your messages face a great amount of competition, so your best strategy is required to ensure they are read.

Psychological Strategies

Once you have made the channel choice, determine the appropriate psychological strategy. Before deciding on a strategy, first understand how the audience perceives you. This is the area that Aristotle referred to as *ethos*. Do they see you as being knowledgeable, honest, trustworthy, and genuinely concerned about them? If you lack credibility with them, you will have a difficult time accomplishing your writing objectives. Second, for persuasive messages, determine how open they are to change, because if they are not open to change, even your best strategy will probably fail.

After you have assessed your credibility and their openness to change, consider the following strategic factors:

- Direct or indirect approach
- Head and/or heart appeals
- Positive and/or negative appeals
- Urgent or delayed action

DIRECT OR INDIRECT APPROACH

With direct approach you give the main point of the message at or near the beginning, followed by details. With indirect approach, you give details first, followed by the main point of the message. As a general rule, use the direct approach for conveying good news or routine messages. Use the indirect approach for conveying bad news or persuasive messages.

For example, if the central message is that construction of a new building is on schedule, that message is given at the beginning, followed by details about various parts of the building. However, if the central message is that the company is going to reduce some benefit it offers to employees, the message would first state that the economy is bad and that the company is having to cut back on expenses. Following these details, the central message would be given: "Effective June 1, we will be discontinuing our educational assistance program."

HEAD AND/OR HEART APPEALS

An appeal to the head is what Aristotle called a *logos* strategy. This type of appeal targets the logical, rational domain of the reader. With a head appeal, you would support your arguments with solid reasons and evidence, along with any other appropriate analyses, explanations, comparisons, and details (including all appropriate who, what, where, when, why, how, and how much information. Example: "We need to get the design right before introducing the product in the marketplace; otherwise, the early adopters will share their negative impressions on the internet."

An appeal to the heart is what Aristotle called a *pathos* strategy. With a heart appeal, you would support your arguments with information that touches the audience's basic human emotions, such as happiness, sadness, pride of accomplishment, or frustrations. Telling a story is often a very effective pathos strategy. Example: "Last Wednesday I had to spend four extra hours to gather all the data I need because Ben didn't get his information to me on time!"

POSITIVE AND/OR NEGATIVE APPEALS

When you are trying to persuade someone to take a certain action, you can include both positive and negative reasons. A positive approach focuses on benefits to be gained, whether tangible or intangible. A tangible benefit might be to earn or save more money; and intangible benefit might be to feel better about yourself. A negative approach focuses on what the person might lose, such as receiving a costly fine for violation of a law. As with positive rewards, negative rewards can also be tangible or intangible. Both positive and negative approaches can be powerful motivators.

URGENT OR DELAYED ACTION

Urgency is referred to as *kairos,* highlighting the benefits of taking action right now, and communicating what will be lost by delaying action. Example: "If we don't act now, we'll miss an opportunity to be first in the marketplace with a product like this."

Table 2.4 can be helpful to you in deciding on a strategy. Place a check mark in the various boxes that you determine to be appropriate for each situation. Check either the direct or indirect order; check one or both of the head- and heart-appeal boxes; check one or both of the positive- and negative-reasons boxes; and check either the urgent or not-urgent box. Then develop your message according to the boxes you have checked.

Table 2.4. Strategy Table

Direct approach key point first, reasons after	OR	Indirect approach reasons first, key point after
Head appeal logic and reasoning	AND/ OR	Heart appeal emotion and empathy
Positive appeal what you'll gain	AND/ OR	Negative appeal what you'll lose
Urgent	OR	Not urgent

When deciding on a strategy, remember that each situation is unique and must be considered individually. Also, a written message might be used as just one part of a larger strategy that includes phone calls, meetings, or discussions over lunch. In such cases, make sure each part is compatible with all other parts.

CHAPTER SUMMARY

Chapter 2 discusses how to plan and outline messages. In the content phase, clarify the purpose of the message, which may be to inform, persuade, or build relationships. Then analyze the audience, considering how they feel about you and your message.

Decide on the content by using a top-down or bottom-up outlining approach. Traditional, tree-diagram, and mind-map outlines are top-down approaches. Bottom-up approaches begin with details, which are then organized into clusters, hierarchies, and sequences, resulting in a complete outline. To evaluate the organizational soundness of an

outline, test each family for inclusion, exclusion, hierarchy, sequence, and language. Finally, decide on an effective strategy for presenting your message. Consider different approaches and appeals to achieve your goal.

WORKS CITED

Baker, William H. "How to Produce and Communicate Structured Text." *Technical Communication* 41, no. 3 (1994): 456–466.

CHAPTER QUESTIONS

1. Describe the four basic phases of writing.
2. Explain the three main purposes of most written messages? Why is the third purpose so important?
3. Why should you analyze the audience before you begin writing?
4. What is WIIFM? Why is it important in writing and speaking to various audiences?
5. Why is outlining important?
6. What is bottom-up outlining? In what context is it most useful?
7. What is mind mapping? Why might you use it instead of traditional outlining?
8. What steps are required to turn a free list into an outline?
9. What is involved in the process of classifying?
10. Indicate whether each of the following is an example of chronological or nonchronological sequencing: quantitative, problem-solution, spatial, narrative, cause-effect.
11. Describe the five outline tests.
12. How can you fix an exclusion-test problem (outline test 2)?
13. List five key ways to analyze and evaluate communication channels.
14. What are Aristotle's three rhetorical strategies? Give an example of each.
15. Explain the difference between direct and indirect order.
16. Explain positive and negative strategies.

CHAPTER ACTIVITIES

1. Think of three different topics, one for each of the following sequences: quantitative, comparative, and cause and effect. Tell why each sequence is appropriate for the topic you have chosen.

2. Assume that you must write a persuasive message to someone else. Describe the audience and tell what strategy you will use and why. For instance, assume that you are going to apply for a scholarship and that you must write a letter to convince the scholarship committee to give you the scholarship.

3. Create a message-richness table that shows the relative message richness of email, telephone conversation, and face-to-face meetings. List the five message-richness factors in the left column of your table, and list the three options across the top row. Rate each of the options on a scale of 1 to 5, with 5 being the highest rating.

4. Using a bottom-up approach, develop an outline on the topic, "Why Go to College." Check the outline with the five tests explained in this chapter.

5. Create a mind map or tree diagram that you could use as an outline for describing your favorite sport or hobby.

6. Select six members (three females and three males) of your class to participate in a short sequencing activity. Have them stand in a row in front of the room. Then rearrange the sequence in four different ways: (a) tallest to shortest, (b) oldest to youngest, (c) by gender and then tallest to shortest, (d) and alphabetic by last name. Discuss what implications this exercise has for arranging information for writing.

7. With a group, evaluate the following outline for a report on modern-day transportation. Modify the outline so it meets the standards of the five outline tests.

Modern-day Transportation

I.   Mode
    A.   Human powered
    B.   Air
    C.   Rail
    D.   Road
    E.   Animal powered
    F.   Electronic communication

II. Elements
    A.   Infrastructure
    B.   Vehicles
    C.   Operation

III. Function
    A.   Passenger
    B.   Freight

IV. History

V.   Impact
    A.   Economic
    B.   Planning
    C.   Environment

8. Describe the channel and strategy you would use in each of the following situations:

    a.   You are a college student; convince a friend to go play golf with you on Saturday.

    b.   You are a college student; tell your friend why you cannot go play golf with him or her on Saturday.

    c.   You are a manager; tell a person you interviewed last week that you are not going to hire him.

    d.   You are a manager; tell a person you interviewed last week that you are going to hire him.

    e.   You are a banker; tell a college student that her application for an auto loan has been disapproved.

    f.   You are a college graduate; persuade an employer whom you don't know to hire you.

    g.   You are the president of a student club; persuade a local business leader to speak at a club meeting.

COMPOSING WRITTEN MESSAGES

After you have gathered, analyzed, and evaluated the information you need to communicate, you are ready to compose. Composing is the task of actually writing the text—word by word, sentence by sentence, and paragraph by paragraph. Especially with long documents, composition takes a great amount of time and work. It also requires a lot of concentration, and creating the right environment can make a major difference in your ability to concentrate. Here are a few ideas to consider related to your writing time, place, and things.

First, try to set aside enough time to complete the writing task. A short email can be composed in a minute or so, but a long, complicated report may require a few days. Also regarding time, write during your high-energy, high-concentration time of the day when your mind is clear and alert. Use your low-energy time for completing tasks that require less concentration.

Along with concern about time, choose the best writing place where you can be alone with your thoughts. Eliminate distractions, such as text messages, emails, phone calls, music, or environmental noise. Some people do best when they have some soft background music, but many do best when there is little or no sound. Eliminate things that make you physically uncomfortable, such as hunger, thirst, or an awkward writing posture or position.

Finally, assemble all the things you need to be productive, such as your computer, notes or reference materials, and access to the internet. Have a good work surface where you can spread out your notes, books, and anything else you'll be consulting during the writing process. For long writing projects, you might also benefit from taping drafts of your work on a wall so you can see all the pages at once. This is particularly helpful for evaluating the overall structure and flow of the material. And don't forget the importance of a good ergonomic chair that enables you to be comfortable for long periods of time without becoming physically fatigued.

Once you have created the right environment, you're ready to go to work. This chapter discusses three general composition steps and gives suggestions for improving both the process of composition and the product, or result, of your composition efforts.

1. Clarify your purpose
2. Follow an appropriate pattern
3. Strengthen the content

Figure 3.1 Create a good environment when working on long documents.

CLARIFY YOUR PURPOSE

Always keep in mind the main purpose of the message you plan to write. Generally the purpose is to inform or to persuade, with an underlying purpose to strengthen your relationship with the reader.

Consider writing a working title to help clarify what you are trying to accomplish. Like a thesis statement, working title helps keep your mind focused while you write, and it helps prevent your text from wandering away from the specific goal you are trying to achieve. For example, the working title of this chapter is "how to compose an effective business message." The following examples provide additional working titles for both informative and persuasive messages:

- Who should be hired to replace a retiring staff member
- What computer equipment will be replaced this year
- Where and when our meeting will be held to discuss the new company policy
- How many new employees will we need to hire next year
- How supervisors should handle an on-the-job injury
- Why I should be given approval to hire a new sales person for my staff

After composing the text, check your writing against the working title to see if you have achieved your purpose. When you are satisfied that your text has accomplished its objective, feel free to change the working title to a final title (or subject line in an email), such as "What computer equipment will be replaced this year" to "Computer Replacements During 20XX."

FOLLOW AN APPROPRIATE PATTERN

For very short messages consisting of two or three sentences, you don't have to worry much about message structure. But for longer messages, take a moment to decide on an appropriate outline and message pattern. For instance, you might decide to use a recommendation-reason order in writing about a billing problem your department has experienced. The first draft of your message might be something like the following:

I believe we should request an adjustment in our A/V Services bill. As authorized by you, I gathered information related to the January bill we were sent by audio-visual services. I asked each of our trainers how much time A/V Services actually spent on their projects. Then I compared our trainers' reported time against the detailed bill sent by A/V Services. (Insert table.) The table shows major discrepancies between the bill and the report from our trainers.

You may also use any pattern that has been established for the kind of messages you are writing. For example, to teach someone a series of new concepts, you could use a concept-example pattern (each new concept is explained and then the concept is illustrated in an example). To write a sales letter, you could use an APA pattern (attention, persuasion, action). To write a report of a performance audit, you could arrange the information using a PR pattern (each problem is followed by appropriate recommendations). In addition, many written messages follow a simple chronological pattern, with the various individual events arranged according to the sequence in which they occurred (first event, second event, etc.).

For writing routine messages, most people use a simple three-part OBC pattern consisting of opening, body, and closing. However, an OABC pattern (opening, agenda, body, closing) is often more effective, both for the reader and the writer. (Agendas are also useful in oral communication such as interviews, presentations, and phone calls.) Because the agenda previews the major information contained in the body, the writer has a good roadmap to follow, and the reader is given a mental structure to use in understanding and organizing the information during the reading process.

You may compose these four OABC parts in any sequence you wish. For instance, you may choose to write the agenda first, followed by the body, followed by the closing, followed by the opening. Or you may go back and forth from one section to another during the composition process. Be flexible and follow your best judgment for each writing situation.

Opening

The opening presents the context of the message to the reader. It should be tailored to help the reader connect to the message; that is, the opening should indicate that the message will be relevant to the reader's world. If you compose the opening successfully, the reader's mind will be prepared to receive what is in the body of your message.

Openings may contain any of the following kinds of information.

- Background information about the topic
- Justification or reason for the text
- Statement of authorization, indicating who ordered or authorized the writing
- An attention getter, or hook

For routine and good-news messages, the main idea you begin with might be (a) the reason for the message, (b) the problem you will address, (c) a major recommendation you are making, (d) an answer to a previous communication, or (e) other key information appropriate to the situation. Here are four examples that give the main idea at the beginning, to be followed by relevant details:

1. Thanks for your July 13 letter asking about employment in our new plant in your city.

2. Since February 1, we have lost three major accounts because of our late product deliveries. I'm convinced that we need to implement the procedures used by our Atlanta operations, as we discussed last week.

3. After months of work, I'm pleased to report that the details have been finalized for our upgraded retirement package.

4. Since talking with you in Denver last week, I have given a lot of thought to your idea concerning acquiring the Bronson property. I'm convinced that such a move would not be in the best interest of our company.

All these statements help you connect with the reader and pull the reader into the message. In short documents, one sentence may be adequate for the opening. In longer, more complex documents, one or more paragraphs will be necessary.

For bad-news or heavily persuasive messages, use an indirect approach, leaving the main point of the message until later. For example, with bad news, you would organize as follows:

1. Open by mentioning the topic of the message, but don't give the bad news.

2. Explain the reasons for your decision or the process involved in making the bad-news decision.

3. Being as positive as is appropriate, give the bad news, which should appear as a logical extension of the information given in step 2.

4. Move to a more positive closing, which might include suggesting other options to help the reader.

Figure 3.2 demonstrates the use of the indirect approach.

Agenda

The agenda is a preview or map of the body of the message. Without an agenda, or preview, the reader has no idea where you are going, and this causes increased reading difficulty. Agendas serve as bridges, or transitions, to subsequent text. Agendas can (1) quantify—tell the number of key content units; (2) identify—specify the subject matter that follows; (3) organize—explain the order or arrangement of the following content units; or (4) symbolize—create a

Example of Bad-news Letter

Dear Adam:

Thank you for your email requesting a change in your final grade for Management Communication 320. I can understand your concern about needing a higher grade for admission into the accounting program. As you requested, I have reviewed the scores on the final two papers you submitted.

After reviewing the first paper, I think the score should remain as it is. For the second paper, however, I would feel fine about increasing the score by five points. These extra points bring your semester total to 348, which is still within the B+ range. Had the score been 360, you would have qualified for an A– grade.

Let me suggest two additional options that might help your GPA. First, you could visit with professors in your other classes and see if they will raise your grades. Second, consider retaking Business Communication 320 and try to improve your grade the second time around.

Best wishes,

Professor John Doe

Figure 3.2 Most bad-news letters employ an indirect approach.

visual mental image. The following examples illustrate the four types of agendas.

Quantify. Since February 1, we have lost three major accounts because of our late product deliveries. The following *three* sections explain the details of these lost accounts.

Identify. Thanks for your July 13 letter asking about employment in our new plant in your city. Let me explain (a) *our hiring dates* and (b) *our policies for employment with our firm.*

Organize. Since talking with you in Denver last week, I have thought a lot about your idea concerning acquiring the Bronson property. I'm convinced that such a move would not be in the best interest of our company. Here are my perceptions of the disadvantages of this idea, *listed in order of significance.*

Symbolize. After months of work, I'm pleased to report that the details are in place for our upgraded retirement package. The key features of this new package are like *four wheels on a car.*

As you can see, each example previews the body of the message, programming the reader's mind to receive the body information in a systematic way. With an agenda that immediately precedes well-organized text, readers are able to read, process, and understand the information more quickly, efficiently, and effectively than they are with text that has no agenda and that is poorly organized.

In spite of the value of inserting agendas in writing, poorly written agendas can interrupt the flow of communication. An effective agenda will not draw undue attention to itself, but will flow naturally. The first of the following three agenda examples is stylistically weak and wordy; the second and third examples reflect more stylistically effective approaches:

Too wordy and mechanical: I will now cover three main topics in this email. They are as follows: (a) social security, (b) health care, and (c) personal savings.

Acceptable style: When you plan for retirement, evaluate your (a) social security, (b) health care, and (c) personal savings.

Acceptable style: When you plan for retirement, evaluate the three areas of social security, health care, and personal savings.

The following three examples illustrate different ways to visually emphasize the elements of an agenda:

Employ bolding, italics, or both for agenda words.

Let me explain the **knowledge**, **skills**, and **experience** required for the police chief position.

Include agenda words preceded by alphabetic markers.

Let me explain the (a) knowledge, (b) skills, and (c) experience required for the police chief position.

Arrange agendas vertically, each preceded by a bullet (most appropriate for longer documents).

Let me explain the three categories of requirements of the police chief position:

- Knowledge
- Skills
- Experience

Be wise in using agendas. They are useful in medium-length and long messages, but short messages often don't need them. For example, a full-page memo and a 13-page report would both benefit from an agenda, but a short two-line email would not. In fact, forcing an agenda into a very short message might be counterproductive. The letter in Figure 3.3 contains an agenda that previews the body paragraphs.

Dear Mr. Dixon:

I am pleased to respond to your request for information about Jason Brown. The following paragraphs describe his (a) communication and (b) people skills.

First, Jason is an effective communicator. He has excellent use of the language and writes clearly and persuasively. In his oral presentations he also excels. When presenting, he connects well with his audience, and his delivery is steady and unhurried.

Second, Jason has outstanding people skills. He always has a ready smile and is very easy to be around. He reads people well and is an exceptional team player. He remains calm and in control even is stressful situations. He quickly wins the confidence of others he meets, and he works hard to maintain his good reputation.

I strongly recommend Jason as one who has excellent potential. If you should hire him, I believe you would be very pleased with the results.

Sincerely,

Pat Alexander

Figure 3.3 OABC messages include an agenda to preview the body of the message.

Body

The body usually comprises the largest portion of the text, often as much as 80 to 90 percent of the total. Thus, make sure the information meets the highest of standards.

Content that is clear, correct, complete, and compelling will be more effective:

- Clear: The message must be logical, coherent, and easy to understand.
- Correct: The information must contain no factual errors and must properly cite all sources.
- Complete: The content must contain all the necessary details needed by the readers, including all applicable 5W2H information.
- Compelling: The material must be relevant and the presentation of it impactful to the reader.

In addition to the quality of the content, give careful attention to the organization of the information, as explained in Chapter 2. For messages that have an agenda, the body will follow the structure stated in the agenda. But even for documents without an agenda, the body information should be well organized.

For example, a trend analysis would likely contain significant numeric data and be organized in chronological order (year 1, year 2, year 3, etc.); an evaluation of three job applicants could be organized in order of quality (best candidate, second-best candidate, etc.); and the explanation of a new policy could be organized chronologically (review of current policy, followed by introduction of new policy) or nonchronologically by topic (an item-by-item comparison of elements in the current and new policies).

The important point is to include the best content possible and to organize it in a logical manner. Too often writers simply organize the content in the sequence it was in when it came into their mind. That is acceptable when creating the free list for bottom-up outlining, but for the actual writing, the material should be well organized.

The following sections give additional information to help you compose effective and well-organized text for the body of informative and persuasive messages.

Informative Messages

The body of informative messages can include many different types of information, such as that which defines, describes, classifies, explains, discusses, compares, analyzes, evaluates, illustrates, applies, or instructs, as shown in the following examples.

- Define civil and criminal lawsuits.
- Describe how the new procedure will affect our workforce requirements.
- Classify various insurance options into different categories.
- Explain our company's benefits package.
- Discuss the advantages and disadvantages of merging with another company.
- Compare the effectiveness of direct sales and internet sales.
- Analyze how a new product release will affect sales of our current products.
- Evaluate the strengths and weaknesses of different computer systems.
- Illustrate how a product is manufactured.
- Apply the principle of delegation in a business context.
- Instruct how to process an insurance claim.

Informative messages must be written in a brain-friendly manner so the material is clear. For instance, you could give a basic explanation, show a visual diagram, tell a story, give

an example, or use a metaphor. In some cases you might also go from the known to the unknown—begin with a reference to what the reader already knows and then explain the new information. For example, to explain a new marketing concept, you could briefly refer to the current marketing strategy, give a conceptual explanation of the new strategy, give an example of the concept in a real-world application, compare the new concept with the current strategy, and then list the benefits that would be achieved by adopting the new concept. Following your presentation of the material, the readers' understanding should be clear enough that they could explain the concept to someone else.

An informative message can often be organized around one or more of the 5W2H factors (who, what, where, when, why, how, and how much). For example, a "when" oriented informative message might be as follows:

> Our training retreat next Tuesday will include the following sessions. We'll begin at 9:00 a.m. with a welcome from our president. From 9:30 a.m. until noon we will receive training on the new federal tax laws pertaining to information privacy. After lunch from 12:00 to 1:00 p.m., we will receive two hours of training on the new changes that have been made to our computer-input screens. Following a half-hour break at 3:00 p.m., we'll participate in a fun team-development activity that will run until 5:00 p.m.

A "why" oriented informative message might look something like this:

> I have organized next Tuesday's training meeting for three main reasons. First, our new company president wants to have an opportunity to meet all of us and give us his vision of the next five years. Second, we all need more training on the new tax laws and on our new computer-input screens. Third, we could benefit from some team-building activities to help us become more effective in working together.

Further, a "how" oriented message could explain the actions taken by various people in the creation and marketing of a new product, and a "where" oriented message could describe the sales effectiveness of different markets across the U.S. (e.g., Northeast, Southeast, Midwest, etc.).

Following your writing of an informative message, ask a colleague or friend to read the message and give you feedback regarding its clarity and effectiveness (Chapter 5 gives additional information on revising and editing).

Persuasive Messages

Unlike informative messages that require no response from the reader, persuasive messages are written to generate action, such as the following:

- Persuade to hire a certain person
- Persuade to purchase a new computer
- Persuade to merge two departments in the organization
- Persuade to refund money you spent on a product

When you persuade, you are claiming that the idea you are proposing is the most appropriate action to take, given the current situation. To be effective, address two main why questions: why should we address this problem and why is your recommendation the best. Build your recommendation on a solid foundation of facts, credible opinions, logical thinking, and examples. In your argument you might cite examples, give hard data, quote experts, and include additional evidence as proof of your claim. Include visually oriented elements, such as photographs and diagrams to create a strong visual message that sticks! Also, take time to address alternate proposals, and explain why they are not as good as yours.

As you attempt to persuade, strive to achieve a win-win outcome. Explain how everyone will be better off if they accept your proposal. And perhaps explain how they will be worse off if they don't. In all cases involving persuasion, look at the situation through the eyes of the audience, and try to anticipate their objections. As you are presenting reasons to support the recommendation, they might be thinking of reasons to reject it. Strive to frame their objections in ways that will actually build your own case.

A persuasive message might also include the results of three basic processes: analysis, evaluation, and synthesis. An easy way to think of these processes is to associate them with three questions: What? So what? Now what?

- Analysis (What?) is the process of tearing something apart so you can understand it. Asking all the 5W2H questions (who, what, where, when, why, how, and how much) helps to complete the analysis step.
- Evaluation (So what?) is the process of judging the relative goodness or badness of something. Asking "so what" helps to isolate the implications of each part of the analysis. Whereas analysis can often be more quantitative in nature, evaluation is more qualitative. Evaluation usually involves some established system for rating, such as textual rating (excellent, good, satisfactory, marginal, unsatisfactory), numeric rating (5, 4, 3, 2, 1), numeric ranking (1st, 2nd, 3rd), or actual measurement (3.06, 6.93, 8.77, 10.41). In most cases, provide the evaluation criteria and the measurement methods used in performing the evaluation.
- Synthesis (Now what?) is the process of putting things together in a new and better way. It is engineering a

solution to the problem. Asking "now what" helps to generate creative thinking about how to improve the current situation.

An example will help illustrate what, so what, and now what processes. Assume that you supervise the work of five people. To understand "what" each person is accomplishing, you analyze their work and discover that Persons A and B are producing an average of ten units per day, Persons C and D are producing an average of seven units per day, and Person E is producing three units per day. Moving on to the "so what" question, you judge the work of Persons A and B to be very good, the work of Persons C and D to be fairly good, but the work of Person E to be poor. In response to the "now what" question, you decide to reward Persons A and B with a higher wage, provide additional training for Persons C and D, and terminate the employment of Person E.

A persuasive argument might also employ either a direct approach (*what* followed by *why*) or an indirect approach (*why* followed by *what*). The direct approach may be used for situations needing only a moderate amount of persuasion, with the indirect approach used for more difficult persuasion situations. Both indirect and direct approaches are illustrated as follows:

Indirect, bottom-up approach, with reasons (the *why*) preceding the action (the *what*):

Reason: Our employee Marilyn is quitting next month. That will leave a vacancy on the assembly line.

Action: *Therefore,* we need to hire someone to replace Marilyn.

Or you could reverse the sequence as follows.

Direct, top-down approach, with the action (the *what*) preceding the reason (the *why*):

Action: We need to hire someone to replace Marilyn, *because . . .*

Reason: She is quitting next month. That will leave a vacancy on the assembly line.

Closing

After the body, close the message. The closing may summarize the document's key points, draw appropriate conclusions, recommend a certain action, reaffirm the main thrust of the message, or provide some other closing comment relevant to the situation. (Figures 3.4 and 3.5 give examples of a letter with and without the OABC pattern applied.) Short documents may need only a sentence or two in the closing section, such as the following:

Thank you for your interest in our firm; we look forward to receiving your application. Please contact me at 593–463–29XX if you have any additional questions.

Longer documents generally need longer closing sections, often with longer summaries and multiple conclusions and recommendations. A conclusion is a generalized finding (e.g., a minority of the employees like the new plan). Remember that a finding is detailed data in the body of a report (e.g., only 22 percent of the employees like the new plan). A recommendation is a forward-looking suggestion (e.g., we should discontinue the new plan). The following three examples include sample summary, conclusions, and recommendations paragraphs.

Summary: As the foregoing analysis shows, the issue of whether to raise the minimum wage is a complex problem. Opponents argue that increasing the minimum wage will do little to help the poor because of the resulting rise in unemployment and inflation. Conversely, supporters of a minimum-wage increase feel that employment and inflation will not rise significantly and that the poverty trap will just become worse without an increase in the wage.

Conclusions. In view of this study, three conclusions can be drawn: (1) Parking is perceived by students to be a major problem at the university, (2) public trans-

---

Before OABC

Dear Mr. Matthews:

Thank you for your resume and letter expressing interest in our Police Chief position. This position requires mature knowledge of all aspects of law enforcement at the local government level, including governmental laws, rules, and regulations; traffic control; crowd control; and emergency police procedures. It also requires knowledge of city government administration.

The position involves the ability to plan and execute police department activities with respect to personnel and equipment, including budget management. Communication is also a vital component, with the key audiences being the mayor, city council members, administrators, police force, and the general public. The minimum experience required for the police chief is eight years of work in law enforcement, including five years at highly responsible administrative or command assignments (level of lieutenant or above).

If your schedule allows, we would like to meet with you at 10 a.m. on April 23 in our conference room (B-130 of the city offices). Please call Penny, my executive assistant, at (803) 357–87XX to confirm this appointment. We look forward to meeting you.

Sincerely,

Sydney Smith, City Manager

Figure 3.4 Without an agenda, readers have to discover the information structure on their own.

After OABC

Dear Mr. Matthews:

Thank you for your resume and letter expressing interest in our Police Chief position. The following paragraphs provide information regarding the (a) knowledge, (b) skills, and (c) experience required for this position.

Knowledge. This position requires mature knowledge of all aspects of law enforcement at the local government level, including governmental laws, rules, and regulations; traffic control; crowd control; and emergency police procedures. It also requires knowledge of city government administration.

Skills. The position involves the ability to plan and execute police department activities with respect to personnel and equipment, including budget management. Communication is also a vital component, with the key audiences being the mayor, city council members, administrators, police force, and the general public.

Experience. The minimum experience required for the police chief is eight years of work in law enforcement, including five years at highly responsible administrative or command assignments (level of lieutenant or above).

If your schedule allows, we would like to meet with you at 10 a.m. on April 23 in our conference room (B-130 of the city offices). Please call Penny, my executive assistant, at (803) 357–87XX to confirm this appointment. We look forward to meeting you.

Sincerely,

Sydney Smith, City Manager

Figure 3.5 An agenda informs the reader of the message structure.

portation is seen as only a partial solution to the parking problem, and (3) students are willing to pay higher parking rates for a high-rise parking facility closer to the center of campus.

Recommendations: In light of the foregoing conclusions, Widget International should take two actions: (1) Purchase eight Model X computers and (2) purchase one digital camera for producing corporate proposals. These actions should be completed as quickly as possible.

In addition to the major OABC sections in a large document, you may use an OABC pattern within subsections of the document. For example, an auditing firm's proposal might have major sections about the tasks to be completed by the firm, the task deadlines, the audit team, and the cost of the audit. An opening and agenda for the third section might be as follows:

> [Opening] We will send to your site a team of experienced and highly trained professionals, ensuring that the work performed will meet your highest expectations. [Agenda] The following paragraphs introduce the audit team, along with their professional credentials.

After the body, which would be a developed version of the agenda, the closing might read as follows:

> [Closing] As you can see, this team of auditors has both the experience and the training to conduct a thorough and efficient audit of your operations, assuring that your audit report will provide the information needed for effectively managing your firm and meeting IRS requirements.

STRENGTHEN THE CONTENT

Once you get the information arranged in an appropriate pattern, consider the following three ways to strengthen the content.

Write with Power

To be effective in communication, you must get your message across with power. This requires more than just transferring information from your mind to the mind of the audience. It requires creativity in how you frame your argument or message. For example, Martin Luther King's "I Have a Dream" speech was a message about the problem of racial discrimination. But he didn't just give a bland list of facts about the history of black people. Rather, he framed the content of his speech as a forward-looking "dream" and used that theme repeatedly to create a mental picture and to stir the emotions of his listeners.

Likewise, you have innumerable ways to convey the message you want to get across in each of your messages. You can convey your facts and opinions in a dry, unimaginative way, or you can develop more powerful and interesting ways that touch the heart, as well as the mind, and motivate the reader to action. Some frequently used tactics follow:

- Give the most important ideas first. People remember best what they encounter first in a message, especially if it is given in a creative and emphatic way.

- Simplify your key points. Three points can be remembered better and longer than a dozen.

- Give simple, clear interpretations of numeric data. Even if you have to present a mass of data, highlight the few key interpretations that you want the audience to remember.

- Include imagery, stories, metaphors, and concrete examples to make an idea come alive in the reader's mind and to match the human brain's preference for visuals.

- Use visuals. A well-designed chart or graph can indeed be worth a thousand words.

- Give a name to a proposed idea. Rather than using words like "company unification strategy," develop a stronger, more creative title, like "All-for-One Plan."

- Emphasize the serious consequences of ignoring problems, and highlight the key benefits of implementing solutions.

- Highlight and contrast the differences in opposites or alternatives, such as Product A vs. Product B, Plan A vs. Plan B, etc.

- Repeat key words or phrases throughout the text to enhance recall.

- Appeal to the heart by including information that touches human emotions or values.

These and many other rhetorical and linguistic tactics can be employed effectively in framing the messages you write. There is no quick and easy way to develop the most effective message tactics, but through pondering, brainstorming, and discussing with other people, you can generate approaches that will enhance the power and impact of your messages.

Avoid Logic Fallacies

When your objective is to persuade, the audience will evaluate your argument before being persuaded to accept your point of view. Any fallacy in your logic will weaken your persuasion. To persuade others to agree with you, base your arguments on clear, unbiased, and careful reasoning.

Non sequiturs (Latin for "it does not follow") are errors in logic that can arise from incomplete, illogical, or careless thinking. Listed below are some examples of *non sequitur* reasoning, also referred to as logic fallacies.

1. *Bandwagon evidence:* Arguing that an idea is good or bad just because a majority of the people believe it to be so. "Everybody is doing it, so we should, too."

2. *Either-or thinking:* Arguing that there are only two options or outcomes when more exist. "It's either Julie or Gavin; take your pick." [The truth is that other people could also be considered.]

3. *Evaluation by association:* Arguing that an idea is good because the person who is proposing it is well known, famous, well liked, or in a position of power; or arguing that an idea is bad because its proponent lacks credibility or is unpopular or not well liked. "Our company president eats at that restaurant, so it must be good."

4. *False analogy:* Arguing that because two things are similar in some ways, they are similar in other ways, without any logical support or evidence to justify extending the comparison. "That book about a boy wizard was really successful, so my book about a boy wizard will sell millions as well."

5. *False causality:* Arguing that because two items occur together, one must be causing the other. "Ever since we hired Isaac in late December, our retail sales have been dropping." [The truth is that retail sales always drop after Christmas.]

6. *Hasty generalization:* Making sweeping generalizations by relying on one or just a few cases as evidence of proof. "Our new store did well in Chicago, so new stores should do well in other areas."

7. *Lack of evidence to the contrary:* Arguing that an idea is good because no one has proven it false, or that an idea is false because no one has proven it true. "No one has been able to convict him in a court of law, so he must not be guilty."

8. *Recency persuasion:* Arguing that something is good simply because it is newer, or of more recent origin, than something else. "This is the newest product development in the Brand X line, so we ought to buy it."

9. *Slippery slope:* Arguing to condemn an idea because it might eventually lead to an undesirable end. "If we vote for a new library, the mayor will want a new city center and then a new police station. So we had better not approve a new library."

10. *Tradition:* Arguing that some action is right or good because of traditional acceptance of the action. "We've always processed insurance claims that way in this department, so there's no reason to change now."

11. *Anonymous Authority:* Making an authoritative statement without reference to a specific reliable source. "Research says that most mergers fail after three years."

In addition to avoiding faulty logic in your thinking, avoid the following negative tactics that damage the decision-making process.

1. *Ad hominem:* Attacking the person rather than the argument. "The people in that department are just a bunch of whiners; why should we listen to them?"

2. *Straw man:* Describing another person's argument in a distorted way that makes it easy to reject. "Company X just wants us to buy its products without any consideration at all for quality or price."

3. *Red herring:* Making a deliberate attempt to change the subject or divert the argument away from the central issue. "I realize that our software testing might be a bottleneck in the process, but what about the fact that our company had its most profitable year ever?"

Two final pitfalls to be wary of when writing are the common and sometimes unconscious tendencies to be self-serving or short-sighted. Focusing only on one's own needs at the expense of others or focusing only on the present rather than on long-term considerations can inhibit clear, objective, and careful reasoning. It can foster *non sequitur* arguments, damage credibility, and produce poor decision-making. Over time, being self-serving or short-sighted can ruin careers, damage relationships, and even destroy companies. At the same time, never underestimate the positive influence that clear thinking and coherent communication can have on individuals and organizations.

Compose Effective Paragraphs

The concluding section of this chapter includes instruction on writing effective paragraphs. Typically the paragraphs you write will be one of three types—introductory, body, or concluding—according to their function in the document.

Introductory paragraphs come at the beginning of a document and provide background information, present the issue or topic, and draw the reader into the document. They also provide a transition into the main body of the document.

Disaster can occur night or day and without warning. It can force you from your neighborhood or confine you to your home. It can result in loss of water, gas, electricity, or telephones and cause major disruptions in normal daily routines. Local public safety officials and relief workers can be called on to help, but they cannot reach everyone right away, especially if the disaster is widespread. The following information will describe actions your family can take to prepare for disaster.

Body paragraphs present the main content of the document including research findings, analysis, explanation, statistics, examples, etc. Most of your paragraphs will likely be body paragraphs.

FEMA's Family Protection Program and the American Red Cross's Disaster Education Program have identified three steps that have helped families survive disasters most effectively. First, families have determined the disasters that could happen, such as floods, fire, tornadoes, and chemical spills. Second, they have created a disaster plan for each of the disaster types. Third, they regularly practice their disaster plan several times each year to ensure that everyone is prepared.

Concluding paragraphs come at the end of a document and provide summaries, conclusions, recommendations, and re-emphasis of key points.

To minimize the impact of a disaster to your family, you should implement the three steps outlined above. To find out more, contact your local office of each of these organizations or visit their sites on the web. Don't be caught unprepared!

As you compose paragraphs, especially those in the body of a document, remember five important standards: coherence, length, organization, unity, and development (remembered with the acronym CLOUD).

COHERENCE

Make sure the content flows logically from one sentence to the next. Coherence is achieved through systematic movement from one related idea to the next. Notice the difference in coherence between the two following paragraphs.

No: During the early years of a new business, expenses are high and income is low. They often operate at a loss for many months. They have to have a good product or service to succeed. If customers don't like the product or service, they will shop elsewhere. The main reason businesses fail in their infancy is lack of ability to make money. Roughly 50 percent of new businesses fail in the first five years. They have to advertise successfully. The main cause of failure is that they don't make enough money early enough in life of the business. It takes a lot of money to start most businesses.

Yes: Roughly 50 percent of new businesses fail during the first five years of operation. The main reason is their lack of ability to make a profit. Even if they have a good product or service, income is limited and expenses are high during these early years, including high advertising costs, high personnel costs, and high production costs. Thus, successful businesses must have a solid source of financing to endure their years of infancy.

In addition to logical coherence, be sure your sentences have appropriate cohesion, both within and between sentences. For instance, inserting a transition bridge at the beginning of the second sentence establishes a clear connection with the first sentence.

No: As the deadline for implementing the federal legislation drew near, company executives became increasingly anxious. Many executives hired outside consultants for assistance. [Writing is somewhat choppy.]

Yes: As the deadline for implementing the federal legislation drew near, company executives became increasingly anxious. *This anxiety prompted* many of them to hire outside consultants for assistance. [The transition bridge links the two sentences and improves cohesion.]

The following samples show different types of transition words.

Addition: *In addition,* she is an LPN. *Further,* she has six years of experience.

Example: *For instance,* she received a recommendation letter from the company president.

Comparison: *Similarly,* Gavin also worked as a systems engineer at A & B, Inc.

Forecasting: Her outstanding education is complemented by the *following* three key experiences.

Consequence: *Because* his father passed away on Sunday, he will not be traveling with us to New York.

Condition: *If* we can get the Williams contract, we'll gain a much greater foothold in the market place.

Time: *Later,* we'll go to dinner at the Riverside Restaurant.

Place: *There* we'll review your redesign plans.

LENGTH

Avoid writing paragraphs that are so long that they look

difficult to read (e.g., longer than six or seven lines for emails and correspondence, and nine or ten lines for longer reports). If you write a paragraph that looks too long and too difficult to read, find the most logical breaking point and divide the paragraph in two.

Sometimes a one-sentence paragraph is best!

ORGANIZATION

Generally use a direct approach , with a topic sentence leading the way. Feel free to also add a summarizing sentence at the end of the paragraph as appropriate. To check your document for direct paragraph organization, skim through the document reading only the first sentence of each paragraph and see if you get a generally good sense of the main information. If you don't, go back through and write better topic sentences for each of the paragraphs.

The following paragraph illustrates the direct approach, with a topic sentence at the beginning; it also contains a summary sentence at the end.

> *Two major flexible work arrangements can help reduce employees' childcare concerns.* First, flextime work schedules allow workers flexibility in their work times. With this arrangement, days are divided into core time (hours when employees *must* be at work) and flextime (the earlier morning and later afternoon hours when employees have flexibility). Second, compressed work schedules allow workers to work more hours during some days and fewer or no hours on others. For example, a person could work for ten hours a day Monday through Thursday and then take Friday off. Both of these flexible arrangements are welcomed by employees with children.

The next paragraph is written with the indirect approach:

> Flextime work schedules allow workers flexibility in their work times. With a flextime arrangement, days are divided into core times (hours when employees must be at work) and flextime (earlier morning and later afternoon hours when employees have flexibility). Compared to flextime, compressed work schedules allow workers to work more hours during some days and fewer or no hours on others. For example, a person could work for ten hours a day Monday through Thursday and then take Friday off. *Both flextime and compressed work schedules give work-time flexibility to employees and are welcomed by employees with young children.*

UNITY

Ensure that all sentences refer to the same content introduced in the topic sentence. For example, if the topic sentence of a paragraph is about shrubs in landscaping, the paragraph content should be about shrubs. If the writer wants to talk about trees as well as shrubs, the topic sentence would need to include both types of vegetation. Notice the difference between the following two paragraphs.

No: Many businesses are recognizing the importance of having employee fitness programs. Often a fitness trainer is hired, either full or part time. Obesity is becoming a major issue in our country. Many people are unhappy and unfulfilled at work, and this leads to high levels of turnover in some industries. Having a good fit between a person's talents and interests is important in long-term employee satisfaction.

Yes: Many businesses are recognizing the importance of having employee-fitness programs. This trend is happening because many people fail to get enough exercise and to eat well, thus contributing to an increasing percentage of our citizens who are out of shape and overweight. Employee-fitness programs often include onsite gym facilities, a fitness trainer (either part-time or full-time), health-improvement seminars, exercise programs, and financial rewards for employees who complete the exercise programs. As a result of these programs, many companies are finding positive results even beyond improved employee health, including reduced health insurance costs, higher morale, and added recruitment incentives.

DEVELOPMENT

Be sure to give adequate supporting detail about the topic sentence. You can develop, or support, the main point of a paragraph in various ways, as shown in the following examples.

Explanations:

—Details: "Let me give you more specific information about the new plan. . . ."

—Logic: "We first observed a 46 percent decline in X; then we noticed a large decrease in Y; therefore, we concluded that . . ."

Illustrations:

—Examples: "For example, last month I noticed several employees returning late from . . ."

—Metaphors: "This is a societal cancer that is spreading its tentacles from the teenage population to . . ."

—Stories: "Last week I had an experience that intensifies the need for urgent action. . . ."

Evaluations:

—Qualitative comparisons: "Let's compare the two weapons side by side. . . ."

—Testimonials: "Captain Parkinson tried this approach and highly endorses . . ."

Applications:

—Past: "The finance department tried this approach last month. . . ."

—Future: "You could use this method in a variety of situations, including . . ."

Notice the difference in development in the next two paragraphs.

No: Good business writers should know how to compose effective paragraphs. Paragraphs are usually the combination of several sentences related to the same topic.

Yes: Good business writers should know how to compose effective paragraphs. Effective paragraphs should exhibit five major attributes. First, paragraphs should begin with a topic sentence, which reveals the central focus of the paragraph. Second, the content of all sentences should relate to the topic sentence. Third, the content of each sentence should logically follow the content of the preceding sentence. Fourth, the topic of the paragraph should be adequately fully explained and developed. And fifth, the paragraph should be short enough that it looks relatively easy to read.

Now read the two following paragraphs and identify the differences in paragraph quality.

Kerry's work has been a problem ever since he was hired. I have talked with him on three different occasions about the need to improve, but nothing has happened. I plan to let him go on July 11. His work affects at least a dozen other employees. His performance record and my notes are attached.

I have decided to terminate Kerry's employment, effective July 11. The main reason for this decision is his inability to keep up with the assembly line. He consistently holds up the line, causing delays for at least a dozen other employees whose work is affected by his slow speed. I have talked with Kerry on three separate occasions about the need to increase his output, but no significant improvement has

occurred. Kerry's performance record and the documentation of my interviews are attached.

The first paragraph is lacking in three of the five paragraph standards. To its credit, it is short enough for easy reading and it does have unity, but it has problems with organization, coherence, and development. For example, it does not begin with the topic sentence, that Kerry is being fired. It also bounces from one idea to the next, with no obvious logical pathway. Further, it fails to develop what the problem is with Kerry's work.

The second paragraph reflects good strength in all five paragraph standards. It begins with the main point, moves logically through the reasoning behind the decision, displays appropriate length, ensures good unity by sticking with the topic of discussion, and gives sufficient detail to understand the reasoning behind the decision to terminate.

SUMMARY

When composing business messages, first clarify the main purpose of the message—to inform or to persuade. Consider writing a working title to guide your thinking. The next step is to use an outline or proven pattern to guide your writing. The OABC (opening, agenda, body, closing) pattern is useful for many messages. The opening helps bring the reader into the context of the message. The agenda forecasts the body of the message. Four types of agendas may be used: quantify, identify, organize, and symbolize.

The body of a message delivers the promise made by the agenda. It is the longest part of the message and contains the most substantive information. It may be organized on either a chronological or non-chronological basis. The closing segment of a document may summarize key points, draw appropriate conclusions, recommend certain actions, or provide some other closing comment relevant to the situation.

The content of a message must be complete, correct, and relevant. It must be free from bias and careless thinking. *Non sequitur* reasoning must be avoided, along with negative argument tactics. In addition to having solid content, the writing must be clear, coherent, and effective. The paragraphs should measure up to the standards of coherence, length, organization, unity, and development (CLOUD).

CHAPTER QUESTIONS

1. What is a working title and how is it used?

2. What are the major differences between informative and persuasive messages?

3. What is the difference between the direct and the indi-

rect approach to writing a message?

4. What do the letters OABC represent? How is OABC used in writing?

5. What are the four types of agendas? Should an agenda be included in all written messages? Why?

6. What are the major benefits of agendas in written messages?

7. What is the difference between findings, conclusions, and recommendations?

8. List five common fallacies found in people's reasoning.

9. Explain the paragraph attributes represented by the acronym CLOUD.

10. List three different ways to develop the main point in a business message.

CHAPTER ACTIVITIES

1. Write a memo in which you briefly describe three websites related to one of your favorite hobbies, sports, or topics of interest. Use the OABC pattern. Include quantifying, identifying, and organizing information in the agenda.

2. Write three versions of the same agenda, each applying a different agenda type, such as quantify, identify, and symbolize.

3. Write three paragraphs to demonstrate that you know how to apply the attributes of CLOUD. Paragraph 1 should be chronologically sequenced (e.g., how to perform a task); paragraph 2 should contrast the differences and similarities between two products (e.g., product A vs. product B); and paragraph 3 should apply a most-to-least sequence (e.g., top three sports teams).

4. Go to the federal government's internet website (http://www.usa.gov/) and find a report published by one of the government divisions, such as the Government Accountability Office (GAO). Select three separate paragraphs in the report and evaluate them using the CLOUD attributes. Then rewrite the paragraphs so they meet all CLOUD standards. Include the name and the web address of the report.

5. On the internet, you have advertised for sale something you own (e.g., bicycle, computer, car). A person has responded to your ad but wants more information. Write a reply that persuades the person to buy.

6. You are going to meet a friend for lunch at one of your favorite restaurants. Write an email explaining all the details, including how to get to the restaurant from your friend's home or apartment. *Note:* You may not include a map or hyperlink in this message.

7. Write two versions of an email to a faculty member, inviting that person to speak at an upcoming meeting of your student group. In one version, use the direct order; in the other, use the indirect order.

8. Your company is going to implement a new training program in all its branch offices around the world. In an email you send to explain the change, what information would you include to ensure that the topic is fully developed?

9. A local politician is proposing that your city build a new recreation center, police station, library, or create a new park or other new facility (you choose which one to respond to). Give three logical reasons why this proposal is a good idea as well as why it is a bad idea. Cite three additional illogical reasons (using non sequiturs) why someone might favor or oppose the idea.

ENHANCING VISUAL APPEAL

Workplace documents that contain too many text-only pages give a negative first impression—few people like to read pages of written analysis with no graphic relief. Yet many professionals focus only on the writing when they create business messages and reports. Numerous research studies conclude that undifferentiated text is less effective than text with various message-enhancement techniques, such as headings, business graphics, varied typography, and space (Frischknecht & Baker 2011). Therefore, expand your communication effectiveness by thinking visually, not just textually.

Even when you can't use actual graphics, you can use visually oriented words and metaphors to create a vivid picture in the reader's mind. Consider, for example, the following two textual descriptions of a digital camera. The first example relies on nonvisual text; the second example uses visually oriented wording.

Example A: This digital camera gives you everything you need for your next photo shoot . . . and it is amazingly small!

Example B: This digital camera gives you everything you need for your next photo shoot . . . and it fits right in your shirt pocket!

"Amazingly small" is helpful, but "fits right in your shirt pocket" gives readers something they can see in their mind. Consider another example of symbolism: "We dropped the pass, even though the ball was right in our hands." This sports metaphor is a visually symbolic way of saying, "A good opportunity came to us, but we didn't take advantage

of it." When using metaphors, make sure the audience has experience with the symbolism used; otherwise, miscommunication will result.

Many writers quit working on their documents after they finish editing the text, overlooking the need for visual enhancement. Very short emails and memos are generally acceptable without visual enrichment because they require so little time to read. But for all other messages you write, take time to enhance their visual design.

The following text describes a four-step procedure that guides you through the design aspects of writing. This procedure, represented by the acronym HATS, stands for headings, art, typography, and spacing (Baker 2001).

HEADINGS

Add headings to your documents to enhance information access—which refers to the degree to which the critical information is easily accessible to the reader. Just as people use links to navigate through internet sites, they can use headings to skim through written business messages and find the information they want to read in detail. However, even though you add headings in a document, write the text as though no headings have been used. This action will help ensure good coherence even if people skip over headings and read only the body text.

For long documents, consider inserting a table of contents as an additional navigation aid. For shorter documents you won't need a table of contents, but headings will still be useful. Two aspects of headings—adequacy and hierarchy—are most important.

Adequacy. All documents, including emails, memos, and letters, should have an adequate number of headings to serve as navigation signposts. These headings will enable the reader to see the general structure of the text and to skim the document, stopping for detailed reading as desired.

Hierarchy. For longer documents, headings should reveal the information structure. Variations in typography (font, alignment, bold, italics, case, and size) and placement (side, center) identify first-, second-, and third-level headings. The following examples show three levels of headings, with various typographical treatments: a major heading (Arial, centered, bold, all capitals, 16 point), a second-level heading (Arial, side, bold, initial capitals, 14 point), and a third-level heading (Times New Roman, side, bold, italic, 12 point). Note: In business writing, one heading should not occur immediately after another heading without text in between.

MAJOR HEADING

Second-level Heading

Third-level Heading

Often headings will relate back to the agenda of the message. The relationship between the headings and the agenda can be specified in various levels, as shown in the three examples that follow. No one way is correct, so just use the approach that works best in each situation, making sure the audience recognizes the connection between the agenda and the body.

Heading inserted as the first word(s) of a paragraph:

Knowledge. This position requires mature knowledge of all aspects of law enforcement at the local government level, including but not limited to . . .

Heading placed on the line preceding the paragraph:

Knowledge

This position requires mature knowledge of all aspects of law enforcement at the local government level, including but not limited to . . . .

Heading placed two lines before the paragraph:

Knowledge

This position requires mature knowledge of all aspects of law enforcement at the local government level, including but not limited to . . .

The wording of headings can take one of three forms: topic, statement, and question. Topic headings are the most commonly used form. Statement headings are used less often, but they convey more information than topic headings and are therefore effective in conveying useful information even if the audience doesn't read the subsequent text. Question headings can be used to help emphasize issues being considered, and are useful in guiding readers who are searching for answers to specific questions. The following examples illustrate the differences.

Topic Heading: Intellectual Property

Statement Heading: Intellectual Property Plays a Key Role in XYZ Company

Question Heading: What Role Does Intellectual Property Play in XYZ Company?

Table 4.1 Visual Communication Alternatives

Information Type	Effective Ways to Present
Who	Photographs, organization charts
What	Line drawings, photographs, concept maps
Where	Geographic maps
When	Flow charts, Gantt charts, PERT charts
Why	Cause-and-effect drawings, concept maps
How	Process charts, line drawings, concept maps or models
How much	Tables, charts (bar, pie, line)

ART

Add artistic and visual aspects to your written messages. Art refers to the use of visuals, such as tables, bar charts, maps, organization charts, and flow-process charts. Visuals often can communicate more quickly than words. Think how difficult it would be to explain in words all the information that is quickly conveyed with a detailed map.

Too often, writers use text as their default means of communicating all kinds of information. Instead, they should first consider the type of the information and then determine what form of display will most efficiently and effectively convey the message. The Table 4.1 gives some options for communicating visually oriented information.

When you insert a visual item in a report, remember three "I's"—*introduce*, *insert*, and *interpret*. First, introduce the visual with a statement like, "Figure 3 illustrates the differences between Site A and Site B." Second, insert the visual within the text as soon after the point of introduction as possible. Third, interpret the visual. The purpose of the interpretation is to tell about the key points you want the reader to learn from the visual. For example, you might say, "Figure 3 shows that production at Site B is more than twice the amount at Site A. Further, production at Site A has fallen by 5.5 percent during the last year." The introduction must always come before the visual, but the interpretation may come before or after, depending on the space constraints of the page where the graphic is placed.

Additional general guidelines for visuals are as follows:

1. Number visuals consecutively. For instance, number tables as Table 1, Table 2, etc. Number other visuals as Figure 1, Figure 2, etc. If the document only has only one table or only one figure, do not number it.

2. Develop a descriptive title for each visual. Instead of using an overly brief title like "20XX Sales," create a title like, "20XX Worldwide Sales of Leadership Training Materials."

3. Be consistent in placing figure and table numbers and titles. Many organizations place the number and title of tables and figures at the top of the visuals. Captions of photos are generally placed at the bottom. You will see variations of these guidelines, however, so adapt to the practices of each organization.

4. Keep graphics simple and easy to understand. Don't try to communicate too much information in one graph. Some people suggest a "five-second standard," which means that the reader should be able to understand the main message of a visual in about five seconds.

5. Use appropriate legends and call-outs to ensure good understanding. A legend is an explanatory list of the symbols or colors used in a chart. A call-out is explanatory text placed beside a graphic, with a line going from the explanatory text to the part of the graphic it is explaining. Legends and call-outs are particularly helpful with complex tables or graphics.

6. Cite appropriate source information in a footnote at the base of the graphic or table. Don't be guilty of plagiarism.

In addition to these general guidelines, a number of specifics for tables, bar and line graphs, pie graphs, and photographs and clip art are important to remember.

Tables

Tables consist of an information grid, with vertical columns and horizontal rows containing numeric or alphabetic information. Tables can consist of very simple and brief displays, such as Table XX in Figure 4.1, which contains only three columns and four rows of data, plus a total. This table also contains only horizontal lines to separate the data (although vertical lines could also be included). Notice that this table employs boldface type to make the headings and total row more visible.

Figure 4.2 illustrates a more complex table with addi-

Table XX. Industry Classification of Research Participants

Industry	NAICS Code	Number
Retail	44–45	84
Construction	23	68
Professional, Scientific and Technical Services	54	50
Health Care and Social Assistance	62	37
Total	**N/A**	**239**

Figure 4.1 A table consists of rows and columns of information, often with column headings and a total row.

Size of Company (# of employees)	Male Employees		Female Employees	
	Percent Yes	Percent No	Percent Yes	Percent No
<5	25.8	74.2	35.0	65.0
6–10	36.7	63.3	37.1	62.9
11–50	41.0	59.0	48.8	51.2
51–100	48.8	51.2	57.3	42.7
101–250	63.5	36.5	67.3	32.7
251–500	61.8	38.2	69.8	30.2
Total	**41.7**	**58.2**	**48.4**	**51.6**

Table XXX. Share of Employees With and Without Paid Sick Leave at Their Current Main Job—2001 (Small Businesses with 500 or Fewer Employees and Having Only a Single Establishment)

Source: Joel Popkin and Company. "Cost of Employee Benefits in Small and Large Businesses." Small Business Administration Home Page. August 2005. 22 May 2007 <http://www.sba.gov/advo/research/rs262tot.pdf >.

Figure 4.2 Complex tables can include numerous columns and braced headings.

tional rows and columns, as well as braced headings (major headings over secondary headings).

Remember five important guidelines as you create tables. First, keep tables rectangular in shape. Avoid the temptation to include cells that jut out from the rectangular shape of the table. Second, generally leave no empty cells. If data is missing for a cell, include a dashed line, N/A (not available), or black or gray fill, thus letting the reader know that the data omission was not accidental. Third, sequence the data in rows and columns in some logical way, such as alphabetical or from high to low. Fourth, use typographic enhancement for emphasis, such as boldfaced headings. Fifth, try to keep the entire contents of each table on one page. If you have to divide a table across pages, however, type "continued from page x" and repeat the column headings for easy reference.

Bar and Line Graphs

Bar and line graphs are the most common informational visuals used in business and government reports. In most cases, the vertical axis (Y axis) of the graph will represent some quantity, such as money, and the horizontal axis (X axis) will represent time, such as months or years. Figure 4.3 shows a bar chart with drug-arrest data for four parts of a city. At the top of each bar is a data label that gives the exact quantity of the bar.

Pictograms are sometimes used as a creative alternative to bar graphs. Instead of showing data as a bar, a pictogram uses small visual symbols (see Figure 4.4).

Figure 4.5 illustrates a line chart with number of self-employed business owners shown on the Y axis and data from 15 years shown on the X axis.

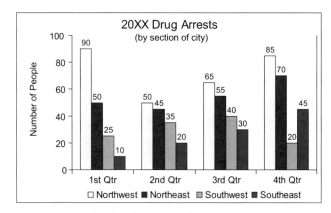

Figure 4.3 The height of the bars in bar graphs signifies the quantity of the data being measured.

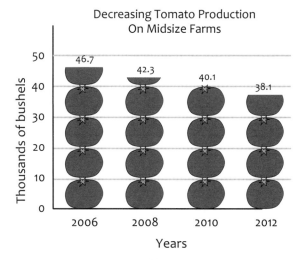

Figure 4.4 Pictograms use small symbols instead of bars to represent the data.

Number of Self-Employed Business Owners

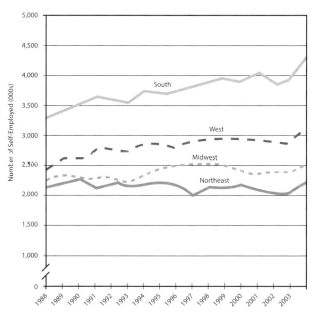

Figure 4.5 Line graphs typically show time on the X axis and quantity on the Y axis.
(Source: Robert W. Fairlie, "Self-Employed Business Ownership Rates in the United States: 1979–2003." Small Business Administration Home Page. December 2004. 22 May 2007 <http://www.sba.gov/advo/research/rs262tot.pdf>.)

Several guidelines are important to remember as you prepare bar and line charts. First, arrange bars in the best sequence, such as from high to low. Second, consider using data labels (except when too many data labels would make the chart look cluttered). Also, use a legend when you have more than one data series. Third, include titles for X and Y axes for clarification. Fourth, generally avoid placing red and green bars beside each other, because color-blind readers cannot tell the difference. Fifth, generally prefer two-dimensional bar charts, but if you do use three-dimensional bar charts, limit their depth to avoid confusion about the real height of the bars.

Likewise, don't deceive by distorting illustrations to your advantage. For example, keep equal time increments along the x and y axes of charts, and keep the height or length of each bar in exact percentage proportion to other bars. For instance, a bar showing 25 percent should be exactly half as long as a bar showing 50 percent. For pictograms, use multiple small images to represent quantity differences, rather than using a small and a large size of the same image. As you can see in Figure 4.6, the larger image is twice as high as the smaller, but is also twice as wide. Visually the larger image is therefore four times the size, creating confusion as to the actual difference between the quantities represented.

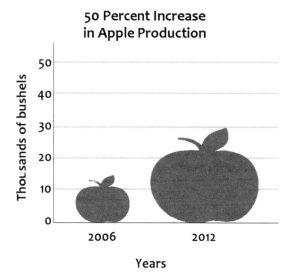

Figure 4.6 Make sure you don't distort illustrations to make the data confusing or deceptive.

Pie Graphs

Whereas bar graphs show quantity by the length of the bars and line graphs show quantity by the vertical placement of the lines, pie graphs show quantity by area. Unfortunately, the human eye does not easily distinguish between the size of two areas of similar size. As a result, bar and line graphs are preferred over pie graphs. Nevertheless, pie graphs are used fairly often in business.

If you decide to use a pie graph, remember three basic guidelines. First, arrange the segments in an appropriate sequence (from largest to smallest in clockwise order), except that the miscellaneous segment should always come last. Also, if possible, begin the largest segment at the top (the twelve o'clock position). Second, label and show the quantity for each segment of the pie. Third, if you wish to draw emphasis to one segment, explode it (detach it and slide it away from the rest of the segments), as shown in Figure 4.7.

Families on Welfare, 20XX

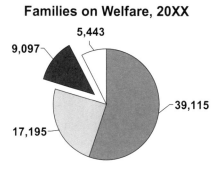

Figure 4.7 Pie chart segments should be arranged in descending order, beginning at the top of the circle and moving in a clockwise direction.

Photographs and Clip Art

You can take photos with digital cameras, use scanners to capture images of photographs and flat objects, such as a coin, use the "Print Screen" button on your keyboard to capture what is on your computer screen, and choose from thousands of photos online or published on CDs. Photo-editing and illustration software packages also give you limitless possibilities. To work with photos and clip art, however, you need to understand the different formats of these computer graphics. Computer graphics are of two types: vector and raster (also known as bitmap).

VECTOR GRAPHICS

Vector graphics are generated on the screen by a computer formula that includes a starting point and a stopping point. Vector graphics are created by *draw* programs. A simple diagonal line on the screen might have a formula something like this:

1. Start at the point where $X = 10$ and $Y = 30$ (10 pixels to the right and 30 pixels down).
2. Proceed to the point where $X = 50$ and $Y = 20$ (50 pixels to the right and 20 pixels down).

A more complex vector image would have multiple vectors, or points, with the last point being the same as the first point, thus creating a closed figure. Closed figures can be filled with colors or patterns (see Figure 4.8).

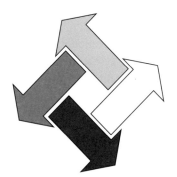

Figure 4.8 Vector graphics usually require only limited storage space and are scalable without loss of resolution.

Vector and raster graphics vary in size and quality. With vector graphics, not every pixel has to be described by the vector formula; thus, vector files are much smaller than raster files. Further, vector graphic files are scalable without loss of quality; that is, they can be enlarged or reduced in size without loss of resolution. By contrast, enlarging raster graphics often produces poor results. For instance, when increased significantly in size, raster graphics become pixilated; that is, their edges become very jagged. As each pixel becomes larger, the visual resolution of the picture decreases. The major advantage of raster graphics is that they can capture the texture and color richness of real-life visuals.

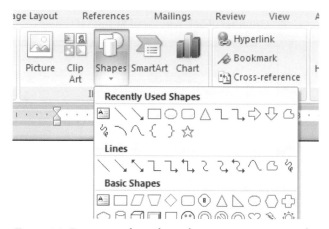

Figure 4.9 Drawing tools can be used to create your own visuals.

With drawing tools, you can create simple graphics of your own (as shown in Figure 4.9). Drawing tools in Microsoft PowerPoint and Microsoft Publisher include lines, connectors, block arrows, flowchart symbols, stars, banners, call outs, and action buttons. These software packages also contain draw tools to align, distribute, rotate, and flip images. More advanced drawings can be made with illustration software like Adobe Illustrator.

Using a combination of four basic shapes—line, circle or oval, square or rectangle (with squared or rounded corners), and triangle—you can draw a variety of simple objects to use in documents or slide shows. All of these shapes are available with common office software, such as PowerPoint and Publisher. After drawing the various parts of an object, select all the parts and group them. In grouped mode, they then stick together as one graphic, rather than as a number of individual parts.

The following house and bus are made from grouped combinations of rectangles, triangles, lines, and shapes.

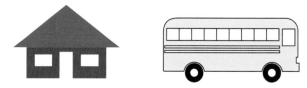

Figure 4.10 Simple figures, like this house and bus, can be easily created with drawing tools.

You can also use these four shapes for developing concept models, as shown in Figure 4.11. Instead of just listing

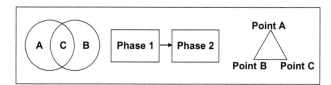

Figure 4.11 Circles, rectangles, lines, and triangles can be used to create concept models.

concepts as text, think of ways to relate them to each other in a graphic way.

Clip art is not used often in most business or government documents because of its bad reputation for being somewhat amateurish. Thus, if you do use clip art, make sure it is professional and adds to your message, rather than detracts from it. Also, avoid using different styles of clip art in the same publication. For example, two pieces of art drawn by the same artist will usually show similar artistic style; two pieces of art drawn by different artists often will not. And as with all graphics, get appropriate legal clearance from the creator before using clip art.

RASTER GRAPHICS

A computer screen is made up of rows and columns of picture elements called pixels (shortened word for *picture element*). Older low-resolution computer screens had 640 pixels across each row and 480 pixels down each column; today's screens have a much higher pixel density and, as a result, have high-resolution screens. Higher pixel density means better picture quality.

Storing raster images requires that each pixel on the screen be described digitally. Thus, a 640 x 480 screen has to have information for all 307,200 pixels (640 multiplied by 480). In addition, if the screen is color instead of just black and white (monochrome), the equation becomes three-dimensional. The third dimension is referred to as bit depth, or color depth. Table 4.2 shows the difference in the amount of computer bytes needed to store an image at different bit depths for display on a low-resolution screen.

Raster graphics are created whenever you scan a photograph, perform a screen capture, take a digital photograph (see Figure 4.12), or use a paint program. When raster graphics are displayed on the internet, they are usually in JPEG, GIF, or PNG format. Photos are usually saved as JPEG files; simpler graphics, such as logos, are often saved as GIF or PNG files. All of these types involve file compression; that is, if a 3.4-megabyte BMP or TIFF graphic (uncompressed formats) is subsequently saved as a JPEG,

Figure 4.12 Photographs are stored as raster images and often require large amounts of file space. The file size of the 300 dpi image on the left (print resolution) is about four times larger than the 72 dpi image on the right (standard screen resolution).

it will be reduced (compressed) in data size, perhaps to about 350 K. Smaller file size results in shorter transmission time, which means less waiting time for internet users.

The following guidelines will help you get the most out of the photos you use in newsletters, handouts, slideshows, and reports.

1. Move or zoom in close to fill the picture with the subject matter. Later, you can perform additional cropping with your photo-editing software (see Figure 4.13).

2. Simplify the subject matter so the message of the photo is clear and obvious. Remove distracting items from the area you are shooting.

3. Photograph tall and narrow objects in portrait (vertical) mode; shoot short and wide objects in landscape (horizontal) mode.

4. Use light appropriately. Usually the sun or other light source should be shining on the front of the object (such as a person's face), rather than on the back. When

Table 4.2 Bit depth and file sizes of raster graphics.

Bit Depth	Screen Equation	Approximate File Size
1 bit (Black and white)	640 × 480	307,200
4 bit (16 colors)	640 × 480 × 4	1,228,800
8 bit (256 colors)	640 × 480 × 8	2,457,600
16 bit (65,536 colors)	640 × 480 × 16	4,915,200
32 bit (16+ million colors)	640 × 480 × 24	7,372,800

Figure 4.13 Many photos require cropping to focus on the most important content.

photographing people outdoors, prefer cloudy days over sunny days that cast harsh shadows. If you must photograph people on a sunny day, use a camera flash to reduce the darkness of shadows on their faces.

5. To enhance a photograph's visual appeal, apply the rule of thirds. Imagine a tic-tac-toe grid on your photo. Place the subject at one of the places where the lines intersect. For example, Figure 4.14 shows two photos of the same office setting. The photo at the right, however, has the man's face positioned at a one-third intersection.

Figure 4.14 Which photo is more interesting? Applying the rule of thirds achieves a more dynamic and interesting image (right).

6. Prefer odd numbers of objects, such as three or five, rather than even numbers like two, four, or six. Thus, a photograph of three people will usually be more visually pleasing than one with two or four.

7. Edit photos to improve the contrast, brightness, and colors and to eliminate problems such as red eye and other imperfections.

8. Generally, use a caption to explain a photo. Use a font that is different from the font used for the rest of the surrounding text. For instance, if the body text of a report uses 11-point Times New Roman, you could use 11-point Times New Roman italics for the photo caption.

Don't forget to get signed legal clearance to use photographs of people and products.

Miscellaneous Graphics

While not as common as the tables, bar charts, line charts, and photographs, other visuals can be used effectively as the need arises, including maps, organization charts, flow-process charts, and project-management charts. Because of the visual nature of geography-related data, for example, maps are often superior to tables and bar charts (see Figure 4.15). When working with all types of information, consider carefully the most effective and efficient way to communicate that information to the audience. Avoid the temptation to settle for text or a table when a map, organization chart, or other type of visual will work much better.

Figure 4.15 Maps are often better than text for communicating location information.

TYPOGRAPHY

Next, consider the typography to use in the document. The most important aspects of typography are reflected on the tool bar of word-processing software, including the font, size, style, and alignment.

Font (typeface)

Serif fonts (such as **Times New Roman**) are often preferred for body text because the serifs (the little finishing marks at the end of their strokes) make each letter more unique and easier to recognize. Sans serif fonts (such as **Arial**) are *sans* (without) such distinguishing little flourishes. Sans serif fonts are often used for headings because they usually have a thicker stroke. This blockier weight makes them easier to read in larger point sizes or from a distance. Because of these differences, sans serif fonts are more easily read than serif fonts in small groups, such as headings or titles, but are not as easy to read as serif fonts in large groups such as paragraphs.

Professional designers recommend the use of only two primary fonts (typefaces) for most documents, one serif and one sans serif. These two faces can then be varied for different levels of headings and different effects in body type.

In addition to serif and sans serif categories, decorative and script typefaces can be used to add personality and flair to a document. However, these are best considered like strong spices in cooking. A small amount sprinkled carefully and with thoughtful intent can add pleasing flavor to a document, but dumping in a random selection can overpower a document's purpose. If you are not sure about including another font, it is better to leave it out.

From the thousands of faces that are available, use one that fits the situation. For example, use an informal font for something like a department party announcement. Use a formal font for a formal reception. Use a neutral font for routine memos and reports.

Come to our department party!
(Comic Sans font)

You are invited to a reception to honor . . .
(French Script font)

This memo will introduce a new procedure . . .
(Times New Roman font)

Finally, don't forget that your purpose is to communicate. An interesting or eye-catching font like the following won't strengthen your document if people can't read it.

DOES THIS HELP COMMUNICATE?

Size (height)

Typography height is measured in points, with 72 points equaling one inch. Normally, use 10–12 point type for general audiences. For an elderly audience, increase the type size perhaps to 14. For slideshows viewed by a large audience, increase the type size appropriately. Use larger sizes for different levels of headings, such as 26-point type for first-level headings, 18-point for second-level headings, and so forth.

Times New Roman 11-point

Times New Roman 18-point

Arial Bold 26-point

Style

You can enhance basic type in several ways to make it more noticeable, including the two most commonly used treatments—**bold** and *italic*. (When you use reverse type—light text on a dark background—you may need to bold all the text of some fonts to ensure that the thin strokes of each character are clearly visible.)

In most cases, avoid underlining text because the line cuts through the descenders of lower-case letters like j, q, g, and y, detracting from their appearance (e.g., typography) and making them more difficult to read. You can also use occasional color for emphasis, or use ALL CAPITAL LETTERS for headings. Do not use all capitals for body text, however, because text in all capitals is hard to read. Use moderation with all typographic enhancement, because too much visual enhancement is distracting.

Alignment

Type can be aligned on the left, center, or right. It can also be aligned on both left and right sides, called full justification. For most business documents, use left alignment, also called ragged right. The following samples illustrate different text alignment.

This is left-aligned text, also called ragged right. It aligns text on the left margin, leaving irregular line lengths on the right side.

- All lines of bulleted text should be left aligned with the first line of text, not with the bullet.

This is centered text. It has ragged left and right sides and is centered on the middle of the text line. Centered text is most often used for headings and formal invitations.

This is right-aligned text, also called ragged left. It aligns text on the right margin. It is used often for aligning page numbers in tables of contents.

This is fully justified text. Both left and right sides of the text are aligned. This alignment style slows down reading but gives a polished formal appearance.

In addition to alignment concerns, typography experts suggest that readability can be improved by reducing the length of text lines (the ideal line length is about 40 characters). To achieve a shorter line length for text-heavy messages, you may increase the width of the side margins, slightly increase the text size, or use a two-column format.

SPACING

Add appropriate white space. Pages with many lines of text without a visual break look gray and uninviting. White space gives visual relief, prevents reader fatigue, and enhances reader friendliness. Space also divides and frames elements on a page. For instance, white space placed around a block of text or a graphic divides it from neighboring elements.

Check two aspects of spacing in your documents: external and internal. External spacing refers to the margins around the edges of the page. For most routine documents, a one-inch margin is standard, but don't be afraid to allow margins of more than an inch for text-heavy documents.

Internal spacing is the space within the text. If your pages appear to be gray, you need to increase the internal spacing. The simplest and most common way is to leave one line of space between paragraphs and before and after tables and graphics. You may also try increasing the line spacing. Keeping paragraphs short is one of the best tactics to ensure an adequate amount of white space on a page.

Also, be aware of stray elements such as headings, orphans, or widows. A heading should always be followed by at least two lines of body text before a page break. An orphan is a paragraph's first line left by itself at the bottom of a page; a widow is a paragraph's last line left by itself at the top of a page. Where possible, avoid both by making sure at least the first two lines appear at the bottom of the first page and at least the last two lines appear at the top of the next page.

The memos below and opposite show the impact of the HATS procedure on a routine document. Figure 4.16 suffers from the following design problems:

Headings: No headings are used in the body of the memo.

Art: No visual techniques are used to assist the reader in making the information easier to read and understand.

Typography: All type is 10-point Arial, a sans serif type. Type style variation is not used to emphasize impor-

---

To: Western Region Store Managers
From: Sara Howard, FastFood Operations Manager
Date: June 10, 20XX
Re: Recruiting, Hiring, Scheduling, and Retaining Employees

On a recent visit to Las Vegas, I found a FastFood store that is getting and keeping a quality work force, a goal which, as you know, is an ongoing problem for our industry. The manager, Carl Wallace, shared with me the success strategy.

Carl has determined that the standard FastFood staff figure of one employee for every $2,500 of monthly sales is not optimal. After experimenting, he found the best figure to be $1,800. At this level, more employee flexibility is achievable.

Maintaining adequate staffing levels is an industry-wide challenge. To solve this problem, Carl has organized his workforce into three teams. Each team is given a $100 monthly budget to use in recruiting, interviewing, and training new employees. If the team's staff level is maintained at 10 throughout a quarter, each member of the team receives a $100 bonus. Another industry problem is employee retention. Annual turnover at Carl's store has decreased 151 percent since implementing his program. Four incentives have helped improve employee retention: Monthly free-food days; 30-day wage evaluations for new employees, quarterly wage evaluations for all employees; monthly performance reviews for all employees; and "Buddies" and other programs to ensure employee satisfaction.

Because of Carl's success, I strongly recommend that you consider implementing one or more of these approaches as appropriate in your store. Please send me an email response to this memo by the first of next month to let me know your specific plans.

Figure 4.16 Messages with no visual enhancement are gray, uninviting, and are often hard to read.

tant text. Alignment of the text creates an unhelpful and uninviting block shape.

Spacing: Internal spacing is too tight, giving the memo a dark, gray appearance which repels rather than attracts the reader.

The redesigned memo in Figure 4.17 incorporates the following improvements:

Headings: Three headings are added in the body of the memo, clearly showing the text structure and reflecting the three main parts of the text.

Art: The financial information is displayed in a bar chart, showing a clear visual comparison between the two sales-to-staff ratios.

Typography: The subject line is bolded, as are the headings in the body. The individual agenda items are set off with

---

Spacing

To: ↓ Western Region Store Managers
From: Sara Howard, FastFood Operations Manager
Date: June 10, 20XX
←—Spacing   — Typography

Re: **Recruiting, Hiring, Scheduling, and Retaining Employees**

On a recent visit to Las Vegas, I found a FastFood store that is getting and keeping a quality work force, a goal which, as you know, is an ongoing problem for our industry. The manager, Carl Wallace, shared with me the success strategy, and I recommend it to you for implementation. Carl's strategy includes (a) determining appropriate staff levels, (b) finding qualified staff, and (c) retaining employees.

/ Art

Determining Appropriate Staffing Levels. Carl has determined that the standard FastFood staff figure of one employee for every $2,500 of monthly sales is not optimal. After experimenting, he found the best figure to be $1,800. At this level, more employee flexibility is achievable (see accompanying chart).
— Headings

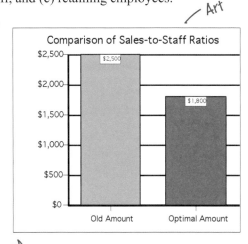

Finding Qualified Staff. Maintaining adequate staffing levels is an industry-wide challenge. To solve this problem, Carl has organized his workforce into three teams. Each team is given a $100 monthly budget to use in recruiting, interviewing, and training new employees. If the team's staff level is maintained at 10 throughout a quarter, each member of the team receives a $100 bonus.

Retaining Employees. Another industry problem is employee retention. Annual turnover at Carl's store has decreased 151 percent since implementing his program. Four incentives have helped improve employee retention:
—Spacing

- Monthly free-food days

- 30-day wage evaluations for new employees, and quarterly wage evaluations for all employees

- Monthly performance reviews for all employees

- "Buddies" and other programs to ensure employee satisfaction
— Typography

Because of Carl's success, I strongly recommend that you consider implementing one or more of these approaches as appropriate in your store. Please **send me an email response** to this memo by the first of next month to let me know your specific plans.

Figure 4.17 Headings and other visual enhancements make messages more inviting and easier to read

alphabetic markers (a, b, and c). A bulleted list has been created in the fourth paragraph, making the information easier to find. Also, the entire document has been typed in 11-point type, a good size for general audiences. Further, the memo body is left aligned, making the text easier to read than fully justified text. The left-aligned body also gives the memo a more friendly appearance. Finally, the response request is bolded in the last paragraph, helping to ensure that the reader doesn't miss the return-requested information.

Spacing: Needed space has been added between the paragraphs, as well as between the various parts of the main headings at the top of the memo. The subject line has been framed in white, quickly revealing the content of the memo. The horizontal space between the bullets and their associated text is closer than word processors' default tabs allow, reflecting a close relationship between the bullets and text.

The HATS design process offers three key benefits.

1. HATS can be easily remembered because of the obvious acronym.

2. It provides a general standard for both designing and editing documents.

3. It improves the audience's reading experience, enhancing both efficiency and effectiveness.

The HATS design steps may take additional time, but your professional reputation will be enhanced because of improved document quality, and your documents will set an example for others to follow.

CHAPTER SUMMARY

A four-step procedure, represented by the acronym HATS (headings, art, typography, and spacing), can guide you through the design aspects of writing. Headings in documents increase the documents' access—the degree to which the critical message information is accessible to the reader. Art and visual elements, such as tables, bar charts, maps, organization charts, and flow-process charts, often can communicate more quickly than words. To work effectively with graphics, you need to know the tools and the principles of effective graphic design. Follow generally accepted guidelines when including tables, bar and line graphs, pie graphs, photographs, and clip art.

The most important aspects of typography include the font, size, style, and alignment. Usually, use one serif and one sans serif typeface for each document. Normally, use 10–12 point type for general audiences. For most docu-

ments, align the text on the left, leaving one-inch top, bottom, left, and right margins.

Documents also need appropriate space. Space gives visual relief, prevents reader fatigue, and enhances reader friendliness. Space also divides and frames elements on a page.

WORKS CITED

Baker, William H. "HATS: A Design Procedure for Routine Business Documents." *Business Communication Quarterly* 64, no. 2 (2001): 65–76.

Frischknecht, Sierra Sloan and William H. Baker. *Enhanced vs. Undifferentiated Text: A Study to Assess the Effects on Readers: Proceedings of the 76th Annual Convention of the Association for Business Communication, Oct. 19-22, 2011.* Montreal, Quebec, Canada. Association for Business Communication, 2011.

CHAPTER QUESTIONS

1. What words are represented by the acronym HATS?

2. What does the five-second standard refer to?

3. What is a legend? A call out? A braced heading?

4. Compare the similarities and differences of bar charts and line charts. Why are line and bar charts generally preferred over pie charts?

5. Describe the differences between vector and raster graphics.

6. Describe the difference between serif and sans serif fonts. Which of these styles is used most often for body text?

7. In photographs, what is the rule of thirds?

8. Explain two guidelines for photographing people outdoors on sunny days.

9. How many typographic "points" are in an inch? What is the ideal type size for most audiences.

10. What type of text alignment should be used with most office documents?

11. What is a "gray page"? Why is it undesirable?

12. What are widows and orphans? Why should they be avoided?

13. What is white space? What are the two main functions of white space?

CHAPTER ACTIVITIES

1. Obtain some quantitative data from the U.S. Census Bureau website or other government or business site approved by your instructor. Using this data, create an

original bar chart and an original table. Cite the source of your material at the bottom of the chart and table.

2. Write a memo that includes and explains the graphics you created for Activity 1.

3. Apply the principles and techniques of HATS in the memo you wrote for Activity 1 in Chapter 3.

4. To help you learn to communicate more visually, sketch a simple visual to accompany an article in today's newspaper. Don't worry about your artistic talent (stick figures are OK); just sketch the best way you know how.

5. Download a photograph from the internet. Save the photo on your computer hard drive as a JPEG and as a TIFF file. Compare the data size of the two different files.

6. Take a digital photograph that demonstrates the rule of thirds. Submit the photograph to your instructor and explain how you have applied the rule of thirds and other composition guidelines.

7. Write a paragraph that uses metaphoric language to explain something that is conceptual.

8. Create a flow chart that shows the steps involved in some process with which you are familiar.

9. Create a Gantt chart that shows the writing assignments to be completed in this class.

10. Find a one-page document on the internet or elsewhere. Evaluate its design, and then recreate the document so it includes effective use of headings, art, typography, and spacing.

11. Using the draw tools of PowerPoint, create a concept model for a topic of your choice.

5

REVISING AND EDITING TEXT

Revising is a critical writing skill. No writers are so gifted that they can write first-draft polished documents, except perhaps for very simple documents. Well-known author William Faulkner (1950), in his Nobel Prize acceptance speech, referred to his years of writing as "work in the agony and sweat of the human spirit." Writing is hard work, and it requires the creation and revision of multiple drafts before the final polished document is produced. Therefore, always plan for revision as a normal step in your writing process.

Why does writing quality matter? At least three potential problems can result if you send messages with errors or other weaknesses:

1. Writing errors damage your credibility. The reader assumes that you either don't know or don't care.

2. If your writing is unclear, the reader must take extra time to understand it.

3. If your writing contains factual errors, the reader may draw improper conclusions.

Remember also that the reader, not the writer, determines whether the writing is successful.

To help with your revision work, this chapter focuses first on getting and giving feedback, and then on revising design, organization, content, and style.

GETTING AND GIVING FEEDBACK

Revising is more than just checking for grammar errors, although it includes that. Above all, good revision focuses on achieving the communication purpose. For example, if

you write a collection letter that does not collect, it hasn't achieved its communication purpose.

When other people ask you to review their documents and give feedback, first understand the purpose of the document. Then understand the audience—their characteristics, feelings about and knowledge of the topic, and their perceptions of the author.

When you ask other people to review your documents, choose reviewers who are knowledgeable and who will be forthright in their feedback. Be open to the feedback they give

Figure 5.1 Ask other people to review your important documents.

you, and apply all the suggestions that you feel are appropriate. Don't become defensive—you don't have to use all the feedback they give, but you should be cordial when it is given.

When proofreading and editing either for yourself or for others, use standard proofreaders' marks (see Figure 5.2). When in doubt about the clarity of a proofreading mark, write additional notes in the margins so the writer understands your concerns or recommendations.

Remember that the writer has no obligation to use the

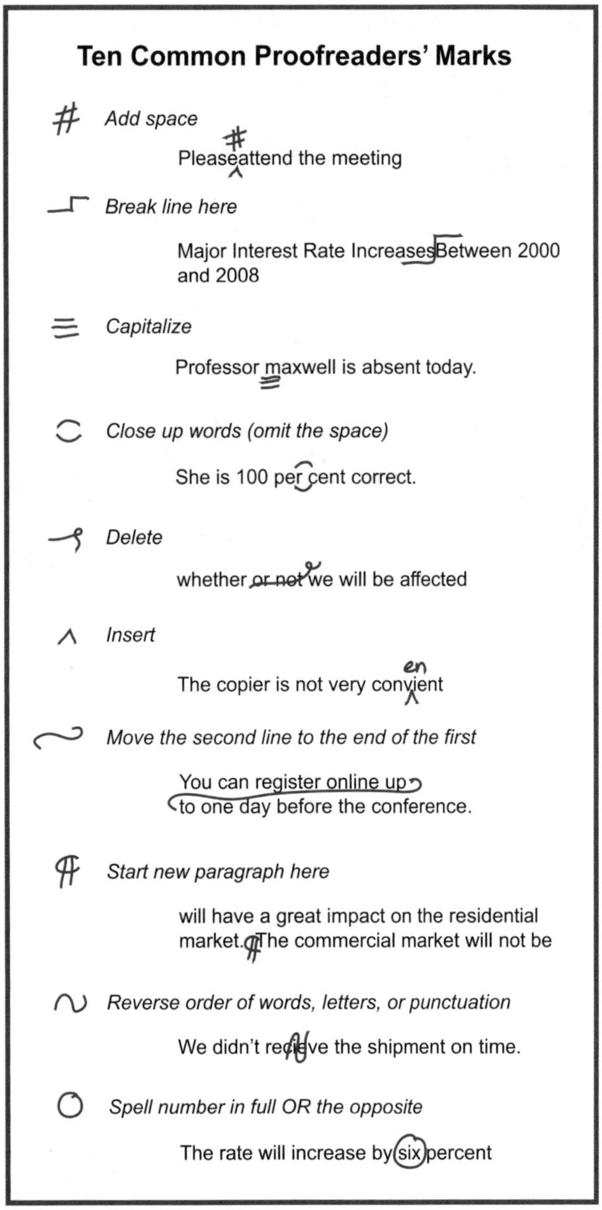

Ten Common Proofreaders' Marks

*Add space*

Please attend the meeting

⌐   *Break line here*

Major Interest Rate Increases Between 2000 and 2008

≡   *Capitalize*

Professor maxwell is absent today.

⌒   *Close up words (omit the space)*

She is 100 per cent correct.

⌿   *Delete*

whether or not we will be affected

∧   *Insert*

The copier is not very *en* convient

∼   *Move the second line to the end of the first*

You can register online up
to one day before the conference.

¶   *Start new paragraph here*

will have a great impact on the residential market. The commercial market will not be

∽   *Reverse order of words, letters, or punctuation*

We didn't recieve the shipment on time.

◯   *Spell number in full OR the opposite*

The rate will increase by six percent

Figure 5.2 Standardized marks help proofreaders communicate efficiently with writers.

feedback given by the reviewer. Different people will react to writing in unique ways, and the writer has to determine which feedback to use and which to set aside. Don't be offended if the writer does not use your feedback.

REVISING DESIGN, ORGANIZATION, CONTENT, AND SENTENCES (DOCS)

This chapter covers four levels of reviewing and revising a document. Remember the four levels with the acronym DOCS:

Level 1—Review the Design

Level 2—Review the Organization

Level 3—Review the Content

Level 4—Review the Style

A rubric is provided at the end of the chapter to guide the DOCS review process.

Level 1—Review the Design

The design review is a high-level examination to check the document for correct formatting and appropriate visual appeal. First, make sure the document format follows generally accepted standards, given the specific document genre. For instance, an email should follow email formatting standards, a job resume should follow formatting standards for resumes, and a report should follow generally accepted standards for reports. Such standards include the width of the top, bottom, left, and right margins; the placement and sequence of information about the sender, the receiver, the date, and the title or subject line; and other related factors. In essence, a business letter should look like a business letter and a report should look like a report.

Second, after ensuring that the appropriate format has been followed, examine the document to see whether appropriate HATS elements have been employed. Initially, quickly glance at the document and ask yourself whether it looks "reader friendly." If it looks uninviting and difficult to read, make appropriate changes in the use of headings, art, typography, or spacing.

- *Headings.* Does it use plenty of headings and subheadings to show the structure of the message?
- *Art and Visuals.* Does it use visual techniques to make important information stand out? Are tables, charts, photographs, and illustrations used to convey numeric, procedural, and other graphically oriented information?
- *Typography.* Are appropriate typefaces used for headings and regular body text (perhaps a serif font for body type and a sans serif font for headings)? Is the font size appropriate (usually 11- to 12-point type height for general-audience documents)? Is text appropriately aligned (left, center, full)?
- *Spacing.* Do the pages have appropriate outside margins, with adequate white space between paragraphs?

Figure 5.3 shows a typical memo you might encounter in a business. Comments have been added showing the application of HATS to the document.

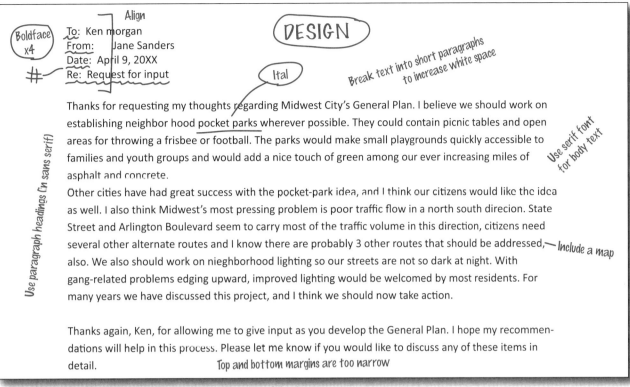

Figure 5.3 A typical business memo that has been reviewed for design.

Level 2—Review the Organization

After the design review, check the organization of the major information blocks in the message. To check the organization, skim the entire document (rather than getting heavily involved at the sentence level) and analyze the overall information architecture.

As you review the organization, first check to see whether a direct or indirect approach has been used. Remember, the direct approach places the key message at or near the beginning of the message. The direct approach is used for most routine and good-news messages, and should be used in the majority of messages. The indirect approach places the key message later in the message, following the explanatory or persuasive information needed to condition the reader's mind. The indirect approach is far less frequently used and is reserved mainly for persuasive and bad-news messages.

After evaluating the overall approach, consider the structure and sequence of the information blocks in the document. Skim the document and review the major informational units. For example, an analytical report might include sections on background issues, the purpose of the research, the methods used for conducting the research, the various findings of the research, and the conclusions and recommendations given as a result of the analysis.

Following an examination of the structure and sequence, make appropriate changes. For instance, the research findings might need to be rearranged from most to least significant, and the recommendations might need to be sequenced according to implementation order. Finally, check to see if OABC structure is used appropriately. OABC may be used as an overall pattern, but it may also be used as a pattern within subsections of longer documents.

Figure 5.4 shows the same memo as Figure 5.3, only this time it has been evaluated for organization.

Level 3—Review the Content

The content review consists of analyzing, evaluating, and refining the content. This can be done globally using the four "C"s and then on a paragraph level using CLOUD.

THE FOUR "C"S

To examine the four "C"s of the document, read the document as normal—sentence by sentence and paragraph by paragraph—from beginning to end. Consider the content from the reader's perspective as well as the writer's. As you read, make sure the content is clear, complete, correct, and compelling (the four "C"s).

Is it Clear?

Clarity examines the presentation of the content. Are the key points of the message easy to comprehend? Are word choice and diction appropriate for the audience? Are tech-

To: Ken morgan
From: Jane Sanders
Date: April 9, 20XX
Re: Request for input

ORGANIZATION

Add agenda

Thanks for requesting my thoughts regarding Midwest City's General Plan. I believe we should work on establishing neighbor hood pocket parks wherever possible. They could contain picnic tables and open areas for throwing a frisbee or football. The parks would make small playgrounds quickly accessible to families and youth groups and would add a nice touch of green among our ever increasing miles of asphalt and concrete.

Other cities have had great success with the pocket-park idea, and I think our citizens would like the idea as well. I also think Midwest's most pressing problem is poor traffic flow in a north south direcion. State Street and Arlington Boulevard seem to carry most of the traffic volume in this direction, citizens need several other alternate routes and I know there are probably 3 other routes that should be addressed, also. We also should work on nieghborhood lighting so our streets are not so dark at night. With gang-related problems edging upward, improved lighting would be welcomed by most residents. For many years we have discussed this project, and I think we should now take action.

Move this text to first body paragraph

Break into 3 paragraphs

Thanks again, Ken, for allowing me to give input as you develop the General Plan. I hope my recommendations will help in this process. Please let me know if you would like to discuss any of these items in detail.

Good use of direct approach

Figure 5.4 A typical business memo that has been evaluated for organization.

nical or esoteric words defined? (*Esoteric* words are words that are not widely understood or used.) Do examples and explanations help in understanding? Are the various parts of the message coherently and logically presented?

One way to see if your document is clear is to perform a usability test. Invite someone who is representative of your intended audience to read the document and mark anything that is confusing or difficult to understand.

Is it Complete?

Completeness pertains to inclusion of all relevant content. Does it answer the basic 5W2H questions (who, what, where, when, why, how, and how much)? Does it examine all sides of the argument? Does it consider all options? Does it cover the subject matter in appropriate depth?

Completeness also pertains to the exclusion of irrelevant material. Does the document contain too much information? Are certain examples or explanations unnecessary? Content that does not contribute, or, worse yet, that distracts from the central message, should be eliminated.

Is it Correct?

Correctness refers to the quality of the content. Is it factual and free from bias and error? Are all financial and other quantities correct? Can all statements of fact be proven? Are all sources properly cited? Are there any ethical violations, such as misrepresentations or exaggerations of the truth, inten-

tional withholding of relevant information, or making of promises that cannot be fulfilled? Does it include any false or malicious statements that would constitute defamation. (Defamation is the dissemination of untrue information about another person, resulting in damage to that person's reputation.) Two main types of defamation are libel and slander. Libel is written defamation; slander is spoken defamation. In addition to making defamatory comments about people, business writers must avoid making false or malicious statements about competitors' products or practices.

Is it Compelling?

Compelling content is effective content. Does the content achieve the desired objective? Do psychological appeals like logos, ethos, or pathos work? Are examples and explanations persuasive?

You can perform the same kind of usability test used for clarity to see if your document is compelling. Have the representative share their response to the document and see if it matches your objective.

REVISING PARAGRAPHS (CLOUD)

Evaluate paragraphs, especially body paragraphs, on five factors, remembered with the acronym CLOUD. Begin by checking the organization ("O") and then checking the C, L, U, and D aspects.

Organization: Generally, body paragraphs should be writ-

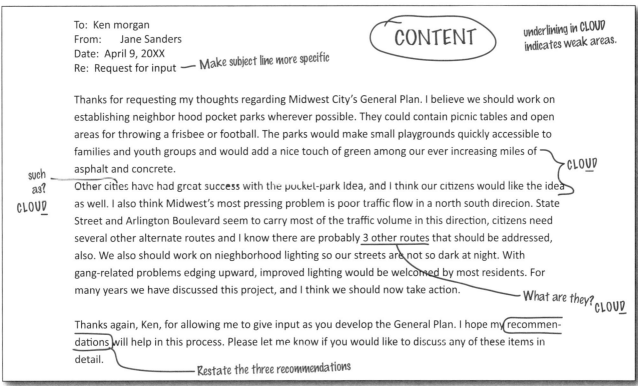

Figure 5.5 A typical business memo that has been reviewed for content.

ten in direct, top-down sequence, with the second and succeeding sentences developing or supporting the topic introduced in the first sentence. The sequence of the sentences will depend on the nature of the information. Sometimes you might also want a summary sentence at the end of a paragraph.

Coherence: Each succeeding thought in a paragraph should flow logically from the thought that precedes it. Thus, sentence 1 should lead logically to sentence 2, which should lead logically to sentence 3, and so forth. Further, show the relationships among the ideas with appropriate transition words.

Length: If a paragraph looks hard to read when you first glance at it, it's probably too long. Many authors suggest that paragraphs in business and government writing generally should not exceed about six or seven lines for memos, letters, and emails and nine or ten lines for longer documents like reports. However, you can usually just trust your eye to tell you whether a paragraph needs to be shortened or divided.

Unity: All sentences should relate to the same topic. If the paragraph is about computer software, it shouldn't include information about computer hardware. If you want to include both software and hardware in the paragraph, introduce both in the opening sentence.

Development: The paragraph's main idea should be ade-

quately developed and supported in the paragraph. Methods of development include statistics, examples, explanations, stories, quotes from authorities, and so forth (see Chapter 3).

Figure 5.5 illustrates the application of the four "C"s and CLOUD to the same memo as before.

Level 4—Review the Sentences

The Level 4 review consists of an in-depth review of sentence details. Above the sentence level, writing quality is judged almost totally on principles and patterns, but at the sentence level, writing must conform to specific rules as well as to principles.

Most professional writers agree that the best reviewing and proofreading occurs on paper. For short, informal emails, reviewing on the computer screen is usually adequate, but for more important documents, review the text on paper as well.

For screen editing, use your software tools to catch writing errors, especially on important documents. Spell checkers are helpful in catching many spelling errors. Grammar and style checkers are also helpful in catching many sentence weaknesses, although not all. Further, they won't always make the right recommendations for correcting the errors.

When proofreading a document on paper, consider three techniques to improve the accuracy of your work.

- Read the document out loud meaningfully to force you to concentrate on each word. (When reading silently, you typically read clusters of words without giving adequate attention to individual words.) If the text doesn't sound like something you'd say in a conversation with the audience, revise it until it sounds good out loud.
- Use a ruler or piece of paper to cover the text below the line you are reading. This technique will also help you to consider individual lines and words instead of larger clusters.
- Have multiple reviewers read the document. One person might catch an error that another person overlooks.

Remember that errors often go undetected in titles, headings, captions, and other areas away from the body text. Therefore, make an additional pass through the document to check these elements.

When evaluating sentences, remember all generally accepted guidelines, rules, and principles. In the appendix of this book you will find guidelines and rules organized under the acronym SPELL (structure, punctuation, errors, language, and length).

STRUCTURE (see pages 197–204)

Make sure all sentences have a clear structure. Well-designed sentences are easy to follow and don't have to be read twice to be understood. Remember SVC (subject, verb, complement) as you evaluate the structure of each sentence.

Subject: Use strong, clear subjects, generally avoiding "it" and "there" as subjects.

Verb: Remember two V's—vicinity and voice. Place each verb close to (in the vicinity of) its subject. Further, use active voice, rather than passive voice, unless you have a good reason to do otherwise.

Complement: Make sure the remainder of the sentence (the complement) is clear and easy to follow. Avoid sentence clutter caused by too many add-on phrases. Make sure all relative pronouns have clear references (her, his, they, this, etc.), place all modifying words close to the words they modify, and ensure grammatic parallelism for words in a series and other structurally parallel phrases.

Also, identify any awkward wording. Where you find problems, reconstruct the sentence for improved wording and structure. For example, you might (a) put secondary information in an introductory phrase or subordinate clause and (b) place the primary information in a main clause, as follows.

No: Over 60 percent of the 1,086 respondents in this nationwide study agree to the fact that the implementation of Regulation 605 in their organizations has improved controls in two big areas of mine safety and health protection. [This 38-word sentence is cluttered and disorganized, making the main message and sentence structure difficult to discover.]

Yes: Of the 1,086 respondents in this nationwide study, over 60 percent agree that Regulation 605 has improved their miners' safety and health. [In this 22-word sentence, the introductory segment serves as a gathering place for background information, which is then followed by the main clause containing the key message.]

In addition to achieving structure clarity, be sure to employ appropriate structure variety. Readers get tired of multiple sentences with similar length and structure.

No: Starting a business requires you to develop a business plan. A business plan includes a description of the business. The description covers marketing, competition, operating procedures, and personnel. A business plan also includes financial data. The financial data section includes a balance sheet, sources of funding, pro-forma income projections, and cash flows. A business plan must also include any other relevant supporting documents. [All six sentences are structured as single clauses with a similar length.]

Yes: If you decide to start your own company, a business plan can be of great assistance to you. Most business plans start with a description of the business, with subsections on marketing, competition, operating procedures, and personnel. Following the description of the business, business plans need a financial data section, usually consisting of a balance sheet, sources of funding, pro-forma income projections, and cash flows. Finally, business plans may include any other sections or supporting documents that the writer considers relevant.

[These four sentences vary in length and structure. The first is an 18-word complex sentence (one dependent and one independent clause). The next is a 19-word simple sentence (one independent clause), with a concluding segment containing four items in a series. Sentence 3 contains 28 words, starting with an introductory phrase, followed by a main clause, and concluding with a four-part series. Finally, sentence 4 consists of 16 words in a simple-sentence construction (independent clause).]

PUNCTUATION (see pages 206–210)

Review each sentence for appropriate punctuation. Be especially watchful for violations of the following punctuation rules:

- Place a comma between all items in a series.
- Place a comma after many introductory phrases.
- Insert a hyphen between two or more words that act jointly to modify a subsequent noun or pronoun (e.g., high-priced product).
- Place a hyphen between all "self" words (e.g., self-assured).
- Include a left parenthesis whenever you use a right parenthesis.
- Place commas and periods inside quotation marks at the end of a quote.
- Use a period with a polite request that asks for an action.

ERRORS (see pages 211–223)

Check each sentence for case, agreement, tense, number, and capitalization rules. Be especially watchful for the following violations that occur frequently.

- Generally use "me" or "I," rather than "myself." (For example, "Submit the report to David or me, and then he and I will distribute copies to everyone." Avoid "Submit the report to David or myself, and then he and myself will distribute copies to everyone.")
- Use the apostrophe correctly with possessive case.
- Avoid placing an apostrophe in the possessive form of "its" (e.g., "The house sustained major damage when its windows were blown out by the tornado").
- Check agreement, making sure that each subject agrees with its associated verbs.
- As a general rule, spell out numbers one through nine; write as numerals everything larger than nine. Be aware of the numerous exceptions to this basic rule.
- For each item in a vertical list, capitalize the first letter of the first word.
- Don't capitalize directions unless they refer to an area (e.g., "out West").

LANGUAGE (see pages 224–227)

Evaluate word usage throughout the document.

- Use words that are appropriately precise, rather than general and ambiguous.
- Use words that are easily understood by the audience that will read the document; jargon may be used if it will be readily understood.
- Make sure all words are correct in usage (e.g., principle vs. principal, affect vs. effect).
- Spell all words correctly (e.g., receive, judgment, questionnaire, separate).

Check the wording of sentences to ensure that the tone is appropriate. Generally, use words that are cordial and conversational, yet professional.

No: We can't ship your parts until March 1. [Wording is negative; focuses on what you can't do.]

Yes: We will ship your parts on March 1. [Words focus on the positive—states what you can or will do.]

No: Your order was received today. It will be shipped within the next two working days. [Words are mechanical and uncaring.]

Yes: We appreciate your order and will ship it to you within the next 48 hours. [Words are warm and friendly.]

No: Per your request that we scrutinize the various purported illegalities suggested in the management audit report, we hereby submit the attached. [Words are too pompous and arrogant; not conversational.]

Yes: Here is our analysis of the three illegal actions described in the management audit report. [Words reflect "conversational language."]

Figure 5.6 In writing, as in speaking, your tone should be appropriate to the situation.

LENGTH (see pages 228–229)

Avoid long, wordy sentences that cause readers to lose their way. Ask yourself, "How can I say the same thing with fewer words?" You can reduce sentence length and wordiness in the following ways:

1. Omit redundant words:

   No: In my mind I thought I would be rehired again.

   Yes: I thought I would be rehired. ["In my mind" and "again" are redundant.]

2. Replace more words with fewer words:

   No: I made the assumption that she was planning to be in attendance.

   Yes: I assumed she would attend.

   No: The negative effect of the pay cut on the motivation of the employees in the marketing department was severe in its impact. [Avoid too many prepositional phrases.]

   Yes: The pay cut greatly reduced the marketing employees' motivation.

   No: We are cognizant of the fact that great demands are currently being imposed on your financial resources. [Avoid overly formal language.]

   Yes: We know money is tight for you right now.

Also consider splitting a long sentence into two shorter ones that are easier to read.

   No: The foregoing standards and OMB Circular A-133 require that we plan and perform the audit to obtain reasonable assurance about whether or not noncompliance with the types of compliance requirements referred to above could have a direct and material effect on a major federal program.

   Yes: The foregoing standards and OMB Circular A-133 specify our audit criteria. These criteria require that we determine if any noncompliance could directly or materially affect a major federal program.

Figure 5.7 shows the same business memo reviewed at the sentence level.

THE FINAL DOCUMENT

After you have finished the DOCS review, apply the changes to your document. Figure 5.8 shows the revised memo. Check the revised document to ensure that all your DOCS changes have been properly implemented.

Revision is a cyclical process; after you've made all your

Figure 5.7 A typical business memo that has been reviewed at the sentence level.

revisions, consider going through a DOCS review again. If you made significant changes to the content or organization, you may have introduced new errors or problems that a second or even a third DOCS review would help eliminate.

The number of revision cycles depends on the nature of the document. For a short email to a few coworkers, a single DOCS review may be sufficient. For an annual company-wide report, several revision cycles may be necessary.

CHAPTER SUMMARY

Revising is more than just checking for grammar errors, although it includes that. Above all, good revision focuses on achieving the communication purpose. When other people ask you to review their documents and give feedback, first understand the purpose of the document and the audience. When you ask other people to review your documents, choose reviewers who are knowledgeable and who will be forthright in their feedback.

To:　　Ken Morgan
From:　Jane Sanders
Date:　April 9, 20XX

Re:　　**Request for Input on Midwest City's General Plan**

Thanks for requesting my thoughts regarding Midwest City's Genveral Plan. From my perspective, the three most pressing needs are to (a) improve traffic flow, (b) install neighborhood lighting, and (c) build pocket parks.

Improve Traffic Flow

I think Midwest's most pressing problem is poor traffic flow in a north-south direction. State Street and Arlington Boulevard carry most of the traffic, and citizens need other options. I have attached a map showing the following three routes that could be considered.

- 800 East from 1200 South to 1600 North
- 1200 West from 800 South to 1600 North
- 800 West from 800 South to 1600 North

Install Neighborhood Lighting

We should also improve neighborhood lighting so our streets are not so dark at night. With gang-related problems edging upward in our city, improved lighting would be welcomed by most residents. For many years we have discussed this project, and I think we should now take action.

Build Pocket Parks

In addition to improving traffic flow and neighborhood lighting, I believe we should establish neighborhood *pocket parks* wherever possible. These small parks could contain small playgrounds, picnic tables, and open areas for throwing a frisbee or football. The parks would be quickly accessible to families and youth groups and would add a nice touch of green among our ever-increasing miles of asphalt and concrete. Other cities, such as Westmore and Johnsonville, have had great success with pocket parks, and I think our citizens would like the idea as well.

Thanks again, Ken, for allowing me to give input as you develop the General Plan. I hope my recommendations to improve traffic flow, improve neighborhood lighting, and establish pocket parks will help in this process. Please let me know if you would like to discuss any of these items in more detail.

Figure 5.8　Compare this revised memo with Figures 5.3, 5.4, 5.5, and 5.7. As you can see, a methodical DOCS review can result in a significantly improved document.

When you revise a document, follow a DOCS process (design, organization, content, sentences). The design review checks the document format and visual aspects (HATS). The organization review checks the overall approach and structure of the information. The content review ensures that the information is clear, complete, correct, and compelling. The content review also checks the quality of paragraphs, including coherence, length, organization, unity, and development (CLOUD). The sentence review assesses adherence to basic sentence rules and principles including structure, punctuation, errors, language, and length (SPELL). A computer's spelling and grammar checkers can help with the sentence-level review.

WORKS CITED

Faulkner, William. *William Faulkner: Nobel Prize Speech* (1950). http://www.rjgeib.com/thoughts/faulkner/faulkner.html (accessed August 1, 2006).

CHAPTER QUESTIONS

1. What three major problems can occur because of writing errors?

2. What are the responsibilities of the writer and the reviewer when a document is being evaluated for quality?

3. Explain the four levels of document review.

4. What does CLOUD represent?

5. Explain the difference between unity and coherence.

6. Should you quality check your documents on the computer screen or with a paper printout? Why?

7. Why does reading text out loud help catch writing errors?

8. What does the acronym SPELL represent?

9. Why should subjects and verbs be kept close together?

10. What two words should generally be avoided as sentence subjects?

11. What two "v" factors should be checked when reviewing sentence verbs?

12. What do the four "C" words of content represent?

13. Why is sentence variety important?

14. Why is the tone of a message important?

CHAPTER ACTIVITIES

1. Revise the following sentences and apply the guidelines and principles introduced in this chapter.

a. The computer that was delivered by UPS last week is being returned because of product damage.

b. One of the citizens' Neighborhood Watch groups in the west section of the city got overly zealous in trying to control vandalism during the early hours of the morning.

c. Sgt. Jackson wrote four DUI tickets, six tickets for excessive speeding, and helped two stranded motorists.

d. We'll discuss not only next month's calendar but we'll discuss the entire year's calendar, also.

e. Please send your travel request, your annual objectives, and budget.

f. It is hoped that the new security measures will prevent further break-ins.

g. There are eight people in the waiting room.

h. What this company needs is more money for research and development.

i. Joseph's brother said he would help the Johnson's move their piano this Friday.

j. Growling angrily, the lion tamer persuaded the lion to return to its chair.

k. Our training activities have had the overall effect of increasing the professionalism of emergency managers and increasing our abilities to prepare for, respond to, and recover from any emergency or disaster that may threaten the lives, property, and environment of our citizens.

l. In the event that you encounter a situation that appears to be suspicious, be sure to call for backup support.

m. Each police officer should keep himself physically fit.

n. All mailmen should complete this training by July 1.

o. In planning and performing our audit, we considered the City of Somewhere City's internal control over compliance with requirements that could have a direct and material effect on a major federal program in order to determine our auditing procedures for the purpose of expressing our opinion on compliance and to test and report on internal control over compliance in accordance with OMB Circular A-133.

2. Write instructions on how to tie a necktie, tie a square knot, change a car tire, or perform some other task. Then

have two or three roommates or friends perform a usability test with the instructions to see if they can perform the task correctly by following your instructions.

3. Study all the SPELL rules and principles in the appendix, and then take a grammar test to assess your competence. Spend additional time studying the rules you miss, and then take another test to see if you have improved.

4. Critique and revise the following paragraph, using CLOUD as your standard.

> Safety-awareness programs and workshops are often used to deal with on-the-job injuries. Some organizations have contests to see how many days their employees can operate without having a workplace injury. Check with your workers-comp carrier for other ideas. They likely have other clients in the same field as yours, and those other companies can provide additional possibilities for improving on-the-job safety. On-the-job safety is a concern to all organizations, and all managers should have the safety and well being of their employees as a top priority. Nothing affects the morale of an organization like the death or serious injury of a key employee.

5. Critique the sentences in the following paragraph. Then write a revised version of the paragraph.

> Bicycling has many advantages. Bicycles provide exercise. They don't require gasoline to operate. They also generate no air pollution. They provide good exercise. They also reduce traffic congestion. They are also less costly to park. They are also highly maneuverable. And they can travel on special paths and trails. They also reduce air pollution.

6. Critique and revise the following message, checking all design, organization, content, and sentence factors:

> Thanks you for your order of 6 DVD's. "If Only They Were More Motivated," "Send Me an Email," and "Oh, No, Not Another Meeting" have been sent. "Slide Show Tips and Techniques," "Performance Appraisal that Really Improves Performance," and "Hiring Employees: Your Most Important Work" will be sent by Mar. 25. With each DVD you'll receive a companion booklet to assist your trainers in maximizing the value of the DVD in your organization. We want you to be 100 percent satisfied with the materials you receive from us. The booklets contain participant materials that may be freely copied for your in house seminars and workshops. We're also inclosing our latest catalogue that includes over fifty new training DVDs. As with all our training materials, these new DVDs carry a thirty day, no questions asked return-policy. Thank you again for your order, we appreciate your patronage.

7. Critique and revise the following message, checking all design, organization, content, and sentence factors:

> To: Chad R. Lakin, Academic Vice President
> From: Jan Sparks, Advisement Center Manger
> Date: November 13, 20XX
> Re: Recommendation
>
> As you know, the enrollment at our community college has tripled in the last 10 years, to a level of 18,000. Projections for the next decade indicate continuing growth, to peak at around 30,000. The resulting workload for our central advisement office has been enormous, causing numerous problems. For example, office space is inadequate. Advisement counselors cannot keep pace with program and policy requirements in all the academic departments, and the work backlog is causing numerous complaints from students and the academic departments. I'm aware that many other schools have decentralized and now have an advisement office in each of their major academic divisions across campus, and it seems we ought to adopt this same model and disperse our advisors across our 6 divisions. There could still be a central advisement officer to work with all the division advisement staff members, thus ensuring close oversight and standardization of procedures, etc. I have talked with all our advisors, and they all seem generally in favor of this proposal, although they have some reservations because of not knowing all the details involved. Please let me know what you think.

Rubric for Evaluating Writing

Writer_____   Topic_____

Rating (10-1)	**Evaluation Factors** Circle (strengths), underline weaknesses, add +/- comments
Design	—*Format* (appropriate for the message) —*Visual appeal* ▪ *Headings:* enable skimming, show information structure ▪ Art: appropriate tables, graphs, photos, bullet/number lists, etc. ▪ Typography: appropriate font, size, style, alignment ▪ Spacing: appropriate margins, text spacing *Comments:*
Organization	—***Approach:*** appropriate direct/indirect approach —***Structure:*** appropriate agenda and information structure *Comments:*
Content	—***Clear, complete, correct, compelling*** —***Paragraph standards:*** good coherence, length, organization, unity, development *Comments:*
Sentences	—**Structure:** (subject, verb, complement) —**Punctuation** —**Errors in grammar** (capitalization, numbers, spelling, etc.) —**Language** (word choice, formality, tone) —**Length** (conciseness) *Comments:*
_____/40 **Total**	

WRITING BUSINESS CORRESPONDENCE

Written business correspondence refers to messages sent as emails or as regular paper memos or letters. Typically, these messages are relatively short and can have a variety of purposes, such as to inform the reader of an upcoming meeting, to request information about a company policy, to persuade the reader to grant a request, or to express condolences after the death of a family member. This chapter will explain the process of writing various types of correspondence, whether traditional paper or electronic versions. The phases of planning, composing, and formatting are covered.

PLANNING

When planning your correspondence, first identify the purpose of the message. Determine exactly what you're trying to accomplish. Ask, "If this correspondence is successful, the reader(s) will do such and such." Usually, the purpose of a letter or memo involves both informing and persuading the reader. After clarifying the purpose, analyze the audience, create a brief outline, and develop a strategy for accomplishing the purpose.

Learn all you can about your audience, including the following.

- Who they are—their personality, demographics, and context (position and responsibilities in the organization, pressing needs, and decision-making authority).
- How they feel about you—how well they know you and what their relationship is with you.

- How they feel about the subject matter—how well they understand the subject and how they feel about it.

After analyzing the audience, use either a top-down or a bottom-up approach to create an outline. Considering the audience's current level of knowledge, determine how much explanation is needed to achieve the objectives of the message.

Also, consider how the content of the letter will affect the reader's emotion, and decide whether to use a *direct* or *indirect* approach. If you are communicating routine or good news, use a direct approach; but if you are conveying bad news or attempting to persuade a difficult audience, con-

Figure 6.1 Before writing, learn all you can about your audience.

sider using an indirect approach. You might also decide to employ multiple messages, such as a phone call and a letter.

For difficult persuasive messages, remember that people are motivated by both positive forces (things they want, such as money, jobs, success, and recognition) and negative forces (things they want to avoid, such as pain, job failure, or embarrassment). Further, remember to appeal to both logic and emotion.

Logic:

Cause and effect: If you act now, you can save 50 percent on the installation cost.

Statistics: Over 80 percent of our business comes from repeat customers.

Fair play: We completed the engineering work on the project according to the agreement; now it is your turn to complete your part of the agreement.

Nothing to lose: If you're not satisfied with the first issue, just call our toll-free number and let us know. We'll cancel your subscription and you'll owe nothing.

Ethics: We all have a responsibility to protect the environment of this community.

Emotion:

Pride: Imagine how you'll feel driving to work in your new car.

Fear: If we don't turn this company around soon, we'll all be out looking for new jobs.

Bandwagon: Nearly two-thirds of the 500 largest companies are using this approach.

Association: Olympic winner Sara Smith uses product XYZ.

If you are writing to someone outside your organization, generally use more formal language, making sure the document is polished both in writing and appearance. If the recipient works inside your organization and is above you on the organizational chart, be more formal and careful with format and appearance. If the message is going to someone who is your equal or who is lower than you are in the organization, you can usually be a bit less formal.

COMPOSING

Composing puts your plan into action as you create messages that are clear, correct, complete, and compelling. Clear messages are easily understood. Complete messages contain all appropriate content, including information regarding what, who, when, where, why, how, and how much. Correct messages contain accurate information with

no errors. Convincing messages are effective in achieving the desired objectives of the message.

Depending on the type of message being written, you will use either a direct or an indirect approach. Use a direct approach when your message will be received without having to first change the reader's mind. Use an indirect approach when you will have to change the reader's mind through persuasion, such as with bad-news messages or sales messages. Research has shown that an indirect message is more effective when attempting to persuade a person to accept a controversial idea (Frischknecht & Baker 2011).

Table 6.1 provides guidelines for writing five different types of messages: good news, routine, mildly persuasive, difficult persuasive, and bad news. Figures 6.2, 6.3, 6.4, 6.5, and 6.6 illustrate examples of these different types of messages.

FORMATTING

Different business documents have various formatting expectations, including such factors as line spacing, margins, and placement of text. The following sections list formatting standards for memos, emails, and letters.

Memos

Memos typically have four parts in their heading, including To, From, Date, and Subject lines. You may also use Re. (meaning "regarding") in place of Subject. The body of the message then begins a double space beneath the subject line.

1. Use one-inch margins.

2. Type the subject line in all capitals or in bold for emphasis. Also, consider extra spacing before and after the subject line for emphasis.

3. Left align the information following To, From, Date, and Re.

    To: Nathan Rogers

    From: Beth Marcos

    Date: January 14, 20XX

    Re: **SAVINGS AND INVESTMENT PLANS**

4. Use To, From, Date, Re. sequence for the heading, rather than To, From, Re., and Date.

5. Spell out the month to prevent month-day confusion. Outside the United States, the day comes before the month; thus, 8/9/20XX is 8 September 20XX, rather than August 9, 20XX. Either 9 August 20XX or August 9, 20XX is acceptable format.

6. Sign or initial beside your name at the top or at the

Table 6.1   Types, Approaches, and Guidelines for Composing Correspondence

Message Type	Approach	Examples	Guidelines
Good news (*Figure 6.2*)	Direct	• Announce a promotion • Grant a request • Announce an achievement	**Opening:** Give the main idea. **Agenda:** As appropriate, forecast the body text, revealing its content and/or structure. **Body:** Develop the body content. **Closing:** Close as appropriate, perhaps referring back to the good news given at the beginning.
Routine (*Figure 6.3*)	Usually direct	• Ask for clarification about a policy or procedure • Announce an upcoming meeting • Request permission to attend an important conference • Request permission to make a small purchase	**Opening:** Give the main idea, sometimes giving a sentence or two of appropriate introduction before the main idea. **Agenda:** Forecast the key body information, revealing its content and/or structure. Consider enhancing the visual access of the agenda items with (a), (b), (c), etc. **Body:** Develop the body information to fulfill the agenda. **Closing:** Close with content appropriate to the subject matter.
Sales, or mild persuasion (*Figure 6.4*)	Usually quite direct	• Convince a person to buy your product or idea • Convince a person to make payment on a financial account. • Persuade a person to accept a different point of view on a matter that has limited risk	**Opening:** Hook the reader's attention with content that interests the reader. Then introduce the key message. **Agenda:** Use an agenda if appropriate (such as introducing key features and/or benefits explained in the body). **Body:** Develop the key features and/or benefits, and include logically or emotionally persuasive content as appropriate. **Closing:** Emphasize the action you want the reader to take.
Difficult persuasion (*Figure 6.5*)	Usually indirect	• Convince people to change their mind about a difficult issue • Persuade people to participate in something in which they have little interest • Convince people to take action on a matter that has significant implications	**Opening:** Effectively frame the troublesome issue or problem being addressed, but don't give the key message yet. **Agenda:** Use an agenda if appropriate to provide structure for the body content. **Body:** Explain your reasoning or other relevant content; then state your key point. Highlight the positives and minimize the negatives of your argument. As relevant, highlight the negatives and minimize the positives of other perspectives. **Closing:** Reinforce the key message, and request appropriate action.
Bad news (*Figure 6.6*)	Usually indirect	• Deny a person's employment request • Announce the elimination of an employee benefit • Announce the firing of an employee • Place an employee on probation	**Opening:** Begin with content appropriately related to the main idea, but don't give the bad news yet. **Agenda:** Omit the agenda (or give a very general agenda). **Body:** Give your reasoning that logically leads to the bad news. State the bad news with as little negative language and negative feeling as possible, perhaps visually burying it in the middle of a paragraph. Highlight any positive information as appropriate. **Closing:** Try to suggest possible alternatives to help the reader, or give other relevant content that is as positive as appropriate.

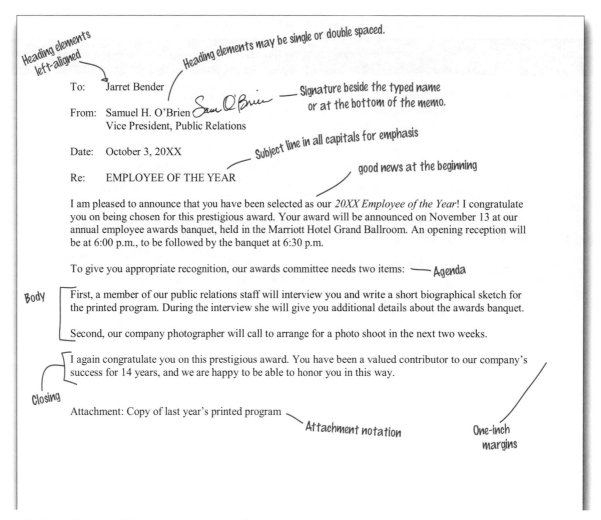

Figure 6.2 A sample memo delivering good news using the direct approach.

bottom of the memo, depending on standard practice in your organization.

7. For multiple-page memos, type the page number on second and succeeding pages.

A sample memo illustrating these formatting guidelines is shown in Figure 6.2.

Emails

Email programs provide space for recipients' names, the subject line, the body of the memo, and attachments.

Recipients can be placed in one of three fields. The *To:* field is for main recipients. The other two fields include recipients for whom the content may be valuable for their information. The *Cc:* field (carbon copy) works just like the *To:* field, and every recipient can see all the email addresses in those two fields. However, email addresses in the *Bcc:* (blind carbon copy) field cannot be seen by any other recipient. The *Bcc:* field is helpful when discretion must be used regarding who is receiving the email.

The subject line should usually serve as a topical intro-

duction to the content. Make sure you write a descriptive subject line, because people often decide whether to read an email on the basis of the subject line.

Other tips to remember with email are as follows:

1. Read your email messages at least once or twice a day. Take appropriate action on each one, and strive to keep your mailbox empty. Avoid piling up hundreds of old messages.

   • Delete all spam (junk) messages instantly, even before reading them if possible. Do not open or reply to spam messages. Try to prevent incoming spam messages with a filter.

   • Read messages and then delete them or file them in another folder if you want to keep them. Do not keep them in your email in-box.

   • Respond to quick-action items immediately and then delete or file them as needed.

   • For action items that will take longer, place them in an action folder, enter them as a new task on

Figure 6.3 Sample routine message in email format.

your prioritized task list, or print them for use as a source document. Then complete the needed action in a timely manner.

2. For sent or received emails that you want to keep, move them into a well-organized email filing system. Follow up as needed.

3. When sending emails, be careful what you write. Remember that email messages are not private. You never know to whom your emails will be forwarded. If you are always careful in both what you say and how you say it, you don't have to worry. For extra sensitive messages, don't send them by email! Handle them in a face-to-face setting or by telephone.

4. Read your emails out loud before sending them. This will help you catch writing and proofreading errors.

5. Even though many emails are informal messages, don't become too lax in your writing. Exercise use correct grammar, spelling, and punctuation.

6. For emails longer than a few lines, consider using OABC

and HATS to enhance readability (see Figure 6.3). If you do not have font variations, you can capitalize, underline, or number headings to set them off from the other text.

7. An agenda is particularly important for messages longer than one screen so the reader will know what to expect on subsequent screens.

8. Write your name or initials at the end of the memo to clearly indicate the end of the document.

Letters

Business letters generally follow one of three formats: the full-block, the modified-block, or the simplified format.

FULL-BLOCK FORMAT

The full-block format is used for most correspondence (see Figure 6.4). The following formatting standards apply.

1. Leave one-inch left and right margins, and begin all lines at the left margin.

2. Single space the text, but double space between paragraphs and all letter parts, except as follows: (a) add extra spaces as needed between the date and the first line of the inside address, and (b) leave 3–5 spaces between the complimentary close and the writer's name at the bottom of the letter.

3. Center the letter vertically on the page.

4. For multiple-page letters, type the name of the recipient, date, and page number at the top of the second and subsequent pages as follows (continue the text three lines below the page number):

Abdul R. Ahmad
March 4, 20XX
Page 2

A space-saving option is to place the three items on the same line across the top of the page with the name at the left margin, the page number centered, and the date at the right margin.

SpeakWorks

1875 South State; Orem, UT 84097 ❖ Phone: 801-717-3499 Fax: 801-717-3499
Online: speakworks.com ❖ Email: info@speakworks.com

March 4, 20XX

1-4 blank spaces between date and recipient address.

Mr. Abdul R. Ahmad
4783 44th Avenue
Anywhere, XX 83924

One line of blank space before and after salutation.

Dear Mr. Ahmad:

Opening hook
As an instructor of speech communication, you can give your students more than just a video recording of their presentations and a few written comments. Now you can capture video AND embed time-stamped comments that students can view online immediately after their presentations. And you can have these advantages for FREE!

Key point introduced after opening hook

Announcing REACT, a real-time, video-based presentation-coaching system! This amazing technology offers numerous advantages for enhanced student involvement and improvement:

Visual enhancement of persuasive information.

Yes ...	No ...
Capture video with online software, *using only your laptop computer, a webcam, and an internet connection.*	*No more hassle with expensive video cameras, DVD's, or other extra technology.*
Capture instructor's feedback during the presentation, *and time-stamp the comments to the specific points in the presentation where they were given.*	*No more handwriting of comments on paper for you, and no more mental disconnect between comments on paper and subsequent viewing of presentations for your students.*
Capture fellow students' feedback during presentations *so they can be involved both in giving their presentations and in coaching their peers.*	*No more disconnected, passive endurance while students wait their turn to present.*
Provide immediate video and time-stamped text feedback *to students after their presentations.*	*No more delay in getting instructor feedback or waiting for video media to be produced.*

If you would like to improve the precision and effectiveness of your feedback, and to provide the feedback online for viewing immediately following students' presentations, REACT is the program for you. Using REACT, you'll see improved performance more quickly, and you'll give your students a distinct edge in their business careers.

Here is what students are saying after they use REACT:

- I loved being able to watch myself present. I have never had that opportunity before, despite being involved with many presentations. Now I can be a part of my own audience and evaluate how I can improve my skills.
- REACT helped me actually see what I was doing from an audience's perspective.

Figure 6.4 A two-page sales letter in full-block format.

One-inch top margin on page 2

Mr. Abdul R. Ahmad   _Heading for page 2_
March 4, 20XX
Page 2
        _2 blank spaces between page heading
            and continuing body text_

- The "line" rating system is great. I loved being able to see exactly how well my presentation was being received.
- REACT is simple and easy to use without prior experience.
- The best part of the REACT system is the ability to give and receive feedback from multiple people at the same time during the presentation.

Action ending
Call XXX-XXX-XXXX today and ask how you can implement this software for free in your classes, or visit us online at speakworks.com. Join thousands of others who have discovered the advantages of REACT!

        One blank space between body and
Sincerely,   _complimentary close_

Suzanne Ashcroft   _3-4 blank spaces for signature_

Suzanne Ashcroft, Sales Manager

Enclosures: REACT promotional brochures   — _Enclosure notation_

Figure 6.4 continued.

MODIFIED-BLOCK FORMAT

The modified-block format is similar to the full-block format, but moves the date, complimentary close, and sender's name closer to the center of the page—all left aligned with each other (see Figure 6.5). The body paragraphs may also be indented one-half inch if you wish. All other guidelines pertaining to the full-block format apply to the modified-block format.

SIMPLIFIED FORMAT

Another variation of the full-block format is the simplified format (see Figure 6.6). The simplified letter format is not used often, but it works well when you're writing to a group (e.g., a committee) or when the recipient's name is gender neutral, such as Chris or Pat. Because the simplified format replaces the salutation of the recipient with a subject line, you don't have to wonder whether to use "Dear Mr. Jones" or "Dear Ms. Jones." The following guidelines apply to letters written in the simplified format.

Writer's address and date begin at center

Letter is vertically centered
on the page

582 Hilltop Road
Somewhere, XX 92827
July 18, 20XX

Mr. Steven Kaiser
8834 Riverside Drive
Anywhere, XX 92827

Dear Mr. Kaiser: — 1 Blank space

Indirect approach

As you recall, your company built two bookcases for me about two months ago. When the bookcases were delivered, four of the shelves had problems. I immediately returned the shelves to you so the problems could be resolved: — No agenda

- For the shorter bookcase, two shelves had surface scratches that could be repaired with sanding and re-staining.
- For the taller bookcase, two shelves showed some separation between the plywood layers. These shelves could not be fixed; therefore, two new shelves needed to be made.

Numerous times during the past several weeks I have stopped at your store to ask about the shelves, but every time I am told, "We'll check on them and get back to you." Then nothing happens! The last time I checked was about a week ago. As usual, your store clerk said she would call me the next day and let me know the status of the shelves, but no call came.

When the bookcases were delivered, I paid you the full price to settle the financial aspect of this purchase. Now I would like to get the two repaired shelves and two new shelves delivered so we can finalize the entire transaction. I do not want to delay this matter any longer! — Main point at end of message

Please check on these shelves today, and then call 609–472–14XX to let me know exactly when you will be able to deliver. I will sincerely appreciate your assistance.

Sincerely,

Signature block left aligns
with writer's address
at top of letter.

Carla Conrad

Figure 6.5 A difficult-persuasion letter in modified-block format.

Picture Place

1490 Lakeside Drive
Anywhere, US XXXXX
Phone: 1-800-229-XXXX
Web: pixplace.com

Letter is centered vertically on the page

July 18, 20XX

———— *1-4 blank spaces between date and recipient address*

Chris Shen
8834 Riverside Drive
Somewhere, XX 83924

One line of space before and after subject line

MALFUNCTIONING K305 CAMERA — *Subject line in all capitals*

Indirect approach   We have received your K305 camera and your description of the recent problems you have had. Our technicians have carefully examined the camera to determine the cause of the problems. Here is what they found. — *For bad news, avoid using an agenda that reveals the bad news.*

First, our technicians discovered a hairline crack in the body of the camera, perhaps due to the camera being accidentally dropped. Second, they found numerous sand particles around various camera buttons and the lens, perhaps from use in windy, sandy conditions. The sand could be cleaned from the various camera parts, but the damage from the crack cannot be repaired. We are returning the camera to you in a separate package.

If these problems had occurred during our manufacturing process, we would have been happy to replace your camera free of charge. Because the problems were caused after purchase, we can offer you a new camera for $89.95 (35 percent lower than the suggested retail price). The new camera will have the same 90-day guarantee you had with your other camera and will capture photos of the same quality you enjoyed in the past.

Before September 1, please call 1-800-229-XXXX to let us know if you would like to take advantage of this offer. With proper care of the new camera, you'll be able to enjoy many years of rewarding photography.

Jen Alta Villa

JENNIFER ALTA VILLA—CUSTOMER SERVICE SPECIALIST

Content focuses on what you can do, not what you can't.

Bad news is placed in the middle of a paragraph for de-emphasis

Bad news is given after the reasons

Figure 6.6 An indirect bad news letter in simplified format.

1. Leave one-inch left and right margins and begin all lines at the left margin.

2. Single space the text.

3. Double space between paragraphs and all letter parts, except as follows: (a) add extra spaces as needed between the date and the inside address, and (b) leave 3–5 spaces between the body and the writer's name at the bottom of the letter.

4. Center the letter vertically on the page.

5. Omit the salutation and replace it with a capitalized subject line.

6. Omit the complimentary close and capitalize your name and title. (Sign your name between the last paragraph and your typed name.)

7. For multiple-page letters, type the recipient's name, date, and page number on the second and subsequent pages.

Chapter Summary

Business correspondence consists of exchanging messages between business people, typically by emails, memos, and letters. When planning your correspondence, identify the purpose of the message, analyze the audience, and develop a strategy for accomplishing the purpose.

Compose the message so it will be clear, complete, correct, and compelling. A direct approach is appropriate for most good-news and routine messages, but a more indirect agenda is better for bad-news messages and for messages that require strong persuasion.

Different business documents, such as reports, letters, memos, and emails, have various formatting expectations, including such factors as line spacing, margins, and placement of text. For letters, three common formats are full-block, modified-block, and simplified. Be aware of these formatting standards, and apply them appropriately in all your documents.

Works Cited

Frischknecht, Sierra Sloan and William H. Baker. *Enhanced vs. Undifferentiated Text: A Study to Assess the Effects on Readers: Proceedings of the 76th Annual Convention of the Association for Business Communication, Oct. 19-22, 2011.* Montreal, Quebec, Canada: Association for Business Communication, 2011.

Chapter Questions

1. What is the difference between a direct and indirect approach in writing business letters?

2. Explain why a good-news message should employ a direct approach.

3. Explain why a bad-news message should use an indirect approach.

4. What is the difference in the vertical positioning of memos and letters?

5. What does the abbreviation "bcc" mean when it is used with an email?

6. Explain the differences between the full-block, modified-block, and the simplified letter formats. When should the simplified letter format be used?

7. Describe three guidelines for managing your emails.

8. What communication factors should you remember when writing to people inside vs. outside your organization?

Chapter Activities

Before submitting any of the following assignments, review them thoroughly for compliance with all design, organization, content, and sentence (DOCS) standards.

1. Write an informative memo to your instructor. Explain what you consider to be the two or three most important aspects of this chapter.

2. Write an email to your instructor. Explain what you consider to be the three most important things you have learned in college.

3. Write a sales message to post on your social-network site. Try to sell something you own, such as a bicycle, motorcycle, apartment contract, computer, or other electronic device. Follow the guidelines for sales messages given in this chapter.

4. Write a complaint letter to a business organization regarding a problem you have had with one of its products or services. Ask for some specific action, such as a refund of your money or a replacement of the product. Write the letter twice, once using a direct approach and once using an indirect approach. Use modified-block format for one letter and full-block format for the other. Explain which approach and which format you like best.

5. Write a letter of recommendation for a friend or classmate who is applying for a job. Address the letter to the Human Resources Department of the company. Use the simplified letter format. Effectively use OABC and HATS. (See sample recommendation letter in Figure 7.10.)

6. You work as a customer service agent for MidWest Air-

lines. On January 1, 20XX, you received the following letter (today's date is January 4). Write an appropriate letter to this individual, but do not grant his request for a free flight.

On December 23, 20XX I was flying MidWest Airlines from Calgary to Chicago on flight 268 with a stop off in Minneapolis. The flight was delayed 2 hours because of bad weather. I took that particular flight because it did not require me to de-plane in Minneapolis. To prevent hassle between flights, I thought this would be the best option, but when we arrived in Minneapolis your people told me the Chicago flight had been cancelled. After much rudeness from your staff I was put up in a hotel for the night.

Then when flying home on Dec. 26, 20XX, the flight I scheduled from Chicago to Calgary was late by two hours. Then when I arrived in Minneapolis, I again found the flight to Calgary had been cancelled. Again after much rude behavior by your staff, I was given a hotel for the night. I then called my family in Calgary to let them know that I was not coming in that night and they had told me that when they called the airline to find out if the flight was delayed, the airline told my family that the flight had landed in Calgary. This was very odd since I was stranded in Minneapolis. I must say that the entire experience flying on your airline was a total nightmare. I will think twice before ever flying with you again. I would like the airline to accept responsibility for bad service and unacceptable behavior from their staff. A free flight would be nice.

Tom Martin
328 Thornhill Road NW
Calgary, AB T2E-6S6

7. Your position is Director of Personnel Benefits for Southwest Clothing Mills, located at 2883 Industrial Way, Oklahoma City, OK 73132. Your company has a tuition-assistance program (TAP) that helps employees complete educational degrees. The company will pay up to half of the tuition for educational programs for students whose applications are approved. To obtain company participation, an employee must submit a letter describing the intended educational program and asking for assistance. The letter must be accompanied by a recommendation letter from the employee's supervisor. This procedure must be repeated each semester; and for subsequent semesters, the employee's letter must include the grades earned for the previous semester. If a participant doesn't maintain a 3.0 GPA, no funds will be made available until that participant's semester GPA once again reaches the 3.0 level—the participant may then reapply for tuition funding.

Letter 1—Bad News

Dave Wheeler, one of your company's accounting clerks, has just completed his bachelor's degree at University of Oklahoma. His degree is in accounting, and you gave him educational assistance for three semesters while he was working on that degree. Now he wants to pursue an evening MBA degree, also at OU. Tuition for the night program is $3850 per semester. Write him a letter denying his request. Your TAP budget for next semester has reached its limit. Plus, you have a policy of helping out with undergraduate programs first and then with graduate programs *if funds permit.* Dave is a good employee (he gets high marks from his supervisor) and you don't want to destroy his motivation, either for his job or for his educational pursuits. Therefore, be very careful in wording the letter.

Mr. David J. Wheeler
7834 Maple Lane
Broken Arrow, OK 73155

Letter 2—Good News

Julia Lockhart has also applied for funding from TAP. This is her first application, and she wants to complete her undergraduate degree in computer science at the University of Central Oklahoma. She has approximately three semesters left, and her GPA for her prior work at the University of Central Oklahoma is 2.89. Grant her request, and indicate that a check for half of the tuition amount will be sent to her as soon as she sends a copy of her tuition billing statement to you. Remind her that for future funding, she must earn at least a 3.0 GPA for the previous semester. Julia is an administrative assistant in the Public Relations Department and has been given a good recommendation by her supervisor.

Ms. Julia Lockhart
835 North First Avenue
Edmund, OK 73028

8. Obtain an employment resume from two of your classmates.

Letter 1—Bad news. Write a bad-news letter to one, indicating that he or she will not be hired. Without offending, give one or more reasons for your refusal.

Letter 2—Good news. Write a good-news letter to the other, stating that he or she will be hired, and explaining the appropriate starting date, starting salary, starting position, supervisor, and department.

PREPARING EMPLOYMENT COMMUNICATIONS

Seeking new employment is one of the most critical things you do, because your employment affects nearly every aspect of your life: how you spend your time each day, how much money you make, where you live, what kind of home you can afford, where your children go to school, who your friends and neighbors are, what professional skills and abilities you learn, what future career opportunities you will have, how prepared you will be for retirement, and more. Thus, take your employment decisions very seriously.

When you are seeking employment, many online information sources can be helpful. For example, consult the *Occupational Outlook Handbook and the Career Guide to Industries,* prepared by the U.S. Government's Bureau of Labor Statistics. Other sites include www.acinet.org, www.ajb.dni.us, www.monster.com, www.monstertrak.com, www.net-temps.com, and www.careerbuilder.com. Also, conduct a general search for "employment" to find numerous sites sponsored by private organizations.

In addition to using online information resources, request help from friends and other contacts in your professional and social network (e.g., LinkedIn or Facebook). Tell them that you are seeking employment, and ask them to let you know if they hear of any job opportunities that might be a good fit for you. Send them a copy of your resume, highlighting your experiences, education, and strengths that make you a good candidate for the type of work you are seeking.

Seeking employment involves a variety of written and oral communications.

Written (different documents may be sent by hard copy, fax, or email, depending on the circumstances):

- Job announcement (employer)
- Application letter (applicant)
- Follow-up letter (applicant)
- Recommendation letter (third party)
- Offer/rejection letter (employer)
- Acceptance/rejection letter (applicant)

Oral (both employer and applicant)

- Interview(s)
- Telephone calls
- Other (e.g., networking, conversation at dinners, and social gatherings)

The materials in this chapter include instruction and samples pertaining to application letters, resumes, interviews, follow-up letters, and recommendation letters.

APPLICATION LETTERS

Application letters (also known as cover letters) are addressed to the person or organization you want to work for. The purpose of the application letter is to introduce you to the prospective employer and to convince him or her to invite you in for an employment interview. The following paragraphs explain the three main parts of an application letter. (A sample cover letter is given in Figure 7.1.)

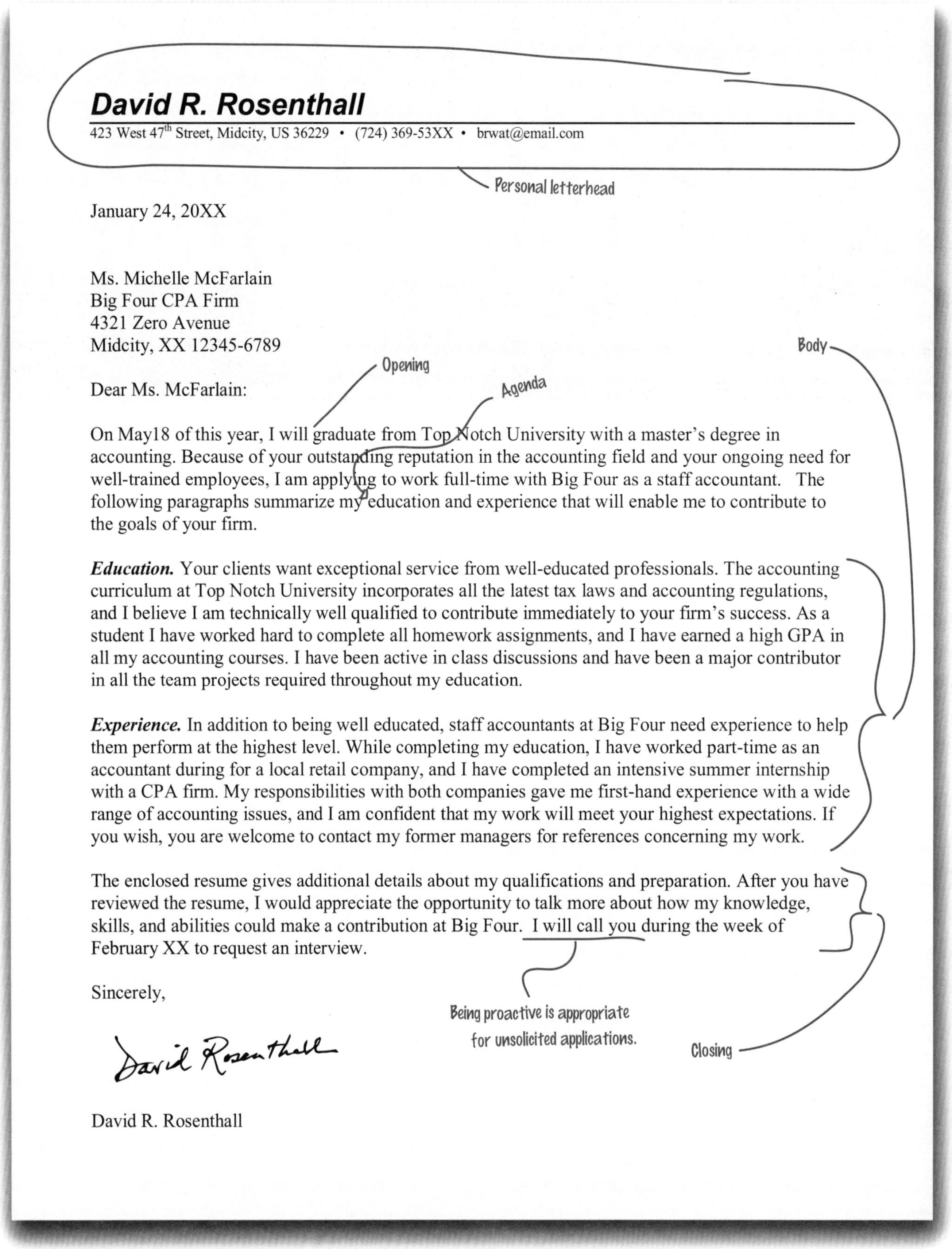

David R. Rosenthall

423 West 47th Street, Midcity, US 36229 • (724) 369-53XX • brwat@email.com

Personal letterhead

January 24, 20XX

Ms. Michelle McFarlain
Big Four CPA Firm
4321 Zero Avenue
Midcity, XX 12345-6789

Dear Ms. McFarlain:

Opening

Agenda

Body

On May18 of this year, I will graduate from Top Notch University with a master's degree in accounting. Because of your outstanding reputation in the accounting field and your ongoing need for well-trained employees, I am applying to work full-time with Big Four as a staff accountant.   The following paragraphs summarize my education and experience that will enable me to contribute to the goals of your firm.

Education. Your clients want exceptional service from well-educated professionals. The accounting curriculum at Top Notch University incorporates all the latest tax laws and accounting regulations, and I believe I am technically well qualified to contribute immediately to your firm's success. As a student I have worked hard to complete all homework assignments, and I have earned a high GPA in all my accounting courses. I have been active in class discussions and have been a major contributor in all the team projects required throughout my education.

Experience. In addition to being well educated, staff accountants at Big Four need experience to help them perform at the highest level. While completing my education, I have worked part-time as an accountant during for a local retail company, and I have completed an intensive summer internship with a CPA firm. My responsibilities with both companies gave me first-hand experience with a wide range of accounting issues, and I am confident that my work will meet your highest expectations. If you wish, you are welcome to contact my former managers for references concerning my work.

The enclosed resume gives additional details about my qualifications and preparation. After you have reviewed the resume, I would appreciate the opportunity to talk more about how my knowledge, skills, and abilities could make a contribution at Big Four. I will call you during the week of February XX to request an interview.

Sincerely,

*Being proactive is appropriate
for unsolicited applications.*

Closing

David Rosenthall

David R. Rosenthall

Figure 7.1 Application letters should tell how your qualifications match the job requirements.

Opening paragraph: Explain the purpose for your communication. For example, tell how you learned of the job opening, explain how employment with the company would fulfill your life's ambitions, or suggest briefly how your qualifications would be an asset to the company. State specifically what job you are applying for. Indicate that the following paragraphs will explain how your credentials match the job requirements.

If you use the OABC framework, include an agenda in the last sentence of the opening paragraph; e.g., "I believe my (a) education, (b) experience, and (c) personal attributes match the requirements of the position you are seeking to fill."

Middle paragraph(s): Explain how your education, experience, and attributes qualify you for employment with the company. Build the body of your letter around the agenda given in paragraph 1. For example, paragraph 2 could show how your education has prepared you for the job you are seeking, paragraph 3 could illustrate how your previous employment experiences add to your qualifications. Convince the reader that you are qualified to be an effective, contributing employee. Improve the access of this information by using paragraph headings.

Last paragraph: Ask for an interview. Refer the reader to the "enclosed resume." Then for unsolicited applications, indicate that you'll call the person to request an interview.

RESUMES

A resume is a self-promotion document to help you obtain a job interview with a prospective employer. Sample resumes are shown in Figures 7.2, 7.3, and 7.4, but feel free to modify your own resume as needed to effectively market yourself. To begin, study the employer's job requirements and then design your resume to closely match those requirements. For example, use the same wording as that used in the job announcement.

Chronological Resume Guidelines

Most job applicants use a traditional chronological resume format, shown in Figures 7.2 and 7.3. The chronological format is the most common format. The content is listed in easy-to-follow time-based order, and most employers are familiar with this format. The following paragraphs provide guidelines for chronological resumes.

1. Create a heading that lists your name, address, telephone numbers, and email address as the first items on the resume. Type your name in a larger font for emphasis. Use this same heading at the top of your cover letter, perhaps reducing the font size of your name so it's not overbearing.

2. Create a professional summary, skills, or strengths section that captures your main attributes and job qualifications, such as "Ten years programming experience, . . ." or "Word, Excel, PowerPoint . . ." When submitting an unsolicited application, consider including an "objectives" statement that clarifies the type of job you are seeking. *Example:* "Seeking sales or marketing analyst position where I can apply my statistical skills."

3. List your education and experience, with the more impressive section first. In other words, if your education is more impressive than your experience, list your education first. Also, list your education and experience entries in reverse-chronological order—last degree or last job first.

   For each college you include, indicate the degree you received, the dates of attendance, your major field of study, and other pertinent information. At this point you may also include specific classes you have completed, academic awards or scholarships you have received, or professional academic clubs or organizations you have affiliated with. As a general rule, omit high school information.

   For each job, list the job title, employment dates, company name and address (city and state), job duties, and the results you achieved. Quantified results statements highlight your accomplishments, such as, "Reduced assembly-line accidents by 38 percent in a one-year period." Results statements are much better than bland responsibility statements like, "Responsible for keeping assembly line running smoothly."

4. Have one or more additional sections to focus on awards, special achievements, volunteer service, or other relevant information. Some people also like to include their hobbies, but recruiters are split on the value of listing hobbies. About half like them included; about half see them as irrelevant. However, almost no one expresses a dislike for hobbies, so you may include them if you would like.

5. Keep your resume to one page if possible; however, if you have good information that warrants two pages, use two pages. Put your name and the page number at the top of any subsequent pages, as shown in Figure 7.4. Leave two blank lines between the page number and the next line of text in your resume.

6. Proofread. Make sure your resume is perfect in spelling, grammar, and punctuation.

AARON DOBSON

573 West Amazon Lane • Anywhere, ST 740XX • (839) 400–XXXX • aadobr@email.com

SUMMARY

Experience: Three years work experience in beverage industry analyzing brand distribution, customer trends, and sales results and opportunities

Administrative skills: Excellent quantitative, communication, and interpersonal skills; fluent in Spanish; worked in cross-functional teams in results-driven environment

Computer skills: Word, Excel, PowerPoint, Microsoft Publisher, and SPSS

EDUCATION

Master of Business Administration, Marketing Emphasis   Apr 20XX
Top Notch University, Big City, ST
- Awarded graduate scholarship
- Scored in 90th percentile on GMAT
- Served as president of MBA Marketing Association
- Developed training presentation for instructor's website

Bachelor of Science, Statistics, Business Analysis Emphasis   Aug 20XX
Minor, Business Management
State University, Anywhere, ST
- Secretary of Student Chapter of American Society for Quality

EXPERIENCE

Sales Analyst   Oct 20XX – Aug 20XX
Soft Drink Bottling Group; Big City, ST
- Developed and implemented Excel tool that tracked distribution voids of 70+ innovative SKU's for 2200 retail, convenience, and food-service customers
- Assumed full responsibility in development and execution of all incentives for sales representatives; increased success rate of incentive targets achieved by 30 percent
- Received Customer Service Award, awarded to only 10 employees each year who exemplified the company's customer-service initiative
- Completed company's management-development program
- Built yearly volume plans of 8.5 million cases for 4 territories and 60+ routes, and analyzed sales and out-of-date, breakage, and sellable returns on a daily basis

Course Assistant   May 20XX – Aug 20XX
Department of Statistics; Big City, ST
- Conducted weekly training meetings for 5-10 department teaching assistants
- Graded exams, homework, and quizzes, and maintained grade database of 200 students
- Assisted professor in lectures for introductory statistics class
- Ranked in the top 20 percent of TA's on student ratings

SERVICE

Volunteer: Annual United Way Day of Caring   Mar 20XX

INTERESTS

Cycling, hiking, literature, music, and international travel

Figure 7.2 A sample resume submitted for a posted position. Employment resumes should reflect careful attention to content and design.

Emily R. Bowen

335 North Norfolk   Hometown, ST 565XX   339–461–XXXX   mle@email.com

Objective

To obtain a summer internship in tax accounting and gain experience with current tax law.

Experience

Accounting Clerk (June 20XX–January 20XX)
TNU Department of Visual Communications, Big City, ST
- Identified weaknesses in AIS that led us to recover over $10,000 of revenue.
- Suggested and implemented billing policies that saved time and increased accuracy by 15%.
- Helped plan and submit a $500,000 yearly budget.

Training Consultant (September to December 20XX)
TNU Center for Service and Learning, Big City, ST
- Worked with small team to evaluate the center's recruiting and training practices.
- Implemented policy changes, brochure redesign, access to additional training materials, and recommended more effective recruiting media.

Education

Top Notch University; Big City, ST (May 20XX)
Major: Accounting (3.8 GPA)
- Academic Scholarship; Dean's List
- Member Beta Gamma Sigma and Beta Alpha Psi
- Relevant course work:
    Completed: Business Communication, 2nd year Spanish, Intermediate Financial Accounting, Financial Statement Auditing, Accounting Information Systems (including Access)
    Currently enrolled: Fundamentals of Tax, and Cost and Managerial Accounting

Figure 7.3 An unsolicited resume like the one above will often contain an objective statement to clarify the position being sought.

Emily R. Bowen

Page 2

Volunteer

Volunteer Service (April 20XX to April 20XX)
Peace Corps, Mexico
- Taught English classes.
- Gave HIV/AIDS awareness training.

Volunteer Counselor (September 20XX–December 20XX)
TNU Unified Sports Program
- Taught children with Down Syndrome how to play sports.
- Built self-esteem and friendships.

Computer Skills

- ACL, Quickbooks, Peachtree
- Microsoft Access, Excel, Word, Outlook, FrontPage, and PowerPoint

Figure 7.4 Subsequent pages in a resume should have a header that includes the page number.

7. Pay attention to appearance. Use an attractive format and use high-quality paper for a professional image.

Functional Resume Guidelines

Some applicants choose a functional-resume format, shown in Figure 7.6. The functional-resume format emphasizes a person's skills and competencies and de-emphasizes their career path. It is often used by individuals who wish to make a career shift, who want to de-emphasize their age, or who don't have an impressive career path. The following paragraphs provide guidelines for functional resumes.

1. Create the heading section just as you would with the traditional chronological format. Include your name, address, telephone number, email address, and so forth.

2. As appropriate for unsolicited resumes, insert an objective that clearly states the types of employment you are seeking.

3. Create a section that highlights the knowledge, skills, and abilities that are relevant to the employment you are seeking. Organize this information under appropriate headings, such as communication, leadership, project management, analytical, technical, and computer skills. As with chronological resumes, include specific results you have achieved, and quantify the results whenever appropriate.

4. Create any additional sections that will be of value to the employer, including education, experience, professional memberships, awards received, and so forth. If you include education and experience, keep them brief, because you will already have listed your critical education and experience information in the previous section.

Other guidelines regarding typography, spacing, length, proofreading, and so forth are consistent for both chronological and functional resumes.

In addition to preparing a resume, some people create a portfolio of additional electronic documents, which they place on the internet (e.g., cetificates, awards, writing samples, letters from previous employers, etc.). Be sure to do your very best design work when developing material to put on the internet. Also, be very careful with any personal information you put on the internet, because many employers conduct internet searches for anything about your past that would disqualify you.

INTERVIEWS

At times during your career you will be interviewed, and at other times you will interview other people. The following sections give tips for both types of settings.

When You Are Being Interviewed

The following guidelines will help you make a good impression in an interview. Review these guidelines, and practice your interview with someone who can effectively represent an interviewer.

1. *Do your homework.* Learn about the organization by searching the internet, looking in the library, or studying information provided by a college placement center. Learn about the organization's products and services, organizational structure, industry challenges and trends, competition, and financial standing.

2. *Be prepared and be on time.* Be prompt—leave early for the interview so an unexpected delay won't make you late. Carry an extra copy of your resume, paper, and a pen for making notes either during or after the interview.

3. *Be sensitive to appearance and body language (yours and the interviewer's).* Dress appropriately and conservatively, avoiding faddish clothing and hair styles. Shake hands firmly. During the interview, be alert, interested, and pleasant. Maintain good eye contact. Avoid nervous mannerisms with hands and feet. Watch for nonverbal cues from the interviewer and adjust accordingly.

4. *Speak confidently, clearly, and fluently.* Listen carefully to the questions and answer them completely, yet concisely. Don't dominate the interview with long answers and explanations. Maintain good voice energy.

5. *Be honest; don't pretend to be something you're not!* Be truthful; never lie. Don't exaggerate.

6. *Tie your answers to the job requirements.* Take advantage of every opportunity to tie your credentials to the knowledge, skills, and abilities required for the job. Remember to sell both your technical qualifications and your human skills. For instance, you might be

Figure 7.5 Interpersonal skills are important as you seek employment.

Trevor L. Carter

986 N. College Park Road; Nome, TX 384XX • 592 - 738 - XXXX • tlcarter95@ email.com

PROFESSIONAL SKILLS

Communication Skills
- Presented to large groups using professionally designed PowerPoint slides
- Developed facility with Spanish language; performed health coaching in Spanish and assisted with translation in office settings
- Wrote comprehensive evaluation report of Walktober program and made recommendations for improvements in future events
- Created and designed weekly newsletters for Walktober participants

Interpersonal Skills
- Acquired donations from various companies through successful verbal and written communication
- Demonstrated proficiency in teaching and informing target population on pertinent topics
- Resolved landlord/tenant disputes, taking legal action when necessary
- Demonstrated strong interpersonal skills; worked well with individuals from various cultural backgrounds

Leadership Skills
- Served as Chair of Walktober program at Jefferson County Health Department and oversaw all details; over 250 employees participated
- Raised over $5,000 of donations in kind from various companies
- Managed property for 210 self-storage units; responsible for coordinating maintenance and repairs

Technical Skills
- Assisted in financial management and budgeting for large self-storage company
- Demonstrated excellent technical-writing skills; wrote three successful grant proposals
- Demonstrated critical thinking; ability to analyze and solve problems, and ability to make effective decisions
- Demonstrated proficiency with Microsoft Office software: Word, Excel, PowerPoint, Publisher

EDUCATION

Bachelor of Science in Community Health (Health Education Emphasis)   Dec 20XX
Achiever State College, Somewhere, ST (3.68 GPA; Dean's list – 4 Semesters)

Related Coursework:

- Principles of Marketing
- Community Health Program Development and Evaluation
- Modifying Health Behavior
- Foundations of Health Education
- Human Diseases/Pathophysiology

EMPLOYMENT HISTORY

Assistant Manager – Alamo Storage; Port Arthur, TX   Dec 20XX - Present

Intern – Jefferson County Health Department; Beaumont, TX   May 20XX - Aug 20XX

Home Health Aide – Southwest Home Care; Beaumont, TX   Aug 20XX - Dec 20XX

PROFESSIONAL MEMBERSHIPS

THEA – Texas Health Education Association

NSNA – National Student Nursing Association

Figure 7.6 A functional resume emphasizes the applicant's qualifications, rather than the employment and education history.

Table 7.1 PAR Stories Consist of a Problem, Action, and Result

Attribute(s)	Problem or Situation	Action I Took	Result(s)

asked an opening question like "Tell me about yourself" or "How would you describe yourself?" For questions like this, give a concise self-summary in which you describe your main personal attributes and your experience and educational qualifications. Then you might end your response with something like the following: "That's why I think I would be an effective employee in your company."

7. *Give compelling answers.* A good answer gives informative, interesting, and convincing details that support your claim that you are a good fit for the job. If your answers are informative, interesting, and convincing, they will have great "sticking value" in the mind of the interviewer and thus will be remembered. If, on the other hand, your answers are vague and general, they will likely be forgotten.

Just as you used results statements for your resume, use them in your interview. Or better yet, have a compelling story to tell for each of your attributes. Consider developing a story for all the areas that might be covered in a job interview, such as your ability to work in a group, your presentation skills, your computer skills, your greatest achievement in life, your greatest challenge in life, and so forth. Begin with the problem or situation, tell what action you took, and tell the results. Use Table 7.1 to develop your own problem-action-result (PAR) stories for the attributes you want to highlight. Then rehearse your PAR stories so you can tell them smoothly and effectively. Here is an example of a PAR story:

Problem: "Our systems analysis department had an old project that should have been completed six months earlier, but the analyst assigned to the project just hadn't delivered. So my boss asked me to take it on."

Action: "I first went to the client to make sure I knew what he wanted. I then went to my boss and requested the full-time service of another analyst for three months. Next I gathered all the data we needed for the project. Then the other analyst and I went to work."

Result: "We finished the project in three months—right on time—and the client was happy with the results."

If you are asked a negative question that could work *against* you, try giving an answer that works *for* you. For instance, you might be asked, "What is one of your greatest weaknesses?" To such a question you might respond with the following PAR story:

Problem: "Well, my dad was an army officer and so we had to move a lot. This meant I was uprooted from my friends every few years, and I became a bit quiet and hesitant to get involved socially."

Action: "But in high school I realized that I needed to change my attitude and be more outgoing. As a result, when we moved to St. Louis at the beginning of my junior year, I went out of my way to develop new friendships."

Result: "A few months later I was elected as vice president of my senior class. So even though I didn't particularly like all those moves my family had to make, I have become more resilient and adaptable as a result."

8. *Have two or three questions to ask the interviewer.* Determine what you want to know about the company, and be prepared with a short list of questions to ask the interviewer.

- Tell me about the organizational culture here.
- What training opportunities are provided for new employees?
- What is the typical promotion pattern of new employees?
- What do you like best about working for this organization?

9. *Be prepared to answer any surprise questions.* If you are asked a surprise question, the interviewer may be looking more for how you think and how you respond than for whether you give an exact answer. For instance, assume the interviewer asks, "How many gas stations are there in the U.S.?" To respond, pause and think for

a minute about the process you might follow to obtain a reasonably close answer. You might say something like, "Well, if we have roughly 300 million people in the country, and if we assume two cars for every three people, that would give us about 200 million cars. And if we assume there is one gas station for every 1,000 cars, that would give us about 200,000 gas stations."

Sometimes you may be interviewed over the telephone, rather than in a face-to-face interview. Preparing for a phone interview is much like preparing for a regular interview, including researching the company, preparing your PAR stories, and so forth. But the actual interview is different in several ways.

First, with telephone interviews you can't see the person or people you are talking with, so you miss out on facial expressions and other nonverbal cues that help set the tone of the interview. Equally important is the fact that they can't see you, so they miss out on your nonverbal cues. Thus, be sure to listen very carefully. When you are responding to a question, speak clearly, answer every question fully, smile and let your warmth come through in your voice, and be respectful. In addition, even though you can't be seen, consider dressing up for the interview; because being professionally dressed will help you remember to act professionally and to speak at an appropriate level of formality.

Second, with telephone interviews you may have various documents spread out in front of you for quick access. For example, place on the table or desk in front of you a copy of your resume, a list of questions you want to have answered, key points you want to emphasize during the interview, PAR stories you want to tell, names of people who will be interviewing you, and any other information you feel would be relevant and useful. Also consider having your computer in front of you, with the company's website displayed. Additionally, be prepared to take notes during the interview, capturing important information immediately, rather than having to wait until after the interview. Finally, have a glass of water nearby in case your mouth gets dry from stress.

When You Are Interviewing Others

The following guidelines are given to help you conduct an effective employment interview.

1. *Take good notes and record your impressions during or immediately after the interview.* Evaluate each person against the factors you are going to use in making the selection decision. Document each interview carefully to protect your firm in case a passed-over person decides to take you to court.

2. *Prepare interview questions in advance.* Review the

Figure 7.7 Interviewers should document each interview for future reference.

resume thoroughly so you'll know as much as possible about the person before the interview begins. Don't ask questions that are answered on the resume.

3. *Start out with a brief warm-up phase to put the interviewee at ease.* For example, ask about a hobby or something else the person feels comfortable talking about.

4. *Avoid illegal questions pertaining to a person's age, race, gender, marital status, religious preference, and any other factor that has no relevance to success on the job.*

5. *Use closed and open questions effectively.* Closed questions can be answered with a yes or no or with a short answer.

   Closed questions: Could you begin employment by next Monday? Do you speak Spanish? How many years did you live in Germany?

   Open questions require more explanation, and they often inquire about feelings, opinions, and values.

   Open questions: How much experience have you had with project management? What would you recommend to improve sales of product X?

Figure 7.8 Good interviewers use effective responding techniques to encourage the interviewee to talk openly.

6. *Use probing questions appropriately.* A common problem with employment interviews is that interviewees often give shallow answers. Probing questions enable you to obtain more in-depth information. They dig beneath the surface of general-level answers and yield answers that are richer in meaning.

   • Could you give me more details about the proposed new-product test center you're working on?

7. *Use behavioral questions appropriately.* A behavioral question is an open question that asks the respondent how he or she acted in a specific situation. It may also be framed as a business case or problem to be solved. The ideal answer for behavioral questions will be given in a problem-action-result (PAR) format, but often the interviewer will have to keep probing until a detailed answer is given.

   Note the difference in the quality of information given by Allen, the interviewee, for each of the following questions asked by Holly, the interviewer.

Closed question that yields almost no useful information

Holly: Are you good at handling irate customers?

Allen: Yes, I have had to do that a lot.

Open behavioral question that generates a shallow answer

Holly: Tell me about a time you had to handle an irate customer.

Allen: Well, I worked at a car rental place for a year, and I had to handle a lot of upset customers in that business. They would have problems with the car, like mechanical troubles, or stuff like that. And I'd have to deal with it.

Open behavioral question, followed by probing questions to generate specific information

Holly: Tell me about a time you had to handle an irate customer.

Allen: Well, I worked at a car rental place for a year and I had to handle a lot of upset customers in that business. They would have problems with the car, like mechanical troubles, or stuff like that. And I'd have to deal with it.

Holly: Tell me in detail how you handled one of those cases.

Allen: Well, this one guy came in and the car he had rented had overheated on the highway, and he had missed an important appointment or

something like that. They're supposed to call us if they have problems, but I guess he called a towing company and had it towed to a repair shop. And he had to spend the next two or three hours waiting for it to be fixed. And then he had to pay over two hundred bucks out of his own pocket. So he was pretty steamed by the time he got back to us.

Holly: So specifically how did you handle the situation?

Allen: Well, he was yelling and carrying on, and so I just called my manager and turned it over to him. I didn't want to get involved. He was so mad.

In this third case, the interviewer finally has something to work with. Allen's first answer was shallow, so Holly kept probing until Allen gave the specifics she wanted. Because of her effective questioning, she now knows that Allen doesn't listen carefully (he didn't answer the questions directly), he doesn't know how to sell himself, and he doesn't know how to handle an irate customer by himself. All of this information was missed in the first case involving the closed question, "Are you good at handling irate customers?"

8. *Be a good listener.* Asking appropriate questions is definitely important, but how you respond and react during the answer is equally important. Your verbal and nonverbal behavior directly affects whether the interviewee will open up and tell you more or become distrustful and withhold information. Here are several responding techniques to foster open communication:

Figure 7.9 Good interviewers are sensitive to both spoken and nonverbal messages.

- Maintain good eye contact
- Smile and nod your head, reflecting understanding
- Say "uh-huh," reflecting interest and attentive listening
- Use "reflective listening." This technique requires you to paraphrase the speaker's response, showing that you really want to understand. It also ensures that what the speaker is saying and what you are hearing are the same thing. Without reflective listening, you're never really sure that true understanding has occurred. Reflective listening is an effective tool in many types of communication settings. Learn it well. Here are three examples:

  - So you're feeling undue pressure caused by the delays in Sam's department?
  - What I hear you saying is that our employees are feeling neglected and unappreciated; is that it?
  - In other words, Kent's work is unacceptable and you think we need to take disciplinary action?

Reflective listening responses ask the interviewee to confirm your understanding of his or her comments. If the paraphrase is accurate, the speaker will affirm its accuracy; if not, clarification can be given.

A variety of question samples follow.

Sample Employment Interview Questions

Personal Characteristics
- Tell me about yourself.
- What are your three greatest strengths? Tell me about an instance that called for you to apply those strengths.
- Why should we hire you over someone else?
- How successful have you been in life?
- What has been your greatest challenge in life? Your greatest accomplishment?

Experience
- What did you like best and least about your previous job?
- Why did you leave your previous job(s)?
- Tell me about your greatest successes in your previous jobs.

Relationships
- What kinds of people are most frustrating to you?
- If I were to call two or three of your friends/previous employers/fellow employees, what would they tell me about you?
- What leadership positions did you have in high school or college?

Education
- Why did you choose such and such as a major? If you could start college over again, would you choose a different major? Why or why not?
- Were you an active participant in class discussions? Why or why not?
- What was your GPA? Is it a fair assessment of your abilities?
- What were your toughest and easiest college classes? Why?
- What were your most valuable and least valuable college classes? Why?

Career Plans
- Where do you see yourself ten years from now?
- Describe your ideal career path.

Knowledge about the Company
- Why do you want to work for our organization?
- What do you know about our organization?

Problem-solving Ability
- You've been out of town for a week. You return to find your in-basket full. How would you handle this situation?
- You've got an irate customer standing at your work station complaining about the poor service he has been given. How would you handle this person?
- How would you determine whether your community needs to build an additional golf course.
- You are now in charge of marketing a new type of running shoe. How will you proceed with this task?

Behavioral Questions
- Tell me about a time when someone was upset and it was your responsibility to resolve the problem.
- Tell me about a time when you had to meet a deadline under difficult circumstances.

- Tell me about the greatest challenge you have had to deal with in life and how you dealt with it.

FOLLOW-UP LETTERS

Within a day or two following an employment interview, send a letter or note thanking the person who interviewed you. A sincere thank-you message is a powerful differentiator in today's electronic world. Include (1) a sincere thanks; (2) something about the interview that you appreciated, found interesting, or particularly enjoyed; and (3) a statement or two reaffirming your interest in working for the organization. Keep the message short. Something as simple as the handwritten note in Figure 7.10 will suffice, as will the typewritten thank-you letter shown in Figure 7.11.

Dear Mr. Anderson,

Thank you for the opportunity to visit with you about employment at XYZ Corporation. I appreciated your discussion of the company's five-year plan and the part I might play in it. I do believe that my strong work ethic, my academic preparation, and my experience make me a good candidate for the position you are filling.

Again, my thanks for a very enjoyable interview. I look forward to hearing from you.

Talia Meyer

Figure 7.10 A carefully worded thank-you note should be sent soon after the interview is completed.

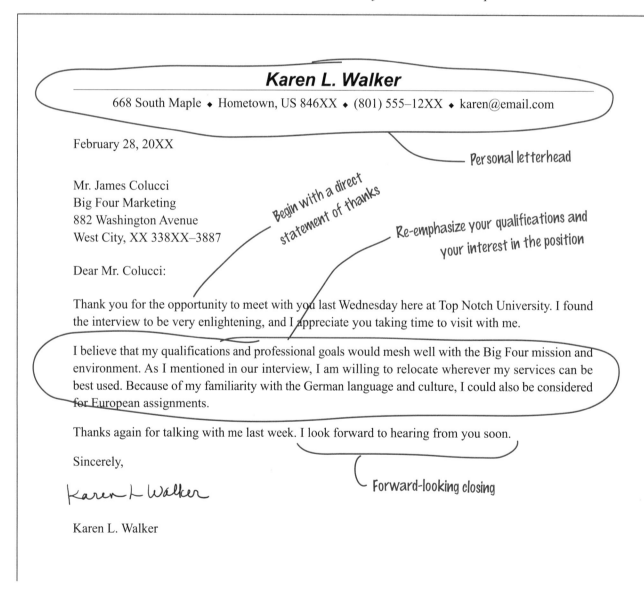

Figure 7.11 Thank-you letters should be concise and should re-emphasize your qualifications for the position.

RECOMMENDATION LETTERS

When job seeking you will often be asked to provide the names of individuals who are willing to serve as a reference—one who knows you and your abilities and who will vouch for your qualifications and competence. As you select these people, choose those who know you well and with whom you have had successful interaction, such as former employers, teachers and professors, and professional colleagues.

Be sure to ask permission from each of your references before giving their names to prospective employers. When you request their permission, ask, "I am applying for employment at ABC Company. If they request a recommendation letter, would you be able to write a good one for me?" If they cannot, eliminate them from your reference list. Whenever you ask someone to write a recom-

mendation for you, provide them with (a) a description of the job you are seeking and (b) a list of your qualifications that make you a good fit for that job—employment, education, experiences, and attributes. Send them a copy of your resume, and highlight the areas that have relevance to the job you are seeking.

When you are asked to write a recommendation letter for someone else, ask for this same information: a description of the job being sought and a list of the person's specific qualifications that makes them a good fit for that job. When planning the recommendation letter, use bottom-up outlining—brainstorm to develop a list of everything you can think of about the person. Then place the various facts into categories and compose the letter, using an OABC pattern and enhancing the document with HATS (see Figure 7.12).

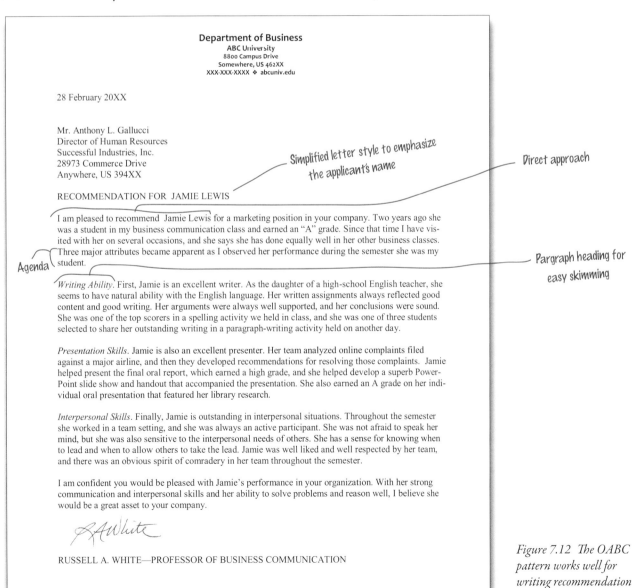

Figure 7.12 The OABC pattern works well for writing recommendation letters.

CHAPTER SUMMARY

Hiring a new employee is one of the most critical things a company does, because employees are the most important asset of any organization. Obtaining employment is also one of the most critical things you do as an individual. Employment communication involves a variety of written and oral communications, including application letters, resumes, and interviews.

The purpose of the application letter is to introduce you to the prospective employer and to convince him or her to invite you in for an employment interview. A resume is a self-promotion document; it is a sales-promotion document and you are the product being promoted. In your resume, present your qualifications in the best possible way to persuade the reader to grant you an interview.

To prepare for your interview, prepare a number of PAR (problem, action, results) stories to help you tell your story better. When interviewing others, prepare effective questions, using open questions and behavioral questions, and use reflective listening to ensure understanding. In addition to preparing for face-to-face interviews, know how to prepare for telephone interviews. Within a day or two following an employment interview, send a letter or note thanking the person who interviewed you.

CHAPTER QUESTIONS

1. Explain the main purposes of the beginning, middle, and closing paragraphs in an employment cover letter.

2. Explain how to decide whether to list your education or your experience first in a resume.

3. In what sequence should your job history be arranged?

4. Should your resume be limited to one page? Why or why not?

5. Explain the main differences between chronological and functional resumes.

6. List three guidelines to remember when being interviewed for a job.

7. Explain how to prepare for a telephone interview.

8. What is a PAR story? Why are PAR stories so important in interviews?

9. What types of questions are illegal to ask in a job interview?

10. Describe the difference between closed and open questions.

11. What is a behavioral question?

12. Describe several responding techniques to demonstrate you are listening to a person you are interviewing.

13. Describe how HATS can be applied to employment resumes.

14. Should the OABC framework be used in composing thank-you letters? Why or why not?

CHAPTER ACTIVITIES

1. Prepare an attractive letterhead to use with your resume and cover letter. Include your name, address, telephone numbers, and email address.

2. Prepare an employment resume for the job you would like to obtain when you graduate from college. Use the examples listed in this chapter to give you ideas, but customize your resume to fit your unique employment situation. First, create a free list of everything in your background that might relate to employment: service, training, leadership, teamwork, special achievements, awards, talents, education, employment, language, computer skills, and any other accomplishments or attributes. Then find a job description for a job that you might like to apply for. Next, using the job description as a guide, categorize the items on your free list according to the job requirements; then sequence the categories as appropriate. Finally, create a polished resume and prepare a cover letter to accompany your resume.

3. Write three PAR stories, each about one paragraph in length. Label the problem, the action, and the results in each story. Also, identify your personal attributes illustrated in each story.

4. Interview two or more of your peers, and have them interview you. After each interview, discuss what went well and what could be improved.

5. Write a thank-you letter to one of the people who interviewed you in Chapter Activity 4. Write an offer letter to one of the people you interviewed. Write a rejection letter to one of the people you interviewed.

6. On the internet, browse the Occupational Outlook Handbook on the U.S. Government's website (http://www.bls.gov/oco/). Read about the outlook for the type of profession you are interested in. Also, visit the additional websites listed at the beginning of this chapter. Write a short memo about what you find.

Chapter 8

WRITING PROPOSALS AND SOLVING PROBLEMS

Organizations are in a constant state of change in an effort to address a wide variety of issues and challenges, such as the following:

- How can we improve our products?
- How can we make more money?
- How can we eliminate waste and reduce expenses?
- How can we make our operations run more efficiently?
- How can we get our employees to work harder and more effectively?
- How can we reach our desired customers better and increase sales?

Very often proposals are an important part of solving problems like these. Thus, Chapter 8 contains two major sections focusing on preparing proposals and solving problems. As you improve your abilities in these two areas, you will increase your power to be a positive influence and to gain greater satisfaction from your professional work.

WRITING PROPOSALS

Proposals are a vital part of business, government, and nonprofit organizations. Because all employees in an organization are accountable to their supervisors or managers, they must obtain permission from their superiors before making major policy, procedure, or program changes; before acquiring new equipment; before hiring new people; and so forth. The way they obtain permission is to present a proposal. In other words, with a proposal they say, "I propose

to do such and such; will you give me permission and funds (if needed) to proceed?"

Proposals are also written to obtain funds from thousands of foundations, endowments, or governmental agencies that give money grants to support worthwhile ventures, such as improving opportunities for certain social and economic groups, supporting scientific research, helping new businesses ventures, and addressing health issues. For example, each year the federal government's department of health and human services gives numerous grants that enhance the health and well being of our society. Individuals and organizations that receive such grants are then subjected to strict reporting requirements to ensure a good return on the granting organization's investment.

Regardless of their common elements, proposals can vary in many ways, as explained in the following sections.

Oral vs. Written Proposals

Proposals may be presented orally, either with a formal stand-up presentation, or with a less-formal conversation or discussion in a meeting. Chapter 12 will help you develop important presentation skills useful with proposals given as oral presentations.

Proposals may also be prepared as written documents and may be formatted less formally as emails or memos, or more formally as reports. In any case, the better the authors can write, the better their chances of obtaining permission and funding. Three different formats are illustrated at the end of Chapter 8. Figure 8.7 is written as a memo proposal,

Figure 8.8 is a proposal report, and Figure 8.9 is a letter proposal.

Internal vs. External Proposals

Proposals may originate and be presented within an organization (an internal proposal) or they may originate in one organization and be presented to a different organization (an external proposal). Figure 8.7 is an internal proposal; Figures 8.8 and 8.9 are external proposals.

Solicited vs. Unsolicited Proposals

Proposals may also be solicited (requested by the organization that has a problem to be solved) or unsolicited (not requested by the organization that has the problem). Solicited proposals often are written in response to an external organization's RFP (Request For Proposal). The RFP will specify the criteria on which the proposal will be judged, the date by which the proposal must be submitted, and other important information that must be addressed when writing the proposal. For example, a proposal submitted to obtain research funds from the federal government will require information about what you propose to achieve, how you plan to accomplish it, who will conduct the research, how much it will cost, when the various research milestones will be accomplished, and so forth.

Typically, proposals submitted in response to an RFP are evaluated in two phases.

Phase 1. The requesting organization will evaluate the proposals to disqualify any that don't measure up to the criteria. For example, business proposals whose pricing is too high or too low or those that don't follow the exact guidelines or structure of the RFP will likely be eliminated during the first phase. For government grants, typical disqualifying factors include a lack of new or original ideas, poorly defined hypotheses, inappropriate methods and research design, inadequate expertise and knowledge or researchers, and poor writing.

Phase 2. The remaining proposals will then be compared and carefully evaluated to see which one best meets the RFP criteria. For instance, an audit proposal from a CPA firm will be evaluated on the reasonableness of its pricing schedule, expertise of the audit team, timeliness of its work, strength of its reputation, professionalism and readability of the proposal, and so forth.

The three proposals at the end of Chapter 8 illustrate both solicited and unsolicited proposals. Figures 8.7 and 8.9 are unsolicited proposals; Figure 8.8 is a solicited proposal. Even if your proposal is unsolicited, you should usu-

ally have a preliminary conversation to prepare the audience to receive the proposal. For example, you could talk with the recipient to find out current needs and problems, and then mention that you would like to submit a proposal to help address those needs. Proposals that come as a surprise generally are not very successful.

Direct vs. Indirect Proposals

Proposals may employ a direct approach (recommendation, followed by background of the problem) or an indirect approach (background of the problem, followed by the recommendation). Although you may use a direct approach with all proposals, you might consider being more indirect with unsolicited proposals. The preliminary information in such cases would describe and discuss the problem, followed by a proposal to analyze and solve the problem

The following two lists give a general sequence for direct and indirect proposals. Individual elements can be reordered or modified as needed.

Direct Proposal (for all solicited proposals)
- General statement of what you propose to do
- Description and discussion of the problem
- Detailed discussion of your proposal (what you will do and how you will do it)
- Benefits
- Time schedule
- Statement of costs
- Your qualifications (if applicable)
- Conclusion and action statement
- Appendixes (as needed)

Indirect Proposal (for unsolicited proposals when the direct approach would be too abrupt)
- Description and discussion of the problem
- General and specific discussion of your proposal (what you will do and how you will do it)
- Benefits
- Time schedule
- Statement of costs
- Your qualifications (if applicable)
- Conclusion and action statement
- Appendixes (as needed)

The three proposals at the end of Chapter 8 illustrate both direct and indirect proposals. Figures 8.7 and 8.9 follow an indirect approach; Figure 8.8 utilizes a direct approach.

Problem-Solving Proposals vs. Research Proposals

Some proposals may seek for permission to analyze and develop solutions to problems or to implement changes after a solution has been developed. Sometimes such proposals come from inside the organization, but outside consulting companies also use proposals in the early stages of performing work for their clients. The remainder of Chapter 8 discusses the various phases of problem-solving to help you not only in working with proposals, but also in performing many other communication activities.

Some other proposals may seek permission (a) to conduct research, either to assist in problem solving or (b) to study some aspect of a topic and disseminate the findings as conference presentations, academic papers, or academic publications in research journals. The latter is the type of work performed by university faculty members and students. Chapter 9 discusses how to conduct and document this type of research.

SOLVING PROBLEMS

Problems are a normal and common part of organization life, and most of your communication in organizations deals with some aspect of problem solving. For example, as you submit a job application you are seeking to solve a problem—to change your employment status from unemployed to employed!

Problems arise for a wide variety of reasons: battles over limited resources, arguments over decisions, frustrations over competing job demands, stress brought on by tight deadlines, insecurity introduced by company layoffs, customer complaints about product-quality problems, and countless other situations. Problem solving can become tedious, but remember that without problems, you would be without a job. You are hired to be a problem solver!

Three general steps are involved in problem solving:

1. Diagnose the problem.
2. Develop a solution.
3. Implement the solution.

To one degree or another, these three steps apply to all problems, simple or complex, and to all organizations, large or small. And you, as a problem solver, must possess sufficient common sense to know what specific actions are appropriate for completing these three steps in different settings.

For example, if you are a marketing manager in a large company and the CEO has set a 10 percent target growth rate for the coming year, you have a complex problem to deal with. With the help of your key staff members, you

Figure 8.1 For more complex problems, involving key personnel is often essential to correctly diagnose the issues.

analyze the current product line, assess the current performance of each product, and set sales targets for each. You also work with the marketing staff to develop appropriate marketing messages for various communication media. Further, you work with production and distribution managers to ensure that product manufacturing and shipping will be synchronized with the new plan. You then activate the plan and follow up closely throughout the year to track progress and implement adjustments along the way.

But if you are an office manager in a local real estate company and one of your secretaries announces she is quitting, you have a much simpler problem. To diagnose the problem, you talk with her and find out she is moving because her husband has been transferred to a distant city. You then advertise the opening and interview the three best candidates. Finally, you select, hire, and train the best candidate. Within two weeks the problem is solved!

Diagnose the Problem

What is a problem? Think of it as the difference between what you think *should be* and what *is*. An opportunity can also be thought of as a problem. It is the difference between what *could be* and what *is*. For example, if you are earning $40,000 a year (what *is*) but you think you *should be* making $80,000 a year (what should be), you have a $40,000 problem. Using this approach, you can define problems in the following manner:

1. Identify what you think *should/could be*. That condition may be something relating to you as an individual, or it might be an organizational standard, mission, or objective.

2. Identify the current status—what *is*.

3. The problem is the difference between 1 and 2 (what *should be* vs. what *is*).

Problems surface in a variety of ways—formal and

informal. Routine reports, continuous-improvement committees, in-house suggestion boxes, suggestions given by customers, grapevine communication, personal observation, and unexpected emergencies are all important information sources. In all areas of your work, be alert to information that signals problems needing your attention.

Once you become aware of a problem, you must gather and analyze additional information so you can perform a proper diagnosis. Too often people start developing solutions before clearly understanding the problem. Therefore, before attempting to solve a problem, take time to analyze and diagnose it. Break it down into small pieces that can be examined in detail.

Simple problems may need very little data analysis for proper diagnosis, but complex problems usually require significant amounts of data and analysis. The data can be either qualitative or quantitative in nature. For example, qualitative information might be as follows:

- People—negative employee attitudes, declining morale, or ineffective training methods.
- Money—spending of funds on questionable purchases, lack of financial oversight lack of budget planning.
- Machines—outdated computers, uncontrolled purchasing of new technology, inappropriate use of new technology.
- Methods—job duplication, job overlap, or lack of needed cross training among different tasks.
- Materials—out-of-style appearance of products, environmentally unfriendly products, or inappropriate management of waste products.

In addition to qualitative data, quantitative data is usually helpful.

- People—increasing employee turnover, increasing in customer complaints, or slow response time to customer requests.
- Money—worsening financial ratios, declining sales revenue, or escalating cost of producing a product.
- Machines—increasing equipment breakdowns or increasing equipment costs.
- Methods—slow manufacturing processes, increasing numbers of product defects, or flawed security measures.
- Materials—poor reliability of product line, increasing number of flaws in raw materials, short shelf-life of products, or shortage of production parts.

For quantitative data, develop a spreadsheet and run appropriate calculations, yielding information such as the following:

- Comparative averages
- Rankings (high to low)
- Trends over various time periods
- Forecasts vs. actual performance
- Budgeted vs. actual performance
- Year-to-date performance (e.g., monthly, quarterly)
- Company vs. industry performance

Also, from quantitative data, develop bar charts, line charts, and other graphics that enable you to analyze the data visually (see Figure 8.2). Often a visual examination will reveal trends, problem areas, and opportunities for improvement.

Introduced in Chapter 3, the following three-part model can be helpful in solving problems:

1. *What?* The first step seeks to understand and describe the problem. This requires careful data gathering from statistical and analytical reports, questionnaires, in-depth interviewing, or other data sources.

2. *So what?* The second step focuses on the importance or impact of the problem. Some problems are so minor in nature or so isolated in frequency that their consequences don't matter much. Some other problems are more serious but require more resources than the solution is worth. Still other problems can't be solved and simply have to be endured.

3. *Now what?* The third step seeks to find a solution to the problem, including relevant solution criteria.

Complete problem statements should address all three parts of the model, as shown below:

What?	We have a 60 percent turnover in our sales associates.
So what?	We are spending too much money and time recruiting, selecting, and training. Customer service is lagging because of limited experienced sales associates. Morale is affected because so many people quit after working here for only a short time.
Now what?	We need to reduce our turnover among sales associates to a level not to exceed 20 percent.

As you think of problem solving, remember the PAR acronym from Chapter 7. You first have a problem situation that needs an action. The result of the action should be a resolution of the problem. A simple fast-food restaurant example will help illustrate:

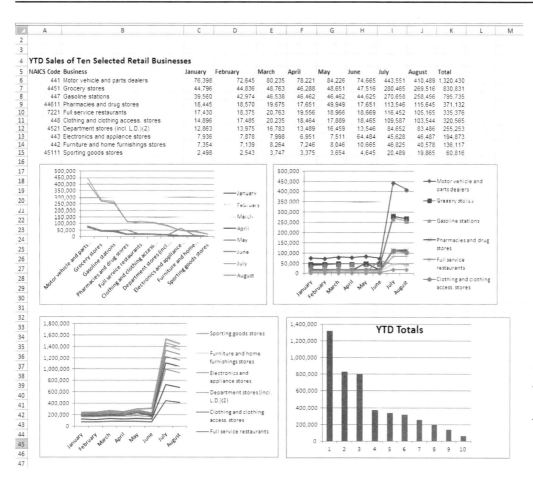

Figure 8.2 Developing graphics to show the data visually can help you identify trends, trouble spots, and opportunities for improvement.

Problem: ABC Fast Food restaurant seeks to provide fast food at a competitive price and to do so in a way that meets customer satisfaction. However, sales revenue has declined 11 percent in the last six months, and the manager, Jim Russell, wants to reverse this trend and achieve a 10 percent improvement in the next six months.

Action: The manager uses a customer survey to gather data so he can understand the reason for the decline. After using his spreadsheet software to analyze the data, he concludes that (a) limited menu selection and (b) increasing advertising by competitors are having the greatest effect on the business. He adds several new menu items and actively advertises the new items.

Result: The result for the subsequent six months is a 13-percent increase in customers.

When diagnosing problems, the 5W2H questions (who, what, where, when, why, how, and how much) help to exam-ine the problem from all angles. Combine *what is* and *what is not* questions. For example, for the question, "What is caus-ing the problem?" also ask, "What is not causing the prob-lem?"

Who? Who discovered the problem? Who is affected by the problem? Who might have caused the problem? Who is concerned about the problem? Who has dealt with problems of this nature in the past?

What? What components of the system have failed? What has changed recently that might have contributed to the problem? What are the symptoms of the problem? What are the causes of the symptoms? What would have prevented the problem from happening?

Where? Where did the problem occur? Where did it begin? Is it occurring in one location or multiple locations?

When? When did the problem occur? When have changes occurred that might have con-tributed to the problem? When must the problem be solved?

Why? Why did the problem occur? Why does the

problem matter? Why did the problem not occur earlier? Why does it happen at some times and not at others? Why did we not prevent the problem?

How? How was the problem discovered? How do the various parts of the system interact with each other? How does the system or process work? How serious is the problem? How urgent is the problem?

How much? How many people or things are involved? How many people are affected by the problem? How much quantity, volume, distance, or time is involved? How many times has the problem occurred?

As you analyze problems, remember the difference between causes and symptoms. The cause is the *origin;* the symptom is the *result*. Too many people try to fix the symptoms, only to find that they reappear because the cause is still present. Only if you fix the cause of a problem will the effect (symptom) disappear. For example, Employee A fails to perform his duties properly. Manager X terminates the employee and hires another, only to find that the problem repeats itself. The real problem is not with the employees but with the manager's failure to train properly. Get the manager to train properly (the cause), and the employee's performance problems will largely disappear (the symptom/effect).

Cause-and-effect analysis is a useful technique for diagnosing problems. It consists of identifying all relevant cause-and-effect relationships. Think of this process as a tree, with the most obvious symptoms up on the leaf level and the causes down in the larger branches and ultimately down at the root level. First, identify a symptom; then ask what caused the symptom. After you identify the cause, repeat the procedure, and keep repeating the procedure until you get to the root cause of all the symptoms. Then focus your main problem-solving efforts at that point.

A cause-and-effect diagram can be very useful for analyzing problems (see Figure 8.3). Using a basic tree-structure format, write the main problem, or symptom, at the starting point of the tree. Then extend various cause-and-effect branches from there, showing the different cause-and-effect chains contributing to the main problem.

Repeatedly asking "what caused this" or "why did this happen" for every symptom will help isolate the root causes that need to be addressed. Thus, each link tells what caused the higher-order problem (symptom). Continue to create additional branch links so long as you can identify meaningful causes and effects. To ensure that you have addressed every possible cause, you might focus various cause-effect chains on what, who, where, when, and how questions. (Note: You can also use a mind-map format for cause-and-effect analysis.) Ideally, if you adequately address the root causes, the main problem will be resolved.

Another tool to consider when diagnosing problems involving personnel is illustrated in Table 8.1. In this table you see that most performance problems can be classified into five main categories. The table also shows the logical

Table 8.1 Personnel Problem Analysis Chart

Description of Problem	Type of Problem	Solution
Person cannot physically or mentally perform as desired.	Ability problem	Transfer or terminate the person; assign someone who can perform properly.
Person could perform properly but doesn't know how.	Training problem	Give appropriate training and practice.
Person knows how and can perform properly, but circumstances are preventing from performing properly.	Environmental problem	Change the environment; eliminate that which is preventing performance.
Person knows how and can perform properly, and nothing is preventing proper performance, but the person is not rewarded for proper performance.	Motivational problem	Give appropriate motivation to achieve proper performance.
Person knows how and can perform properly, nothing is preventing proper performance, and the person is appropriately rewarded for proper performance, but does not want to perform properly.	Morale problem	Counsel and terminate if performance doesn't improve.

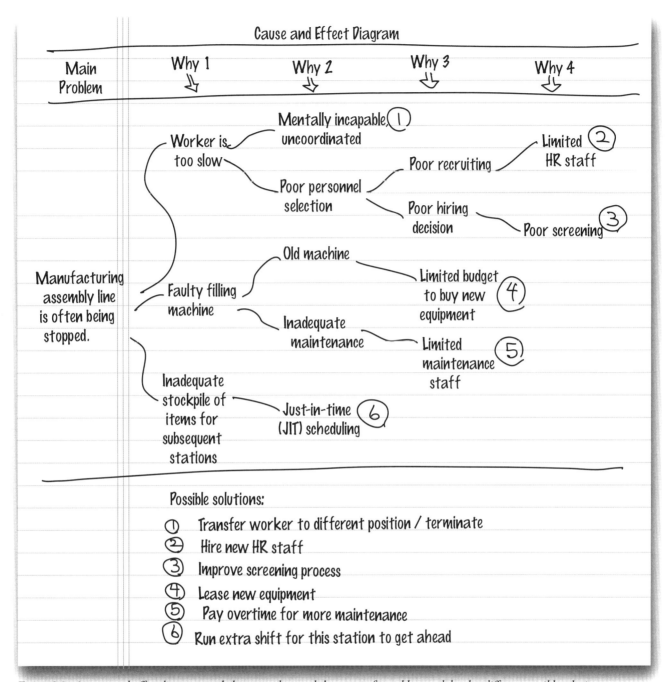

Figure 8.3 A cause-and-effect diagram can help you understand the causes of a problem and develop different possible solutions.

types of solutions that can be implemented to solve the problems. Using this chart will help ensure that you don't misdiagnose a problem and implement a solution that doesn't fit the situation.

After the diagnosis, decide how to best frame the problem. The purpose of framing a problem or issue is not just to inform others of the problem, but also to energize them to take action. Thus, think creatively about how you can achieve both objectives in your framing statement. For instance, the following statements all stem from the same problem, but notice how some focus just on the "what" of

the problem, while others attempt to emphasize the larger "so what" or "now what" aspects of the problem.

- What: One employee is having difficulty keeping up with the assembly line pace.

- What: The assembly line has been completely shut down three times in the last month.

- What: Problems with one machine are causing the entire assembly line to stop.

- So what: The filling machine station is costing the corporation approximately $12,000 each month.
- So what: Frequent assembly-line shutdowns are causing frustration throughout the entire organization.
- Now what: We need to solve the problem of assembly-line shut downs.
- Now what: We need to stop the filling-machine breakdowns.

After you experiment with various framing statements, choose the one that will best inform and generate positive and active involvement from the people who will participate in the decision-making process.

Develop a Solution

Once you have diagnosed and framed the problem, work on the second phase—the solution. Sometimes a solution will be relatively simple. At other times it may be very complicated, requiring multiple solutions to solve each little piece of a large problem. Each problem is unique and each problem requires at least some creativity to customize an appropriate solution. Effective problem solving requires creative thinking, and brainstorming can help with this process. Following brainstorming, evaluate the alternative ideas you have generated and then select the best idea for implementation.

Brainstorming can foster creativity and develop potential solutions to a problem. It can be used in countless ways, including identifying problems, designing ways to implement solutions, improving existing products, or creating new services. Brainstorming is the process of thinking of as many different ideas as possible, with little initial concern for the feasibility of the ideas. Brainstorming can force people to think outside the normal way of doing things and to develop different ways of solving problems. The idea behind brainstorming is that quantity will yield quality; in other words, if you come up with enough ideas, at least one or two likely will be good ones.

When brainstorming, don't assume that there is only one right solution. Usually you can develop a variety of solutions. Often, a combination of ideas proves to be best. Today's problems are complex, and complex solutions are needed to solve them.

Brainstorming can be performed alone (personal brainstorming) or with a group (both oral and written).

PERSONAL BRAINSTORMING

Group involvement can be highly effective in developing potential solutions to problems, but the process of coming up with truly creative solutions to problems is often best accomplished by individuals as they consider and ponder the problem for extended periods of time. During this incubation period the human brain exhibits great capacity to engage in divergent thinking and come up with creative solutions to problems.

Further, you may choose to solve a problem alone when (a) your knowledge of the problem is greater than that of the group, (b) time pressure prohibits getting group input, (c) group members are unaffected by or don't care about the problem or outcome, (d) you prefer to have total control over the outcome, or (e) the group doesn't work well together. In these cases, the old saying that "two heads are better than one" does not apply.

The creativity process includes four basic steps:

1. Understand: Comprehend the problem and its related issues.
2. Incubate: Engage in divergent thinking, pondering endless possibilities, to discover possible solutions.
3. Develop: Discover, or uncover, one or more potential solutions.
4. Refine: Polish and customize the idea to fit the need.

Creativity cannot be forced or rushed; it can take days, weeks, or even months, emerging only after persistently pondering a problem. It can, however, be fostered in a variety of ways. The following suggestions work for many people who rely heavily on creativity in their professional work.

- *Thoroughly study the problem.* Fully comprehend the central problem/objective and all its related aspects.
- *Enrich your knowledge base.* Read widely. Become exposed to as much of the world as possible—different companies, different industries, different fields, different cultures, and different methodologies. The idea is to increase the data in your mental database so you can increase the numbers of mental interconnections.
- *Eliminate distractions.* Go to a place where you can shut out distractions.
- *Set aside large chunks of time to ponder.* Creativity doesn't happen quickly.
- *Arise early.* The morning is usually the time when your mind is most alert and uncluttered. To prepare for the early awakening, go to bed early.
- *Utilize the Alpha sleep state.* Load your mind with the elements and the problem the night before, and let your mind work on the problem between deep sleep (Delta sleep) and wide awake (Beta state). This Alpha state can be described as a relaxed-awake state with your eyes closed.
- *Keep the problem constantly on your mind.* Many people

have found the solution to a problem simply by constantly thinking about it over a long period of time. As they go throughout their normal daily routines, new insights and ideas will often emerge at unpredictable times.

GROUP BRAINSTORMING (ORAL)

Involve a group when you need more than your own abilities to solve a problem. Two heads are better than one in many situations. A group brainstorming session can be carried out in four steps.

1. **Select the group.** The ideal group size is about 6 to 12 people. Groups smaller than 6 may lack the necessary diversity to produce the desired results, and groups larger than about 12 sometimes break into subgroups or intimidate less-assertive members. Group members should have a good knowledge of the problem and its context. They should also feel free to suggest creative ideas and not be inhibited by organizational politics or other group pressures.

2. **Select a facilitator, or serve as a facilitator yourself.** The facilitator explains the process, coordinates the generation and recording of ideas, and probes for better and deeper thinking.

3. **Select one or two recorders.** These people write the group's ideas on a chalkboard or on sticky notes or cards to be taped on a wall or chalkboard. Each idea should begin with a verb and capture a few key words that communicate the essence of the idea. Time is of the essence when ideas are flowing, so the recorders must write quickly, yet neatly and clearly. They should number each item for easy reference later on.

4. **Conduct the brainstorming session.** The facilitator clarifies the group's charge, explaining how the session

Figure 8.4 Group members should be encouraged to be creative in their brainstorming ideas.

will be carried out and emphasizing the importance of uninhibited thinking. Group members should be encouraged to be creative, not worrying about feasibility. They should just let free thinking flow, have fun, and feed off other people's ideas. To stress quantity, the facilitator might say, "Let's try to get 50 new ideas in the next 15 minutes." The group should be encouraged to build on the ideas of others and to look at problem solutions from different points of view.

During the brainstorming, you can allow ideas to come randomly, or you can try a structured go-around, which means that in an orderly way (e.g., from left to right around the room), each person has to offer a suggestion. This forces each person to participate, rather than allowing some people to remain silent while others do all the talking. Here are some additional ways to help generate ideas.

- *Think of people (who):* For all types of problems, think of moving people around or using them in different ways.

- *Think of location (where):* For training, think of moving to a different location.

- *Think of timing (when):* For operational problems, think of moving an operation to an earlier or later phase.

- *Think opposites:* When one idea is given, think of the exact opposite. For example, if you're trying to solve a financial problem, create solutions that would save money as well as ideas that would generate more money.

- *Think of other professions or occupations:* For an operations problem, think of the way an operations problem might be solved by the fast-food industry, by a farmer, by a clothing manufacturer, or by an airline.

- *Add more of the same:* If one person suggests an incentive in a marketing problem, think of adding more incentives.

- *Delete an element:* For a marketing problem, think of dropping, rather than adding, a product.

- *Think of external factors:* For human problems, think of ways to change the environment as well as people.

Another approach might be to think of ways to improve in each of the five M's of management resources:

Manpower:	Reassign, train, fix the environment, motivate, replace.
Money:	Add/expand, eliminate, reduce, maintain, control, modify (redirect, change to profit system, etc.).
Machines:	Repair, replace, upgrade, add, omit.

Materials: Improve, reduce, replace, combine, separate.

Methods: Eliminate, mechanize, automate, combine, separate, standardize, formalize, refine, modify, centralize/decentralize.

When idea generation starts to slow down, push for deeper thinking, for less-obvious ideas, for creative thinking from a different angle. Brainstorming often occurs in spurts—the ideas flow readily, then slow down, then speed up when someone comes up with a novel idea, and so forth. When it seems that new ideas have stopped completely, explain that other ideas might occur to group members during the next few hours or days and that those ideas should also be shared with the group facilitator.

GROUP BRAINSTORMING (WRITTEN)

Oral brainstorming with a group has many benefits, but it also has weaknesses. For instance, (a) social inequities within a group may keep some members from participating, and (b) only one person can participate at a time. To solve these problems, you might try gallery writing. Gallery writing is effective in generating useful ideas as well as solving social shortcomings of oral brainstorming methods.

- Tape several large sheets of paper on the walls of the meeting room. Space the papers at least several feet apart.

- Invite all members to write their ideas on one of the large sheets.

- Have all members then wander around the room reading other people's ideas and writing additional ideas that are spawned by the ideas they read.

An alternative written approach is the nominal group technique (NGT), where each person writes one or more ideas on a small card. After the ideas are publicly displayed, members then submit individual anonymous votes for those they think are best.

Evaluate the Alternatives

After generating a number of possible solutions to a problem, you must decide which option or options to implement. Figure 8.5 shows that whereas the initial phase of brainstorming fosters divergent thinking (diverse thinking), the decision-making phase brings about convergent thinking (moving toward one point and unifying the group thinking). Deciding on a single solution can be accomplished by an entire brainstorming group, by a smaller group that meets separately, or by the manager alone. However, involving subordinates achieves two distinct advantages. First, decisions made by a group are, on average, better than decisions made by individuals. Second, people will generally support decisions better when they have participated in the decision-making process.

To involve either part or all of the group, one method is to give each member a certain number of votes to cast. For instance, if 50 ideas have been generated, give each member five votes (10 percent of the total). The group members then go to the chalkboard, wall, or poster papers and vote (using a simple tally mark or sticky dot). After this voting, you can easily see where the group's preferences lie by noting where the largest clusters of votes have been recorded.

Another method is to take the group through the following four major steps.

1. ***Organize and refine the list.*** Group related ideas from the brainstorming list. Combine overlapping and related ideas. Refine the list so each idea is clear and as mutually exclusive as possible. Any item with one of the following flaws can be dropped from the list, unless it can be modified to eliminate the flaws:

   - Doesn't satisfy critical needs
   - Poses too much risk
   - Is illegal or unethical
   - Is contrary to the organization's philosophy or culture
   - Is not financially feasible

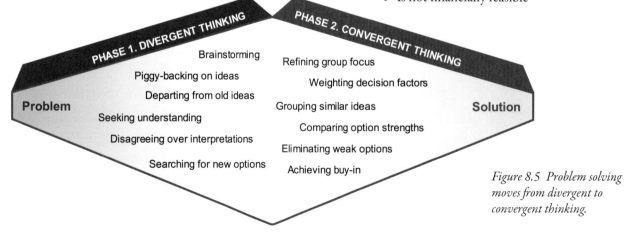

Figure 8.5 Problem solving moves from divergent to convergent thinking.

Table 8.2 Quantitative and Qualitative Evaluation Factors

Quantitative (How Much)	Qualitative (How Well)
• Financial results • Production speed • Number of production units • Percentage of market share • Number of errors • Number of sales	• Acceptance by affected personnel • Ease of implementation • Technical compatibility • Societal acceptability • Legal or ethical compliance • Compatibility with corporate culture • Compatibility with the organization's mission or values (refer to the mission statement) • Risk (financial, human, technology, legal, etc.)

- Doesn't meet time requirements
- Is technically incompatible with existing systems
- Is unacceptable to affected personnel
- Is too difficult to implement

2. ***Establish evaluation criteria.*** The evaluation criteria will serve as a basis for deciding which ideas to implement and which ones to reject. Most of the criteria will focus on *how well* (such as how well the group will accept an idea) or *how much* (such as how much money an idea will save). Some of the criteria will be quantitative; others will be qualitative. You might include such items as listed in Table 8.2.

Sometimes getting agreement on the criteria is a difficult task. This process can require your best negotiation skills and can take considerable time. When generating the criteria, write every person's suggestions on the list. Then ask why each criterion is important to the group or to the person. Be sure there is a good reason for including each criterion on the list. Work with the list and with the group until you produce a list that everyone can live with, even though not all may totally agree with it.

3. ***Weight the criteria.*** You might use a scale from 10 to 1 to indicate the relative importance of each criterion, with 10 being the most important and 1 being of little importance. For example, legal compliance and acceptance by affected personnel might be a 10, ease of implementation might be an 8, and timeliness might be a 5. Be honest with yourself in differentiating between critical *needs* and nice-to-have *wants*.

4. ***Objectively select the best ideas from the brainstorm list.*** Different methods can be used to accomplish this task. For example, as mentioned previously, you can involve the entire brainstorming group, allowing each member three votes, or you can have the subcommittee perform the selection function.

A decision table, or decision matrix, can be useful at this point in the process. This table compares alternatives according to important criteria. Table 8.3 compares three

Table 8.3 A Sample Decision Table

Criteria*	Weight	Alternatives		
		Smith	**Warenski**	**Lee**
U.S. Citizen	X	Yes	Yes	Yes
Technical knowledge	10	8	7	6
Experience	9	9	7	6
Leadership potential	7	6	6	4
Education	5	3	4	5
Total	**31**	**26**	**24**	**21**

Notice that the criteria are listed in descending order (top to bottom) according to weight and that the alternatives are listed in descending order (left to right) according to the total scores. This logical sequencing enhances readability and comprehension.

different potential employees. Note that qualitative and quantitative data can be included in the table.

Whereas identifying the causes of a problem is reverse (or backward) thinking, identifying the best solution to the problem requires forward thinking (what will be the effect of this cause, rather than what was the cause of this effect). The best alternative should cause the right kinds of effects to occur and solve problems to the maximum degree possible.

If the numeric totals don't reflect what you hoped for, one of two things has happened. First, bias may be affecting the process. If so, step back, take a broader view of the situation, and do what is *best* for the situation, not just what is preferred for personal reasons. Second, reconsider weighting one or more of the criteria. Perhaps experience, which can't be taught, is more important than technical knowledge, which can be taught. Reconsider every element of the decision table and make changes as necessary.

Implement the Solution

When you have authorization to proceed, determine how to implement the solution. This is a critical phase, because even a great idea can fail if it is poorly implemented.

Make sure all groups that are affected are represented in the implementation plan. Listen to their ideas, their suggestions, and their concerns. Modify the implementation plan as appropriate to address their legitimate concerns. If at all possible, don't force the plan on them. Obtain their cooperation so they will help you make it successful. Remember the old saying: "A man convinced against his will is of the same opinion still." And in addition to *what* you plan to change, remember that *where, when,* and *how* you introduce that change are also important. The better you anticipate the negative effects of your planned changes, the smoother the implementation phase will be.

Lewin's force-field analysis (SkyMark 2012) helps identify the forces working for and against your implementation plans. Draw a large "T" on a page. Across the top of the T, write the goal. On the left side, list the positive forces; on the right side, list the negative forces (see Figure 8.6). Weight each force on a 5–1 scale—with 5 representing a strong force—and total the positive and negative forces to see their overall impact. Then work to strengthen the driving forces and to reduce the negative forces. Examples of forces include the following:

- Available resources
- Traditions, personal interests, attitudes, values, desires
- Organizational structures and relationships
- Current policies, procedures, and practices
- Financial costs and benefits

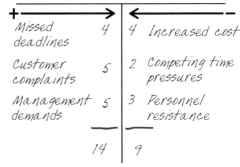

Goal: New Delivery Process

+ →		← −
Missed deadlines	4	4 Increased cost
Customer complaints	5	2 Competing time pressures
Management demands	5	3 Personnel resistance
	14	9

Figure 8.6 A force-field chart helps identify the forces working for and against implementation plans.

Your implementation strategy should work to increase the positive forces and decrease the negative ones.

Implementing new programs or procedures can follow one of four plans: pilot, phase-in, parallel, or cold turkey. With a pilot plan, you try out the new program in one segment of your organization, preferably with a group that likes the program and wants to try it out. After the initial pilot program, implement throughout the organization, using the knowledge and experience you gained from the pilot.

The phase-in plan involves implementing different phases of the new program at different time periods, say on January 1, March 1, and May 1. The parallel plan is often used when replacing manual systems with automated systems. For the trial period, employees actually have to run both systems. This gives the automation team a chance to identify and fix remaining bugs before implementing the system throughout the organization. The cold-turkey plan is just what the name implies: On Day X (e.g., June 1), the old program or procedure is discontinued and the new one takes its place.

CHAPTER SUMMARY

Proposals are a vital part of business, government, and nonprofit organizations. Proposals are written to obtain permission, and sometimes funding, to proceed with plans explained in the proposal. Proposals all have a common general goal—to propose something—but they can vary in many ways. Proposals may be presented orally or in writing. They may also be solicited or unsolicited, and direct or indirect in their approach.

Many proposals seek to conduct problem-solving projects. Three general steps are involved in solving problems: diagnose the problem, solve the problem, and implement the solution. When diagnosing problems, remember the difference between causes and symptoms. The cause is the origin; the symptom is the result. Too many people try to fix the symptoms, only to find that they reappear because the cause is still present.

Brainstorming can foster creativity and develop potential solutions to a problem. The idea behind brainstorming is that quantity will yield quality; in other words, if you come up with enough ideas, at least one or two likely will be good ones. Brainstorming can be performed alone (personal brainstorming) or with a group. Whereas the initial phase of brainstorming fosters divergent thinking (diverse thinking), the decision-making phase brings about convergent thinking (moving toward one point; unifying the group thinking). A decision table, or decision matrix, can be useful in deciding on the best decision. Seek for a solution everyone can live with.

When you have good buy-in from all stakeholders, decide how to implement the ideas. Make sure all groups that are affected are represented in the implementation plan. Modify the implementation plan as needed to address their concerns.

WORKS CITED

SkyMark. Force Field Analysis. 2012. http://www.skymark.com/resources/tools/force_field_diagram.asp.

CHAPTER QUESTIONS

1. What is an RFP?

2. What are the usual sections found in a written proposal?

3. Describe the difference between causes and symptoms.

4. What is a cause-and-effect diagram? How is it used?

5. List three factors a manager should consider in deciding whether to involve the group in making a decision?

6. The idea behind brainstorming is that _____ will yield _____.

7. List three ways to enhance your creativity.

8. What is gallery writing? What are the advantages of gallery writing over traditional brainstorming?

9. What is the difference between divergent thinking and convergent thinking?

10. What is a decision table? Why is it useful in decision making?

11. What are the five categories of personnel performance problems?

12. Describe the role of proposals in organizations.

13. What is a force-field analysis?

CHAPTER ACTIVITIES

1. Conduct an internet search on the words "proposal writing," and browse through a few of the sites that you find. Write a brief summary of your findings.

2. Conduct an internet search on the words "sample proposal." Review a few of the proposals, and examine the content, organization, and writing of the proposals. Write a brief summary of your findings.

3. Conduct an internet search on the initials "RFP." Review a few of the RFP's, and write a brief summary of your findings.

4. Using the internet, gather information regarding three comparable products, such as three computers, three cameras, or three cars. Analyze and compare the three alternatives. Develop a decision table to show your comparison.

5. Think of a problem in your school or community. Create a cause-and-effect diagram to diagnose the problem. Then develop solutions for each of the problem causes.

6. On the internet, find a site that includes complaints filed against a business organization. Analyze some of the complaints and develop solutions for the causes of the problems.

To: Department Managers

From: Training Department

Date: June 15, 20XX

Subject: **CNE Certification Course**

Background

Our CNE Certification Course was developed in 20XX to meet the needs of all units with networks. The company has not charged a registration fee for the course and has paid the participants for the hours spent attending the two-day course and completing the subsequent testing. The participants have been given six weeks to complete the course. If this deadline has not been met, a $25 penalty has been assessed through payroll deduction.

During the past two years, 25 percent of the systems personnel have not completed the course. This high non-completion rate results in heavy resource use without our organization realizing appropriate benefits. We believe the current registration and pay practice fails to promote individual commitment or accountability for course completion. The following sections include our proposal to address this problem, followed by sections on benefits, costs, and timing.

Proposal

To solve the problem, we propose that the registration/pay practice for the CNE Certification Course be changed so each participant's personal financial investment will be linked to course registration *and* completion. The systems personnel who are committed will register; those who are not committed will not register.

- The person must be a competent employee to register. Employees wanting to register must obtain their department manager's signature on the registration form to indicate competency.

- A $50 registration fee will be paid by the employee participant.

- The unit will pay one-half the number of hours spent in the two-day course at regular hourly wage. The participants will not be paid for testing.

- The participants will complete the course within six weeks. If the deadline is met, $25 will be refunded. If the course is not completed within six weeks, the entire registration fee will be forfeited. Non-completion will be grounds for disciplinary action by the department manager.

Benefits

Two key benefits will be realized if we implement this new practice. First, the new registration/pay practice will promote the registration of systems professionals who are committed to course completion. Uncommitted employees will likely not register under this proposed arrangement. Second, this proposal will decrease the cost to the employees' units and help recover course supply costs incurred by the Training Department.

Cost Analysis

The following table highlights the major cost differences for the Training Department between the current and proposed practices.

Figure 8.7 Example of an unsolicited internal proposal.

-2-

COST COMPARISON BETWEEN CURRENT AND PROPOSED PRACTICE

Cost Category	Current Practice	Proposed Practice
Employee wages (average wage of $11.50/hour)	16 hrs (course) + 2 hrs (test) x $11.50 = $207.00	16 hours (course) x 1/2 x $11.50 = $92.00
Supplies	$12.00	$12.00
Handouts	$2.00	$2.00
Refreshments	$3.00	$3.00
Total Costs	$224.00 per participant	$109.00 per participant
Revenue	$0 if deadline met or $25.00 if not	$25.00 if deadline met or $50.00 if not

The foregoing figures indicate the financial benefits of adopting the new proposal. Our organization's typical cost for a completing employee would drop from $224 under the current practice to $84 ($109 expense minus $25 revenue) with the proposed practice—a per person savings of $140. The proposed procedure clearly makes sound financial sense.

Time Line

We hope to implement this new practice for the next CNE Certification course, scheduled for August 16 and 19. Because course publicity must be available by July 6, allowing time for registration and scheduling of participants' replacement personnel, we will appreciate your decision concerning this proposed change by June 25.

Conclusion

We feel that the CNE Certification Course proposal is a wise move from both a financial and a personnel standpoint. If you have any questions concerning this proposal, we would be happy to meet with you either prior to or during your June 20 meeting where this proposal will be discussed.

Figure 8.7 continued.

*Clean*MASTER

945 GreyFox Circle
Brownsville, Texas 956XX
Phone (XXX) 546–1234
Pager (XXX) 546–5678

February 5, 20XX

Mr. Jose Garcia
Brownsville Medical Plaza
1040 West Jackson
Brownsville, TX 95620

Dear Jose:

As you requested, we are submitting the following proposal to perform carpet cleaning for your medical facility. The proposal contains information about all aspects of our work, including our satisfaction guarantee.

CleanMaster's cleaning processes have been perfected over decades of work in every type of situation imaginable. With CleanMaster, you can be confident that your work will be completed with the best procedures and products available and that the work will cause as little disruption to your business as possible.

As you study our proposal, please feel free to call me if you have any questions or need additional information. We look forward to hearing from you.

Sincerely,

James A Rogers

James A. Rogers
Professional Cleaning Specialist

Enclosure: Proposal

Figure 8.8 Example of a solicited external proposal.

Proposal to Perform Carpet Cleaning for

Brownsville Medical Center

1040 West Jackson
Brownsville, Texas

*Clean*Master, Inc.

945 Grey Fox Circle
Brownsville, Texas 78520
Phone (XXX) 546–1234
Pager (XXX) 546–5678

February 5, 20XX

Figure 8.8 continued.

Proposal to Perform Carpet Cleaning for Brownsville Medical Center

Basic Proposal

CleanMaster proposes to perform work for Brownsville Medical Center's Women's Center as follows:

Area	Number
Second-floor hallways	3
Second-floor Nurses Station	1
Labor and Delivery Section hallway	1
Total area to be cleaned	Approximately 4,155 square feet

Procedures to be Followed

This project will be performed using CleanMaster's patented carpet cleaning process, which includes the following:

1. Spray carpet with CleanMaster's detergent soil decomposer to break down dirt and residues that accumulate in carpet.
2. Apply special spot removal detergents on darker stains.
3. Scrub carpet with high-performance scrubber to loosen dirt from carpet fiber.
4. Rinse carpet and extract the dirt, pumping it into the CleanMaster cleaning system waste tank.

Benefits

Selecting CleanMaster provides numerous benefits for Brownsville Medical Center, among which are the following:

- Guaranteed clean carpets that are so essential in a medical facility.
- Limited disruption of important work routines as nurses carry out their medical responsibilities.
- Friendly and genuinely concerned CleanMaster employees who are available 24 hours a day.
- Affordable pricing to have limited impact on your budget.
- CleanMaster's Satisfaction Guarantee: "Do it right the first time or do it over—no questions asked."

Qualifications of Brownsville CleanMaster

CleanMaster has been doing business in the Brownsville area for 23 years. During this time, we have performed professional work for all types of commercial and healthcare facilities. As part of the nationwide CleanMaster organization, we receive regular training in all the latest techniques to improve the cleaning process and give our customers the level of cleaning service they expect.

Although CleanMaster is a national organization, we and our families live here in the Brownsville area, and we want to earn your trust. Our desire is to have you become a repeat customer, and we know that will happen only if you are satisfied with our work. We will strive very hard to earn your trust and perform to your level of satisfaction.

Figure 8.8 continued.

2

Time Line

To disrupt your normal work procedures as little as possible, we propose to perform your work late on a Saturday night, preferably February 13. Performing the work at this time will enable us to complete the project and have your carpets dried before normal business hours the following day.

Pricing

Based on our initial measurement of your cleaning area, we are prepared to clean approximately 4,155 square feet of carpet. The cost of labor, materials, transportation, and equipment resources applied to this project is $494.45, plus $40.79 tax, making a total of $535.24. This price is valid through May 30, 20XX. If you wish to discuss this pricing structure further, please call me at one of the numbers listed on the cover of this proposal.

Conclusion

We appreciate the opportunity to perform cleaning services for Brownsville Medical Center and hope you will consider our proposal carefully. During your decision process, feel free to communicate with us as needed so we can answer your questions and provide any additional information you need.

Figure 8.8 continued.

ABC Consulting, Inc.

Specialists in Complaint-Management Systems
5850 Park Lane Road
Commerce, US 84XXX
723.266.21XX ◆ 723.266.23XX

13 March 2008

Mr. Lukas Steiner
FlyHigh Airlines
7500 Airport Drive
Somewhere, US 554XX

Dear Mr. Steiner:

In spite of your best efforts to meet the needs of every customer, sometimes things just don't go quite right and someone has a bad experience with your company. In the past, that customer might complain to a few friends and then let it go. But today, more and more disgruntled customers are using the web to publish their gripes to the whole world. The result is embarrassing publicity and lost business for you. That's where we come in.

What We Do

We specialize in reducing customer complaints through enhanced complaint management and improved customer service. We have worked with several airline companies and have a superior track record of success. Our team of specialists will work with your organization as follows:

— Analyze customer complaints on all complaint-related websites.
— Develop creative solutions to significantly reduce the most frequently recurring complaints.
— Develop complaint-management methods for effectively working with dissatisfied customers.

Who We Are

ABC was formed to help reduce customer complaints through improved customer service. Four highly trained specialists, assisted by additional support staff, work on all of our complaints-management projects:

- *Daniel Michalkova*: Co-founder of ABC Consulting, Inc. and a recipient of a Master of Science degree in Statistics from Yale University, Daniel has extensive experience in analyzing data and providing recommendations for many prominent companies.
- *Alene Church:* Customer service specialist for 15 years and a graduate from the MBA program at New York University with an emphasis in Human Resources, Alene has contributed significantly in numerous projects for both enhancing customer service and improving overall business techniques.

Figure 8.9 An outside unsolicited proposal in letter format. Note the Gantt chart that shows the project timeline.

Mr. Lukas Steiner   Page 2   13 March 20XX

- *Christine Taylor:* Upon receiving an MBA degree with an emphasis in Finance from Virginia University, Christine was recruited by Boon Consulting, where she received *Employee of the Year Award* consecutively for three years. Because of her experience in improving companies' efficiency, structure, and profits, she was assigned to a project for Mideast Airlines, which ultimately resulted in a decrease of company complaints by 58 percent.
- *Larry Tryon:* Research specialist and MBA graduate from Harvard University with an emphasis in marketing, Larry is the former Operations Manager of Speedy Airways and has a strong background in the airline industry.

Our Deliverables

Upon completion of the project, we will present to the management of FlyHigh Airlines written and oral reports containing:

- Detailed analyses of all complaints found on the internet
- Recommendations for significantly reducing the most frequent problems
- Recommendations for establishing an effective complaint-management system to prevent complaints from being posted on the web

Our Timeline

Complaints-analysis projects are conducted in four major phases, with typical duration times as specified in the following chart:

Project Phases	Week									
	1	2	3	4	5	6	7	8	9	10
1 Gather data	███	███								
2 Analyze data			███	███	███					
3 Develop recommendations						███	███	███		
4 Prepare & deliver reports								███	███	███

We would appreciate the opportunity to work with your organization in increasing your customers' satisfaction and helping prevent negative publicity from dissatisfied customers. After you have had a few days to consider our proposal, we will call to request the opportunity to meet with you for further discussion.

Sincerely,

Daniel Michalkova, Partner

Figure 8.9 continued.

CONDUCTING AND DOCUMENTING BUSINESS RESEARCH

Secondary and primary research constitute the two main types of research conducted in business. Secondary research includes reviewing information that has already been published, such as books, journals, and electronic databases. Primary research requires the gathering of original data, using such methods as surveys (e.g., questionnaires, interviews, or focus groups), observation (e.g., watching consumers' behavior in a retail store), and experimentation (e.g., introducing a new product in one geographic area and not in another). This chapter discusses these two main types of research and provides guidelines for documenting secondary sources.

SECONDARY RESEARCH

In previous decades, secondary research was conducted by slowly searching through printed indexes of journals, books, and reports. With today's databases, you can instantly search millions of records electronically. This section of Chapter 9 provides guidelines for searching and for documenting the information you find.

Conducting Secondary Research

First, write down the topic you wish to search, making sure the scope of your topic is appropriately specific. Next, determine the databases that will likely yield the desired information. Databases can be broad in coverage or more narrowly focused. EBSCO, for instance, contains articles from thousands of journals in business, finance, manage-

ment, and accounting. EDGAR, on the other hand, is more focused and contains financial reports of U.S. corporations.

In addition to selecting the appropriate databases to search, determine the types of publications that will most likely contain the information you need. The four main publication categories include scholarly journals, trade journals, popular magazines, and newspapers.

Scholarly journals contain many research-based articles that have been carefully reviewed by the author's professional peers before being cleared for publication. Many have been subjected to a "blind review," which means that the reviewers did not know the identity of the author during the review period, thus allowing the reviewers to be unbiased and objective in their critique. Scholarly journals contain highly reliable information, but they often don't contain information on the latest issues, because of the time it takes to perform the research and conduct peer reviews.

The remaining three types of publications contain more

Figure 9.1 Vast electronic databases are available for conducting secondary research.

current information, although it may at times be less reliable because it has not been peer reviewed. Trade journals target a specific market or industry, such as the beverage industry. Popular magazines cover a wide array of topics and are published for general audiences. Newspapers cover current news for general audiences and include editorial opinions on varied current issues.

You can also search well-known internet sites such as Google or Yahoo. However, remember that when using the internet, you must be cautious about the quality and accuracy of the information you find. Because publishing on the internet is so easy and so accessible to everyone, you will find poorly written and incorrect information along with that which is good.

Here are a few questions to help you determine the quality of internet information.

The Author: Who is the author? Is the author a credible authority on the topic? Is the author included or cited in other publications on the topic? Can the author be contacted?

The Sponsoring Organization: Who is the sponsoring organization? What is the mission of the site? Can the organization be contacted? Does it have a reason to be politically, culturally, religiously, or ideologically biased?

The Site: Is the site active and kept up to date? Does the site have any broken links or dead-end components? What is the URL's three-letter ending—gov, edu, org, or com? Most sites with gov endings contain reliable data. Many sites with edu endings are also reliable, but some can be unreliable, such as writings from politically biased professors. Most sites with org endings are owned by non-profit organizations, and they can be either reliable or not, depending on their mission. Finally, sites with com endings are for-profit businesses whose purpose is to make money. Therefore, they have a bias in favor of their own survival and profitability.

The Information: Is the information verified with accompanying citations and a bibliography? How current is the information? Are there links to other reliable sources? Is the information well organized and well written? Are there obvious typographical, grammar, spelling, and other writing errors?

To conduct electronic searches, you can search for single words or for phrases. If you use single words, you could search for a word like "debt," or for a combination of single words, like "debt" and "credit." If you search for a phrase, you search for words that are grouped together, such as "credit card debt" (use quotations marks to indicate a phrase). In the first example, the search would find all sources that include the words "debt" and "credit." However, in the second example, the search would only find sources that have the entire phrase "credit card debt."

Variations of these searches are available, such as searching for words that are in relative proximity to each other, or using truncated words (words with one or more of their last letters omitted) with wild cards (a question mark or an asterisk) to search for different forms of a word, such as *crim**. Searching for *crim** would find word variations such as *crime, criminal,* and *criminology,* but it would also find all occurrences of *crimson* and *crimp.* In addition to word-search variations, you also have some document-formatting choices. For example, with some databases, you may choose between summaries or full-text documents, or between all texts or only scholarly texts.

When conducting electronic information searches, you need to know about Boolean operators, which help narrow your searches. Without using these operators, you'll end up with millions of "hits" and mountains of useless data. The main Boolean operators are AND, OR, and NOT. Here is how they work. Assume that you are trying to find all the articles about women's basketball. If you use just the search term basketball, you'll get articles dealing with men's basketball and women's basketball. Thus, you should narrow your search command to include women's AND basketball. If you want to narrow your study to include women's basketball injuries, you just include one additional AND criterion—basketball AND women's AND injuries. Figure 9.2 illustrates the narrowing effect of each additional AND criterion.

After each search, check the articles you have found to see if they contain an appropriate number of articles and the appropriate material you are looking for. If they don't, select more precise key words or modify your Boolean operators to be more restrictive. The articles you find might contain terms that work better than the ones you initially thought of, so learn as you go and continue searching until you get what you're looking for.

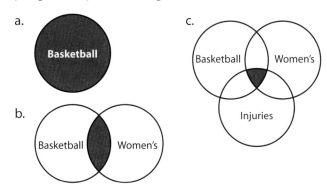

Figure 9.2 Search results are shaded green for "basketball" (a), "basketball" AND "women's" (b), and for "basketball" AND "women's" AND "injuries" (c).

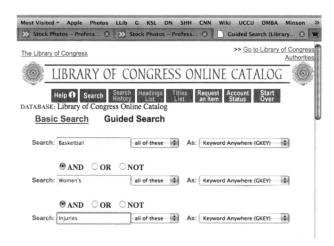

Figure 9.3 The Library of Congress Online Catalog employs Boolean operators to help you focus your information searches.

When you find an article you want to use, select the PDF version if it is available. The PDF version will give you a literal image of the printed pages, including correct page numbers, whereas the HTML version won't give you accurate pagination. Without accurate page numbers, you won't have all the information needed for complete documentation.

Figure 9.3 illustrates a guided search screen from the Library of Congress Online Catalog. As you visit this screen, you enter your key words in the appropriate blanks and then indicate whether you want the AND, OR, or NOT Boolean operators to be used.

Many college professors require an academic proposal before approving students' secondary research topic, and your initial investigation will provide the information you need. In this proposal, describe the topic and its importance, list the research questions you hope to answer, and tell how and when your research will be completed, and request permission to proceed with the research. A short academic proposal is included at the end of this chapter (see Figure 9.8).

Documenting

Including information obtained from other people adds credibility to your own writing, but you are required by law to acknowledge that the work came from someone else and to indicate where you found it. The following sections will explain the why, what, and how of documentation.

WHY DOCUMENT

Documentation is important for at least three reasons: to give credit to the people who created the original work, to tell people how to find the original source, and to comply with copyright law. From a legal standpoint, the owner of an original "expression," or creative work, has the right

to determine who can make copies of the work. Just as a patent protects an invention and a trademark protects a name, symbol, or design, a copyright protects music, writing, art, movies, and software. Text that is written by anyone is automatically protected by copyright, even if a formal copyright has not been granted by the United States copyright office.

If you represent other people's unique work as your own, you are being untruthful and are guilty of plagiarism, and the penalties can be serious. For a college student, plagiarism can result in a failing grade for a report, a failing grade for an entire course, or even expulsion from school for extremely serious violations. In a professional setting, plagiarism can result in disciplinary measures, including dismissal from employment, and in a tarnished reputation.

Plagiarism can occur in various ways. If you copy someone else's text verbatim (word for word) and you don't give due credit, you are guilty of plagiarism. If you paraphrase someone else's work and you don't give due credit, you are guilty of plagiarism. If you blend other people's facts or ideas with your own facts or ideas without giving due credit, you are guilty of plagiarism. You can avoid all the problems of plagiarism by knowing what needs to be documented and how to document.

WHAT TO DOCUMENT

You will generally use three techniques when integrating outside material into your work—quoting, paraphrasing, or summarizing. Regardless of the integration technique you use, you must document the source. Understanding the differences and similarities among these techniques may help you better recognize what must be documented in your own work.

- *Quoting:* You quote when you use exact words, sentences, or phrases from others' unique material. Writers generally quote when the exact wording is important. Quotations must always be surrounded by quotation marks, even if you're quoting only a single word. As a rule of thumb, keep direct quotations to a minimum and use more paraphrasing and summarizing.

- *Paraphrasing:* Paraphrasing occurs when you substitute your own words for the words used in others' unique material. Writers paraphrase when they want to avoid quoting the original material word for word yet convey the same meaning of the original work. While paraphrases do not need to be surrounded by quotation marks, you still need to document paraphrases so readers know the material comes from an outside source.

- *Summarizing:* Summarizing occurs when you condense a larger amount of material into its main points. Writers summarize when they want to highlight general ideas or main points, leaving out unnecessary detail. As with paraphrases, summaries do not need quotation marks, but they must be documented so readers know the material comes from another source.

The following examples illustrate the differences between quotations, paraphrases, and summaries (taken from Middleton, Diana. "Students Struggle for Words." *Wall Street Journal.* 3 Mar. 2012. Web. 8 Sep. 2012).

Quote: "While M.B.A. students' quantitative skills are prized by employers, their writing and presentation skills have been a perennial complaint. Employers and writing coaches say business-school graduates tend to ramble, use pretentious vocabulary or pen too-casual emails."

Paraphrase: M.B.A. students' quantitative skills are valued by employers, but the employers say the students' writing and presentation skills are lacking—they ramble, use flowery vocabulary, and write overly informal emails.

Summary: Employers compliment M.B.A. students on their quantitative skills but complain about their writing and speaking skills.

These three integration techniques may be used both individually and in combination with each other. For example, you may summarize a paragraph and quote a few exact words within your summary. Good writers use all three techniques, while ensuring that their writing flows coherently and cohesively. For examples of quotes, paraphrases, and summaries, see the example papers at the end of this chapter (Figures 9.9–9.12).

Figure 9.4 Citing the work of other people can add credibility to your writing, but you must be sure to give appropriate credit.

Although this section has stressed the importance of documenting outside material, some information from outside sources does not need to be documented. For instance, information that is considered to be common knowledge does not have to be attributed to anyone. For instance, you could state without documentation that cancer is a major health problem in the United States, because that is common knowledge. But if you state that a study conducted in 2011 found a 15 percent increase in a certain type of cancer, you would have to cite the source of that unique information. If you are ever unsure whether outside information needs to be documented, choose to document just to protect yourself.

HOW TO DOCUMENT

Documentation generally consists of two parts: (1) informing your audience with an in-text notation whenever you reference other people's information and (2) providing detailed information about where the original information can be found. The in-text notation serves as a pointer to the more detailed information located in footnotes, endnotes, or a bibliography or reference page.

To standardize the process of documentation, different organizations and groups have developed documentation styles. For example, styles that are widely used by business writers and authors in the social sciences are APA (from the American Psychological Association), MLA (from the Modern Language Association), and Chicago (from the University of Chicago Press). These style guidelines are compiled into style guides that writers can use for properly documenting newspaper articles, journal articles, websites, books, and other sources. Find the details of these style guides on the internet by searching for "APA style," "MLA style," "Chicago Style," or simply "style guides."

All three styles provide guidelines for in-text citations, meaning that within the body text you insert a brief documentation reference. Then at the end of the document, you provide a complete alphabetized list of all the references. For APA, the in-text citations should include the author's last name, year of publication, and pertinent page numbers as appropriate. For MLA, the in-text citations should include the author's last name and page reference as appropriate. For Chicago, in-text citations should include the author's last name, year of publication, and page numbers as needed.

Regardless of the style you choose for a document, be familiar with that style's guidelines and apply them consistently. Many style guides are printed in book form, or you can find style guides online by searching "style guides" on the internet.

In addition to the three APA, MLA, and Chicago in-

Figure 9.5 Consult print or digital style guides to ensure that your documentation style is appropriate and consistent.

text citation styles, Chicago provides an alternate form— the documentary-note style—that uses footnotes or endnotes. This style includes two parts: numbered superscripts (such as [3]) in the body text and corresponding footnotes (at the bottom of the pages) or endnotes (at the end of the entire document) listed in the sequence in which they occur in the body. For your reference, example articles using these four styles are found at the end of this chapter. (To save space, some conventional vertical spacing standards have not been followed.)

Organizations you work for may have their own style guide, or they may use APA, MLA, or another style guide, such as the AMA Manual of Style, published for the medical field. If your organization does not use a specific style guide, just choose a style guide that you like best and apply it to your work—you can find details for many style guides on the internet. Don't let your lack of familiarity with a style guide keep you from documenting! If necessary, you can even develop your own style guide, so long as it complies with the legal requirements of documentation law.

While integrating other people's work and related documentation into your writing, you must still keep a coherent and cohesive flow. Here are four steps that can help you: introduce, insert, interpret, and include.

- *Introduce.* When you use the work of others, introduce it with words that signal your use of outside material. For example, you could state, "In her article on stock portfolios, Smith emphasizes . . ."
- *Insert.* After introducing outside material, integrate it into your writing, using quotes, paraphrases, or summaries. Also, include appropriate documentation notations. For instance, place the author and date in parentheses, such as (Smith 20XX); or include a superscript that refers to a footnote or endnote, such as Smith[1]. This signal points to the detailed source information in the references or bibliography section.

- *Interpret.* Clearly indicate the key point you are trying to make with the cited information, such as the following: "Smith's research helps illustrate the seriousness of the obesity problem in our country." An option is to include the interpretation as part of the introduction: "In her article on stock portfolios, Smith (20XX) emphasizes the importance of diversification."
- *Include.* Once you have used an outside source in your work, include the detailed reference information in your references or bibliography section. Usually located at the bottom of a page (as a footnote) or at the end of your material, the list includes one entry for each source you reference. Each entry gives specific information about the author, title, dates, and publishing information so the readers can find the original material if needed.

Not all references will fit neatly into the rules of the different documentation styles. Thus, as needed, make appropriate adaptations, applying the spirit of documentation law—give appropriate credit and clearly define the location of the material so the reader can find it.

PRIMARY RESEARCH

As mentioned previously, primary research involves gathering original data, sometimes using questionnaires, check lists, or interviews, and sometimes using observational research or experimental research methods. The following guidelines will be helpful whenever you have to conduct primary research. Modify the guidelines as appropriate in the various projects you undertake.

1. Clearly define your research goals and objectives. In a clear, concise statement, write down what problem you are trying to solve or what objective you are trying to accomplish. Use this statement as a guide throughout the research process.

2. Identify the best method for accomplishing your research objective. You have a number of options: interviews (face-to-face or telephone), mailed or emailed questionnaires, focus groups and expert panels, observation, or experimentation.

   Whatever method you use, you must achieve two major standards with your research.

   Validity. The first research standard is validity; that is, research must measure what it purports to measure. For example, if you are trying to determine whether an adverse environmental problem in a community is causing cancer, your research must truthfully achieve that goal. Valid research provides truth about the research problem. Its conclusions are true conclusions based on solid facts and findings. Validity is the highest research

Figure 9.6 Focus groups are assembled to conduct qualitative research about a product or idea.

standard, and no compromise should be tolerated. Research that is not valid fails at the most basic level and should be disregarded.

Reliability. The second standard of research is reliability; that is, research must be repeatable with consistent results. For example, if you conduct research regarding the viability of a software product in a given marketplace, a subsequent study should yield the same findings as the first. A medical study that finds a correlation between eating disorders and self-esteem should produce the same findings in a subsequent study.

3. Identify the population for your study, such as everyone in a certain geographical area, a certain slice of the population in a certain area, or a set of transaction records during a given time period.

4. Determine whether you can contact everyone in the population or whether sampling will be required. If sampling is required, consult a reputable statistician to assist you in determining the needed sample size and in drawing the sample. Three options are listed as follows:

   - *Random:* From a list of the entire population, randomly draw the needed sample of participants.

Figure 9.7 Drawing names or numbers from a hat is the traditional method of achieving random sampling.

- *Stratified Random:* From a list of the entire population, randomly draw the needed sample, making sure that the sample represents the total population according to certain factors, such as gender, income level, or geographical area. For example, if 40 percent of the population is female, make sure that 40 percent of the sample is female.

- *Systematic Random:* From a numbered list of the entire population, randomly draw the first participant and then draw every nth sample participant after that until the needed sample size is achieved. For example, given a population of 5,000 and a needed sample size of 500, randomly draw a number from 1 to 10. If 7 is chosen, thereafter select number 17, 27, 37, 47, etc. to achieve the goal of 500 participants.

5. Create your data-gathering instrument, whether it be a questionnaire, a log, or interview form. You may distribute and administer questionnaires in paper form, but you can make the process much easier by distributing the questionnaire on the internet. Using appropriate survey software, create the questions and then send the complete questionnaire to the people in your population. As the recipients complete the questionnaire on their computer, they return it by email and the software automatically places their data into a spreadsheet ready for analysis.

Questions on your instrument can be constructed in at least seven different formats.

Closed—Ask for factual information.

How many complaints have you received during the past month?

☐ 0   ☐ 1–5   ☐ 6–10   ☐ Over 10

Either/Or—Force respondent to choose one of two options.

Which of the following two sources would you go to when purchasing a new computer?

☐ Buy online   ☐ Purchase locally

Restricted multiple choice—Choose one of several options.

Which of the following applies to you? (Choose only one.)

☐ I feel unhappy in my present job.

☐ I am generally satisfied with my present job.

☐ I am excited about my present job.

Unrestricted multiple choice—Choose all that apply.

Which of the following software packages do you use? (Mark all that apply.)

☐ Word

☐ Excel

☐ PowerPoint

☐ Other (please indicate: _____)

Ranking—Rank each option from high to low. No two items may receive the same ranking.

Rank the following printer models according to your preference (1 = the highest ranking):

Rank　　*Product*

_____　　ColorPro I

_____　　PrintMaster

_____　　LaserLine 320

_____　　PrintTech II

Rating—Evaluate all options on a numeric or semantic differential scale. Different options may receive the same rating. Rating is generally preferred to ranking for three reasons: (1) Ranking is a difficult process; (2) ranking does not allow respondents to give two options the same value, even though the respondent might feel the same about them; and (3) a ranking can be derived from a rating-type question, simply by averaging all the respondents' ratings and sorting them from high to low.

How satisfied are you with the following products you buy from our firm? (Circle 0–6 for each item.)

Satisfied　　　　　*Dissatisfied*

0　1　2　3　4　5　6　　Product A

0　1　2　3　4　5　6　　Product B

0　1　2　3　4　5　6　　Product C

0　1　2　3　4　5　6　　Product D

Open—Ask a question that allows the respondents to pursue whatever avenue of response they desire.

How do you feel about the new health coverage program offered by our firm: _____

_____

_____.

The following seven guidelines can help improve your success in developing questionnaires that will get the results you want:

- Make sure your instrument has a clear title and

clear instructions (answer all the 5 W questions). Give examples as needed for clarification.

- Ensure anonymity of participants wherever possible. Indicate, "All information you provide will be kept strictly confidential."

- Offer some incentive, if necessary, to increase the likelihood of getting a questionnaire completed and returned. Consider giving a small financial reward, a copy of the survey results, or a small gift.

- Make questions as easy to answer as possible. For example, ask for a check mark rather than a complete sentence. Use the same type of question-and-answer format for as many questions as possible, such as a series of multiple-choice questions (a, b, c, d) rather than a combination of multiple-choice, true-false, fill-in-the-blank, etc.

- Organize the questions and group related questions in the same section of the questionnaire.

- Keep the instrument short, simple, and clear. If using paper, restrict the questionnaire to one page, front and back. Long questionnaires discourage people from responding.

6. Pilot test your data-gathering instrument with several members of the population being studied. This step will help ensure that you obtain the information you are seeking and will polish your instrument (clarity, spelling, and efficiency).

7. Gather the data. If necessary, complete a second or third follow-up to get a high response rate. For example, send out a follow-up questionnaire two to three weeks after the initial mailing.

8. Carefully examine each response to ensure that the data is valid. Sometimes respondents don't understand a question or fail to completely and correctly complete the questionnaire. Omit invalid data.

9. Use the correct statistical procedure for analyzing the data. If necessary, consult a reputable statistician for help with this task.

After you complete your primary or secondary research, write a report that clearly describes your research process and communicates the research results. Chapter 10 provides different report formats that you may follow. Throughout the data-gathering process, be sure to document your findings, especially for secondary research. Complete and accurate records are vital in substantiating claims that may be challenged later on. Also, report the findings and conclusions accurately, avoiding the temptation to embellish the facts or to hide disappointing results.

CHAPTER SUMMARY

Secondary and primary research constitute the two main types of research conducted in business. Secondary research involves reviewing information that has already been published, such as books, journals, and electronic databases. Primary research involves gathering original data, using questionnaires, check lists, or interviews. It can also involve observational research (such as watching and documenting people's behavior) and conducting experiments, with control and experimental groups. When conducting electronic information searches, you need to know about Boolean operators, which help narrow your searches.

When quoting, paraphrasing, or summarizing the unique work of other people, you are required by law to document—to indicate the source of the original work. Text that is written by anyone is automatically protected by copyright, even if a formal copyright has not been granted by the U. S. Copyright Office. Documentation is important for three reasons: to give credit to the people who created the original work, to tell people how to find the original source, and to comply with copyright law.

To standardize the process of documentation, different organizations and groups have developed documentation styles. Three common styles are APA, MLA, and Chicago. All three styles provide guidelines for in-text citations, meaning that within the body text you insert a brief documentation reference. Then at the end of the document, you provide a complete alphabetized list of all the references. In addition to the three in-text citation styles, Chicago provides an alternate form—the documentary-note style—that uses footnotes or endnotes. With this form you place a number in the body of the text and then type the complete reference as a footnote or endnote.

When conducting research, you must achieve two major standards—validity and reliability. Often you will be required to sample a population, because contacting everyone in the population would be too expensive and take too long. Strive to select your sample randomly so everyone in the population will have an equal chance of being selected. Gathering information can involve surveys by mail questionnaires, email questionnaires, telephone, or other techniques. A variety of questions can be employed to obtain the desired information.

CHAPTER QUESTIONS

1. What is the difference between primary and secondary research?

2. What is Boolean logic? What are the three main operators of Boolean logic?

3. What is plagiarism? Why is documentation important when you quote or paraphrase other writers' work?

4. What are the main differences between the two types of Chicago-style documentation?

5. What is the difference between validity and reliability? Which is more important?

6. Describe the three main types of random sampling.

7. What is an unrestricted multiple-choice question?

8. What are the disadvantages of ranking questions?

9. What are the advantages of rating questions?

10. List four ways to improve the response rate of a mailed questionnaire.

CHAPTER ACTIVITIES

1. Write an academic proposal for your instructor. Clearly explain your topic and conduct a preliminary search for related articles using electronic databases such as EBSCO and ProQuest. Attach or include a list of the articles that will most likely provide the information you need.

2. Conduct a secondary research study of a current business topic related to your professional field. Gather your data from the most current sources (e.g., within the last two years). Create an outline and test the outline using the five-step outline-checking process explained in Chapter 2. As directed by your instructor, create a references page, works cited page, or bibliography according to APA, MLA, or Chicago documentation style.

3. Using the information you obtained from Chapter Activity 2 in Chapter 9, write a 2,000–2,500 word article for a business magazine or journal. Document all of your quotations and paraphrases, using APA, MLA, or Chicago standards.

4. Conduct a research project on some local problem, such as parking on campus, cost of textbooks, traffic congestion, or campus security and safety. Using a questionnaire form created in Google Docs or other survey software, develop an electronic questionnaire and have a number of your friends or fellow students complete the questionnaire. Analyze the results.

To: Professor Alison Sam
From: Richard Rawlins
Date: February 28, 20XX

Re: Proposal to Research Affordable Housing in Kansas

For my academic research project I propose to research affordable-housing problems in Kansas.

In the United States, housing is categorized as affordable when residents spend no more than 30 percent of their income on housing. Affordable housing is essential because it allows individuals and families to contribute to a community in many vital ways. Further, affordable housing enables families to allocate appropriate amounts of resources to other basic needs such as food, transportation, and healthcare. Without affordable housing, an area can quickly lose its vital lower-wage workforce, and businesses that depend on lower-wage workers have difficulty filling employment vacancies.

Kansas has two main affordable-housing problems. First, minimum-wage earners don't make enough money to afford housing in most areas of the state. For an average two-bedroom rental unit, a minimum-wage earner would need to work more than two full-time jobs. Second, Kansas has an undersupply of affordable housing. Latest figures estimate that there is a 22,000-unit shortage of affordable housing for low-income families.

PROBLEMS TO BE INVESTIGATED

At this stage of my research, I plan to investigate the following questions:

1. To what extent is affordable housing a problem in Kansas?
2. What economic factors are influencing the affordable-housing issue in Kansas?
3. How is the Kansas State government organized to address affordable-housing needs.
4. What can Kansas learn from other states that have been successful in addressing affordable housing issues?

METHODS OF RESEARCH

My research will rely heavily on scholarly articles, government statistical data, and agency reports regarding affordable housing. A ProQuest search on this general topic yielded 298 scholarly documents, 29 of which have been published since the beginning of the year, showing that the topic is significant and timely. After narrowing my search to Kansas, I found 14 articles, some of which are included in the attached bibliography.

SCHEDULE

I intend to complete my library research by March 14, 20XX, after which I will begin work on preparing a presentation to share my findings. I will present an oral report on March 23, 20XX. For that presentation I will prepare a handout and PowerPoint presentation.

REQUEST FOR APPROVAL

I ask that you approve my topic, methods, and schedule. I would appreciate any comments or suggestions you may have regarding this proposal. Please contact me at rlr@abcuniv.edu if you have any questions about my research ideas and plans.

Figure 9.8 Academic proposals are used to obtain professors' permission to conduct secondary research.

Good News for Bad News

On six occasions in only four years, three different Yahoo! CEOs faced the unpleasant task of communicating mass layoffs to employees (Associated Press, 2012). Negative consequences of the bad news included decreased employee morale (Efrati, 2011), criticism from investors (Henn, 2012), and mixed responses in stock price (Letzing, 2012; Vascellaro, 2012).

Difficult situations like this are not uncommon—from announcing layoffs to reporting disappointing earnings, most managers occasionally have to deliver bad news. While managers may not be able to prevent all the negative consequences of bad news, an appropriate direct or indirect approach may help.

Appropriate Approach
When managers write a message, they follow either a direct or an indirect approach. As one textbook author states, with a direct approach the writer presents the major idea of a message first and then presents supporting ideas. An indirect approach is just the opposite—the writer presents the supporting points first, followed by the central idea (Baker, 2011, p. 24). In the context of bad news, the central idea is the actual bad news, and the supporting points are the reasoning that led to the bad news.

When composing bad-news messages, Baker (2011) suggests that when "conveying bad news . . . consider using an indirect order . . ." (p. 67). Because bad news is often unexpected, an indirect approach helps readers to understand the reasons behind the news before receiving the bad news itself. When managers sense that their audience is not "prepared to receive the message," they should consider an indirect approach (Baker, 2011, p. 24), which has been found to be more persuasive than a direct approach (Frischknect & Baker, 2011). If the bad news is "routine," however, managers may use a direct approach (Baker, 2011, p. 68). Thus, depending on the readiness of the audience, managers should vary their approach.

Dampened Consequences
When managers must convey bad news to wide and diverse audiences, they don't have the luxury of customizing a direct or indirect approach for each recipient. Researchers have tried to determine which approach leads general audiences to receive bad news and still favorably view the messenger and the messenger's company. In her experiment with credit-refusal letters, Locker (1999) found that giving a brief explanation before bad news increased readers' acceptance of bad news, but it did not impact how favorably readers viewed the writer. In a later experimental study, Jansen and Janssen (2011) modified Locker's methodology and found that readers not only accepted bad news slightly better with indirect messages, but also viewed the messenger and the messenger's company slightly more favorably.

One scholar has argued against the indirect approach, but his concern seems to focus more on content than on approach. His criticism of using a buffer before giving bad news targets buffers that are unrelated to the bad news (Brent, 1985, p. 6); however, he states that he can "tolerate some delay" when the initial supporting points are related to the main idea and when the indirect structure is appropriate for the message and circumstances (Brent, 1985, p. 8). Given that his criticism focuses on unrelated buffers and not on the indirect approach itself, the prevailing philosophy seems to be the best approach—when conveying bad news to a varied audience, managers' best option is to use the indirect approach.

Conclusion
Internal memos from Yahoo! show that when informing employees of pending layoffs, CEOs used both indirect and direct approaches (Carlson, 2008; Swisher, 2012). While we may never know the exact circumstances that led the CEOs to use the different approaches, we do know that the approach used may have made a difference in how employees and stockholders accepted the bad news and subsequently viewed the CEOs and the company. When placed in similar circumstances where bad news must be communicated, managers should consider using an indirect approach to bring about the most positive consequences.

Figure 9.9 A short article illustrating the use of APA style documentation.

References

Associated Press. (2012, April 4). AP news in brief at 5:58 P.M. Edt. *Associated Press Newswires*.

Baker, W. (2011). *Writing & speaking for business* (2nd ed.). Provo, UT: BYU Academic Publishing.

Brent, D. (1985). Indirect structure and reader response. Journal of Business Communication, 22 (2), 5-8. Retrieved from https://www.lib.byu.edu/cgi-bin/remoteauth.pl?url=http://search.ebscohost .com/login.aspx?direct=true&db=ufh&AN=5777777&site=ehost-live&scope=site

Carlson, N. (2008, October 21). Jerry Yang's layoff memo. *BusinessInsider.com*. Retrieved from http://articles.businessinsider.com/2008-10-21/tech/30101126_1_earnings-release-long-term -employees

Efrati, A. (2011, December 5). Yahoo battles brain drain–Internet company braces for wave of exits after holidays. *Wall Street Journal*. Retrieved from http://www.online.wsj.com

Frischknecht, S. & Baker, W. (2011, October). Enhanced vs. undifferentiated text: A study to assess the effects on readers. In L. Gueldenzoph Snyder (Ed.), *Proceedings of the 76th Annual Convention of the Association for Business Communication.* Paper presented at the Association for Business Communication, Montreal, Quebec, Canada. Retrieved from http://businesscommunication.org /conventions /abc-convention-proceedings/2011-annual-convention-proceedings/

Henn, Steve. (Speaker). (2012, April 4). Latest round of Yahoo layoffs the most severe. *NPR: All Things Considered*. [Radio] Steve Henn. NPR.

Jansen, F. & Janssen, D. (2011). Explanations first: A case for presenting explanations before the decision in Dutch bad-news messages. *Journal of Business and Technical Communication* 25(1), 36-67. doi: 10.1177/1050651910380372

Letzing, J. & Efrati. A. (2012, April 4). Yahoo pushes reset. *Wall Street Journal*. Retrieved from http://www.online.wsj.com

Locker, K. (1999). Factors in reader responses to negative letters. *Journal of Business and Technical Communication* 13(1), 5-48. doi: 10.1177/105065199901300101

Swisher, K. (2010, December 15). Here's Carol Bartz's internal layoff memo to beleaguered Yahoo troops. Retrieved from http://allthingsd.com/20101215/heres-carol-bartzs-internal-layoff-memo- to-beleaguered-yahoo-troops/

Vascellaro, J. (2012, February 27). Bartz remakes Yahoo's top ranks. *Wall Street Journal*. Retrieved from http://www.online.wsj.com

Figure 9.9 continued.

Good News for Bad News

On six occasions in only four years, three different Yahoo! CEOs faced the unpleasant task of communicating mass layoffs to employees (Associated Press). Negative consequences of the bad news included decreased employee morale (Efrati), criticism from investors ("Latest"), and mixed responses in stock price (Letzing; Vascellaro).

Difficult situations like this are not uncommon—from announcing layoffs to reporting disappointing earnings, most managers occasionally have to deliver bad news. While managers may not be able to prevent all the negative consequences of bad news, an appropriate direct or indirect approach may help.

Appropriate Approach

When managers write a message, they follow either a direct or an indirect approach. As one textbook author states, with a direct approach the writer presents the major idea of a message first and then presents supporting ideas. An indirect approach is just the opposite—the writer presents the supporting points first, followed by the central idea (Baker 24). In the context of bad news, the central idea is the actual bad news, and the supporting points are the reasoning that led to the bad news.

When composing bad-news messages, Baker suggests that when "conveying bad news . . . consider using an indirect order . . ." (67). Because bad news is often unexpected, an indirect approach helps readers to understand the reasons behind the news before receiving the bad news itself. When managers sense that their audience is not "prepared to receive the message," they should consider an indirect approach (Baker 24), which has been found to be more persuasive than a direct approach (Frischknect and Baker). If the bad news is "routine," however, managers may use a direct approach (Baker 68). Thus, depending on the readiness of the audience, managers should vary their approach.

Dampened Consequences

When managers must convey bad news to wide and diverse audiences, they don't have the luxury of customizing a direct or indirect approach for each recipient. Researchers have tried to determine which approach leads general audiences to receive bad news and still favorably view the messenger and the messenger's company. In her experiment with credit-refusal letters, Locker found that giving a brief explanation before bad news increased readers' acceptance of bad news, but it did not impact how favorably readers viewed the writer. In a later experimental study, Jansen and Janssen modified Locker's methodology and found that readers not only accepted bad news slightly better with indirect messages, but also viewed the messenger and the messenger's company slightly more favorably.

One scholar has argued against the indirect approach, but his concern seems to focus more on content than on approach. His criticism of using a buffer before giving bad news targets buffers that are unrelated to the bad news (Brent 6); however, he states that he can "tolerate some delay" when the initial supporting points are related to the main idea and when the indirect structure is appropriate for the message and circumstances (Brent 8). Given that his criticism focuses on unrelated buffers and not on the indirect approach itself, the prevailing philosophy seems to be the best approach—when conveying bad news to a varied audience, managers' best option is to use the indirect approach.

Conclusion

Internal memos from Yahoo! show that when informing employees of pending layoffs, CEOs used both indirect and direct approaches (Carlson; Swisher). While we may never know the exact circumstances that led the CEOs to use the different approaches, we do know that the approach used may have made a difference in how employees and stockholders accepted the bad news and subsequently viewed the CEOs and the company. When placed in similar circumstances where bad news must be communicated, managers should consider using an indirect approach to bring about the most positive consequences.

Figure 9.10 A short article illustrating the use of MLA style documentation.

Works Cited

Associated Press. "AP News in Brief at 5:58 P.M. Edt." *Associated Press Newswires* 4 Apr. 2012. Web. 15 Aug. 2012.

Baker, William H. *Writing & Speaking for Business.* 2nd ed. Provo, UT: BYU Academic Publishing, 2011. Print.

Brent, Douglas. "Indirect Structure and Reader Response." *Journal of Business Communication* 22.2 (1985): 5-8. *EBSCO.* Web. 15 Aug. 2012.

Carlson, Nicholas. "Jerry Yang's Layoff Memo." *Business Insider* 21 Oct. 2008. Web. 15 Aug. 2012.

Efrati, Amir. "Yahoo Battles Brain Drain—Internet Company Braces for Wave of Exits after Holidays." *Wall Street Journal.* Wall Street Journal, 5 Dec. 2011. Web. 15 Aug. 2012.

Frischknecht, Sierra Sloan, and William H. Baker. "Enhanced vs. Undifferentiated Text: A Study to Assess the Effects on Readers." *Proceedings from the 76th Annual Convention of the Association for Business Communication,* Montreal, Quebec, Canada, 19-22 Oct. 2011. Ed. Lisa Gueldenzoph Snyder. 2011. Web. 8 Sept. 2012.

Jansen, Frank, and Daniël Janssen. "Explanations First: A Case for Presenting Explanations before the Decision in Dutch Bad-News Messages." *Journal of Business and Technical Communication* 25.1 (2011): 36-67. *Business Source Premier.* Web. 8 Sept. 2012.

"Latest Round of Yahoo Layoffs the Most Severe." *NPR: All Things Considered.* Steve Henn. NPR. 4 Apr. 2012. Radio.

Letzing, John, and Amir Efrati. "Yahoo Pushes Reset." *Wall Street Journal.* Wall Street Journal, 4 Apr. 2012. Web. 8 Sept. 2012.

Locker, Kitty O. "Factors in Reader Responses to Negative Letters." *Journal of Business and Technical Communication* 13.1 (1999): 5-48. *Business Source Premier.* Web. 8 Sept. 2012.

Swisher, Kara. "Here's Carol Bartz's Internal Layoff Memo to Beleaguered Yahoo Troops." *All Things D.* 15 Dec. 2010. Web. 15 Aug. 2012.

Vascellaro, Jessica E. "Bartz Remakes Yahoo's Top Ranks." *Wall Street Journal.* Wall Street Journal, 27 Feb. 2012. Web. 8 Sept. 2012.

Figure 9.10 continued.

Good News for Bad News

On six occasions in only four years, three different Yahoo! CEOs faced the unpleasant task of communicating mass layoffs to employees (Associated Press 2012). Negative consequences of the bad news included decreased employee morale (Efrati 2011), criticism from investors (Henn 2012), and mixed responses in stock price (Letzing 2012; Vascellaro 2012).

Difficult situations like this are not uncommon—from announcing layoffs to reporting disappointing earnings, most managers occasionally have to deliver bad news. While managers may not be able to prevent all the negative consequences of bad news, an appropriate direct or indirect approach may help.

Appropriate Approach

When managers write a message, they follow either a direct or an indirect approach. As one textbook author states, with a direct approach the writer presents the major idea of a message first and then presents supporting ideas. An indirect approach is just the opposite—the writer presents the supporting points first, followed by the central idea (Baker 2011, 24). In the context of bad news, the central idea is the actual bad news, and the supporting points are the reasoning that led to the bad news.

When composing bad-news messages, Baker suggests that when "conveying bad news . . . consider using an indirect order . . ." (2011, 67). Because bad news is often unexpected, an indirect approach helps readers to understand the reasons behind the news before receiving the bad news itself. When managers sense that their audience is not "prepared to receive the message," they should consider an indirect approach (Baker 2011, 24), which has been found to be more persuasive than a direct approach (Frischknect and Baker 2011). If the bad news is "routine," however, managers may use a direct approach (Baker 2011, 68). Thus, depending on the readiness of the audience, managers should vary their approach.

Dampened Consequences

When managers must convey bad news to wide and diverse audiences, they don't have the luxury of customizing a direct or indirect approach for each recipient. Researchers have tried to determine which approach leads general audiences to receive bad news and still favorably view the messenger and the messenger's company. In her experiment with credit-refusal letters, Locker (1999) found that giving a brief explanation before bad news increased readers' acceptance of bad news, but it did not impact how favorably readers viewed the writer. In a later experimental study, Jansen and Janssen (2011) modified Locker's methodology and found that readers not only accepted bad news slightly better with indirect messages, but also viewed the messenger and the messenger's company slightly more favorably.

One scholar has argued against the indirect approach, but his concern seems to focus more on content than on approach. His criticism of using a buffer before giving bad news targets buffers that are unrelated to the bad news (Brent 1985, 6); however, he states that he can "tolerate some delay" when the initial supporting points are related to the main idea and when the indirect structure is appropriate for the message and circumstances (Brent 1985, 8). Given that his criticism focuses on unrelated buffers and not on the indirect approach itself, the prevailing philosophy seems to be the best approach—when conveying bad news to a varied audience, managers' best option is to use the indirect approach.

Conclusion

Internal memos from Yahoo! show that when informing employees of pending layoffs, CEOs used both indirect and direct approaches (Carlson 2008; Swisher 2012). While we may never know the exact circumstances that led the CEOs to use the different approaches, we do know that the approach used may have made a difference in how employees and stockholders accepted the bad news and subsequently viewed the CEOs and the company. When placed in similar circumstances where bad news must be communicated, managers should consider using an indirect approach to bring about the most positive consequences.

Figure 9.11 A short article illustrating the use of Chicago in-text style documentation.

Bibliography

Associated Press. "AP News in Brief at 5:58 P.M. Edt." *Associated Press Newswires*, April 4, 2012.

Baker, William H. *Writing & Speaking for Business.* 2nd ed. Provo, UT: BYU Academic Publishing, 2011.

Brent, Douglas. "Indirect Structure and Reader Response." *Journal of Business Communication* 22 (1985): 5-8. https://www.lib.byu.edu/cgi-bin/remoteauth pl?url=http://search.ebscohost.com /login.aspx?direct=true&db=ufh&AN=5777777&site=ehost-live&scope=site.

Carlson, Nicholas. "Jerry Yang's Layoff Memo." http://articles.businessinsider.com/2008-10-21/tech/30101126_1_earnings-release-long-term-employees.

Efrati, Amir. "Yahoo Battles Brain Drain—Internet Company Braces for Wave of Exits after Holidays." *Wall Street Journal.* December 5, 2011. http://www.online.wsj.com.

Frischknecht, Sierra Sloan and William H. Baker. "Enhanced vs. Undifferentiated Text: A Study to Assess the Effects on Readers." In *Proceedings of the 76th Annual Convention of the Association for Business Communication*, ed. Lisa Gueldenzoph Snyder. Montreal, Quebec, Canada: Association for Business Communication, 2011. http://businesscommunication.org/conventions /abc-convention-proceedings/2011-annual-convention-proceedings/.

Henn, Steve. "Latest Round of Yahoo Layoffs the Most Severe." *NPR: All Things Considered.* Steve Henn. NPR. April 4, 2012. Radio.

Jansen, Frank, and Daniël Janssen. "Explanations First: A Case for Presenting Explanations before the Decision in Dutch Bad-News Messages." *Journal of Business and Technical Communication* 25 (2011): 36-67. http://jbt.sagepub.com/content/25/1/36.

Letzing, John and Amir Efrati. "Yahoo Pushes Reset." *Wall Street Journal*. April 4, 2012. http://www.online.wsj.com.

Locker, Kitty O. "Factors in Reader Responses to Negative Letters." *Journal of Business and Technical Communication* 13 (1999): 5-48. http://jbt.sagepub.com/content/13/1/5.abstract.

Swisher, Kara. "Here's Carol Bartz's Internal Layoff Memo to Beleaguered Yahoo Troops." http://allthingsd.com/20101215/heres-carol-bartzs-internal-layoff-memo-to-beleaguered-yahoo-troops/.

Vascellaro, Jessica E. "Bartz Remakes Yahoo's Top Ranks." *Wall Street Journal*. February 27, 2012. http://www.online.wsj.com.

Figure 9.11 continued.

Good News for Bad News

On six occasions in only four years, three different Yahoo! CEOs faced the unpleasant task of communicating mass layoffs to employees.[1] Negative consequences of the bad news included decreased employee morale,[2] criticism from investors,[3] and mixed responses in stock price.[4, 5]

Difficult situations like this are not uncommon—from announcing layoffs to reporting disappointing earnings, most managers occasionally have to deliver bad news. While managers may not be able to prevent all the negative consequences of bad news, an appropriate direct or indirect approach may help.

Appropriate Approach

When managers write a message, they follow either a direct or an indirect approach. As one textbook author states, with a direct approach the writer presents the major idea of a message first and then presents supporting ideas. An indirect approach is just the opposite—the writer presents the supporting points first, followed by the central idea.[6] In the context of bad news, the central idea is the actual bad news, and the supporting points are the reasoning that led to the bad news.

When composing bad-news messages, Baker suggests that when "conveying bad news . . . consider using an indirect order. . . ."[7] Because bad news is often unexpected, an indirect approach helps readers to understand the reasons behind the news before receiving the bad news itself. When managers sense that their audience is not "prepared to receive the message," they should consider an indirect approach,[8] which has been found to be more persuasive than a direct approach.[9] If the bad news is "routine," however, managers may use a direct approach.[10] Thus, depending on the readiness of the audience, managers should vary their approach.

Dampened Consequences

When managers must convey bad news to wide and diverse audiences, they don't have the luxury of customizing a direct or indirect approach for each recipient. Researchers have tried to determine which approach leads general audiences to receive bad news and still favorably view the messenger and the messenger's company. In her experiment with credit-refusal letters, Locker found that giving a brief explanation before bad news increased readers' acceptance of bad news, but it did not impact how favorably readers viewed the writer.[11] In a later experimental study, Jansen and Janssen modified Locker's methodology and found that readers not only accepted bad news slightly better with indirect messages, but also viewed the messenger and the messenger's company slightly more favorably.[12]

One scholar has argued against the indirect approach, but his concern seems to focus more on content than on approach. His criticism of using a buffer before giving bad news targets buffers that are unrelated to the bad news;[13] however, he states that he can "tolerate some delay" when the initial supporting points are related to the main idea and when the indirect structure is appropriate for the message and circumstances.[14] Given that his criticism focuses on unrelated buffers and not on the indirect approach itself, the prevailing philosophy seems to be the best approach—when conveying bad news to a varied audience, managers' best option is to use the indirect approach.

Conclusion

Internal memos from Yahoo! show that when informing employees of pending layoffs, CEOs used both indirect and direct approaches.[15, 16] While we may never know the exact circumstances that led the CEOs to use the different approaches, we do know that the approach used may have made a difference in how employees and stockholders accepted the bad news and subsequently viewed the CEOs and the company. When placed in similar circumstances where bad news must be communicated, managers should consider using an indirect approach to bring about the most positive consequences.

Figure 9.12 A short article illustrating the use of Chicago documentary-note style.

Endnotes

1. Associated Press. "AP News in Brief at 5:58 P.M. Edt." *Associated Press Newswires*, April 4, 2012.

2. Amir Efrati. "Yahoo Battles Brain Drain—Internet Company Braces for Wave of Exits after Holidays." *Wall Street Journal* 5 Dec. 2011. http://www.online.wsj.com

3. Steve Henn. "Latest Round of Yahoo Layoffs the Most Severe." *NPR: All Things Considered.* Steve Henn. NPR. 4 April 2012. Radio.

4. Jessica E. Vascellaro. "Bartz Remakes Yahoo's Top Ranks." *Wall Street Journal*. Wall Street Journal, 27 Feb. 2012. http://www.online.wsj.com

5. John Letzing and Amir Efrati. "Yahoo Pushes Reset." *Wall Street Journal*. Wall Street Journal, 4 Apr. 2012. http://www.online.wsj.com

6. William H. Baker. *Writing & Speaking for Business.* 2nd ed. Provo, UT: BYU Academic Publishing, 2011, 24

7. Ibid., 67.

8. Ibid., 24.

9. Sierra Sloan Frischknecht and William H. Baker. "Enhanced vs. Undifferentiated Text: A Study to Assess the Effects on Readers." In *Proceedings of the 76th Annual Convention of the Association for Business Communication,* ed. Lisa Gueldenzoph Snyder (2011). http://businesscommunication.org /conventions /abc-convention-proceedings/2011-annual-convention-proceedings/

10. William H. Baker. *Writing & Speaking for Business.* 2nd ed. Provo, UT: BYU Academic Publishing, 2011, 68.

11. Kitty O. Locker. "Factors in Reader Responses to Negative Letters." *Journal of Business and Technical Communication* 13 (1999): 5-48. http://jbt.sagepub.com/content/13/1/5.abstract

12. Frank Jansen and Daniël Janssen. "Explanations First: A Case for Presenting Explanations before the Decision in Dutch Bad-News Messages." *Journal of Business and Technical Communication* 25 (2011): 36-67. http://jbt.sagepub.com/content/25/1/36

13. Douglas Brent. "Indirect Structure and Reader Response." *Journal of Business Communication* 22 (1985): 5-8. https://www.lib.byu.edu/cgi-bin/remoteauth.pl?url=http://search.ebscohost.com /login.aspx?direct=true&db=ufh&AN=5777777&site=ehost-live&scope=site

14. Ibid.

15. Nicholas Carlson. "Jerry Yang's Layoff Memo." http://articles.businessinsider.com/2008-10-21/tech/30101126_1_earnings-release-long-term-employees.

16. Kara Swisher. "Here's Carol Bartz's Internal Layoff Memo to Beleaguered Yahoo Troops." http://allthingsd.com/20101215/heres-carol-bartzs-internal-layoff-memo-to-beleaguered-yahoo-troops/

Figure 9.12 continued.

WRITING BUSINESS REPORTS

Reports constitute an important part of business writing for most managers and professionals. Reports aren't written nearly as often as emails and other short texts, but reports are very important because they provide information used in making major management decisions.

OVERVIEW OF BUSINESS REPORTS

A business report is a written explanation of information needed by management for decision making. For instance, a report from strategy analysts will be used by business managers to determine how and where a company should expand. A report written by the author of this book was used by managers to decide on computer equipment and software by a major insurance company. Another report was used to determine the future of an entire coal-mining operation.

In many cases, the impact of one major report will be greater than the impact of a thousand emails and other short messages. Small decisions may be made without written documentation, but major decisions most often involve a written report.

Reports vary in many ways. Some are short, some are long; some are informal, some are formal; some are written with a focus on the future, and some are written to report on the past. Reports can be classified into the following categories.

Figure 10.1 Most major decisions involve written reports.

- *Periodic reports* are written on a regular basis, such as monthly or annually. For example, a sales report is generated at the end of each month to give important data for production and marketing decisions.

- *Progress reports* give an update on the status of an ongoing project. For instance, an analyst writes a report to inform his or her manager about the progress that has been made during the preceding month.

- *Problem-solving reports* are generally one-time reports that focus on a unique situation, such as the need to fix a major product defect.

- *Compliance reports* indicate whether an organization or unit is complying with legal or management policies.

The creation of a report has several steps, which can be grouped into three different phases: Data gathering, composition, and revision.

Phase I: Gather the Data

First you must determine the specific need or purpose. The purpose might be to solve a problem, achieve a new objective, or report on the progress of a project.

Next, decide on research methods and procedures to achieve the need. Whereas first you focus on *what,* now you must determine *how.* You can gather information from printed materials, such as journals or magazines, or by sending out questionnaires, conducting interviews, or conducting experiments. Primary research consists of gathering original information; secondary research consists of gathering information from material already published by someone else.

If primary research is involved, you will conduct interviews or send out questionnaires, or gather information in a variety of other ways. If secondary research is involved, you will search through published materials written by others and glean the useful information they have written.

Once information is gathered, examine and analyze it so you can understand the insight it gives. After data analysis, draw conclusions and develop recommendations for future actions.

Phase II: Compose the Report

In this phase you will actually write the report. The report tells the story of the steps you took in Phase I:

- **Purpose and Major Recommendations** (Why the report is needed and what is recommended)
- **Procedures** (How the research was conducted)
- **Analysis** (What you found)
- **Conclusions** (What you concluded)
- **Recommendations** (What should be done now)

Refer to Chapters 2 and 3 for guidance on how to create an outline and create the basic composition. Refer to Chapter 4 to review principles of visual design and graphics.

Phase III: Review and Revise the Report

In this final phase, give your report a comprehensive review, using DOCS as the rubric. You will probably find it more effective if you review the report for each element of DOCS individually, rather than attempting to check for all the elements at the same time.

Figure 10.2 Questionnaires are frequently used in conducting business research.

DESIGN

Start by checking the entire report for design and visual aspects, including the format of the report and the appropriate use of HATS.

Check the headings—include an appropriate number of headings to serve as guideposts for reading and skimming. (Figure 10.3 provides examples of different heading levels.)

Check for appropriate art and graphic elements that help make vital information easy to understand. With all information written as text, ask yourself if some graphic representation could more effectively convey the information. Make sure all visuals are numbered, unless only one table or only one figure is included.

Evaluate the typography of the body text, headings, captions, and special words. Make sure all headings and body text are easy to read; be sure also that the font type, font size, alignment, and font style (bold or italics) create a hierarchy of headings that is obvious to the reader. Be sure the type used in graphics is large enough to be read easily. Check text alignment for consistency (left alignment is usually preferred for most text).

Finally, review the use of white space. Check margins and ensure that the information does not look crowded on the page. Break up long passages of text that look difficult and uninviting to read.

ORGANIZATION

Once you've worked on the design aspects, review the organization of the report, making sure to include an agenda to forecast the structure of the report. As a general rule, prefer a direct approach, putting the main conclusions and recommendations of the report near the beginning.

CONTENT

After checking the organization, review the content to make sure the information is clear, complete, correct, and

TITLE

Headings serve several important functions in business and professional writing. First, they serve as signposts, revealing the content of the subsequent text. Without headings, readers have to read each sentence to know what information is contained in the text. Second, headings and their accompanying spacing serve a visual function. Without headings, a page of text would look uninviting and difficult to read. With headings, text looks more inviting and readable. Third, headings reveal the architecture of the information. Fourth, headings help writers focus their composition, preventing them from meandering into unrelated content. Professional writers should learn to use headings effectively.

First-Level Heading

Headings serve several important functions in business and professional writing. First, they serve as signposts, revealing the content of the subsequent text. Without headings, readers have to read each sentence to know what information is contained in the text. Second, headings and their accompanying spacing serve a visual function. Without headings, a page of text would look uninviting and difficult to read. With headings, text looks more inviting and readable. Third, headings reveal the architecture of the information. Fourth, headings help writers focus their composition, preventing them from meandering into unrelated content. Professional writers should learn to use headings effectively.

Second-Level Heading

Headings serve several important functions in business and professional writing. First, they serve as signposts, revealing the content of the subsequent text. Without headings, readers have to read each sentence to know what information is contained in the text. Second, headings and their accompanying spacing serve a visual function. Without headings, a page of text would look uninviting and difficult to read. With headings, text looks more inviting and readable. Third, headings reveal the architecture of the information. Fourth, headings help writers focus their composition, preventing them from meandering into unrelated content. Professional writers should learn to use headings effectively.

Third-Level Heading

Headings serve several important functions in business and professional writing. First, they serve as signposts, revealing the content of the subsequent text. Without headings, readers have to read each sentence to know what information is contained in the text. Second, headings and their accompanying spacing serve a visual function. Without headings, a page of text would look uninviting and difficult to read. With headings, text looks more inviting and readable. Third, headings reveal the architecture of the information. Fourth, headings help writers focus their composition, preventing them from meandering into unrelated content. Professional writers should learn to use headings effectively.

Paragraph Heading. Headings serve several important functions in business and professional writing. First, they serve as signposts, revealing the content of the subsequent text. Without headings, readers have to read each sentence to know what information is contained in the text. Second, headings and their accompanying spacing serve a visual function. Without headings, a page of text would look uninviting and difficult to read. With headings, text looks more inviting and readable. Third, headings reveal the architecture of the information. Fourth, headings help writers focus their composition, preventing them from meandering into unrelated content. Professional writers should learn to use headings effectively.

Figure 10.3 Different heading levels are indicated by varying placement, size, capitalization, and font.

compelling. Consider testing the effectiveness of the report by asking other people to read it and to indicate whether they think it will accomplish its intended purpose. Check all body paragraphs for coherence, length, organization, unity, and development.

SENTENCES

As the final part of this phase, review each sentence for SPELL writing quality. Check the structure to ensure a clear flow between subject, verb, and complement. Make sure subjects and verbs are close together, and ensure that verbs are in the active voice. Check also for correct parallelism. Proofread for correct punctuation, watching especially for correct comma usage, hyphenations between compound adjectives, and other frequently occurring punctuation errors. Check the grammar to ensure that all rules have been

followed with regard to case, agreement, tense, numbers, and capitalization. Check sentences for language, making sure appropriate words have been used, considering formality and word precision. After the language check, evaluate sentence length, omitting any unnecessary words and ensuring that sentences are written as concisely as possible.

Depending on the complexity or significance of the report, you may want to repeat this phase or have others conduct a DOCS review of the report.

Often, but not always, managers will want not only a written report, but also an oral presentation. Chapter 12 provides guidelines for structuring and delivering oral presentations.

SHORT REPORTS

Many report-writing assignments will involve only short reports, often written in memo or letter format (see Figure 10.4). The following guidelines walk you through the process of writing a decision report, which requires the evaluation of multiple options. A sample decision report in memo format follows the list of guidelines.

1. Give adequate background information regarding the context of the problem. State the central problem you're trying to solve or the central objective of the report.

2. In most cases, use a direct approach. At or near the beginning, state your recommendation: "We recommend that XYZ company…." Then indicate, "The following analysis gives support for this recommendation." If you use an *indirect* approach, save your recommendation until after the analysis.

3. Identify the critical factors to be considered in solving the problem (e.g., cost, personnel acceptance, ease of implementation, ease of maintenance, and customer service). Determine the relative importance of each factor in quantifiable terms. Additional criteria may be included, such as "The selected option must cost no more than $12,500," or "The selected alternative must be implemented by the end of this calendar year."

4. Define and introduce alternative solutions to the problem, arranged in an appropriate sequence (e.g., most to least preferred). Follow this same sequence in subsequent sections that evaluate the options.

To: Laurie Peterson, Director of Administrative Services

From: Joseph Bigler, Purchasing Agent

Date: March 4, 20XX

Subject: RECOMMENDED NEW CAR PURCHASE FOR SALES FLEET

In your February 21 Automobile Replacement memo, you asked for information about several vehicles that might be acceptable replacements for the oldest car in our sales fleet. This memo contains the information you requested. The vehicles and models chosen for evaluation include the following:

- **Mazda Model X**
- **Ford Model Y**
- **GM Model Z**

After evaluating the three alternatives, I recommend the **Mazda Model X**. The Model X equals or surpasses all the vehicles analyzed in all the evaluation categories.

The following text includes (a) a list of the critical factors used in the evaluation and (b) a comparison of the three vehicles.

Critical Factors

Four factors were used in choosing the best alternative. Each factor was weighted according to its importance in the car-selection process. The total weighting of the factors equals 100.

- **Price and Depreciation**—the purchase price and three-year resale price. (Weighting = 30)
- **Safety**—safety features, including anti-lock brakes and air bags. (Weighting = 30)
- **Fuel Efficiency**—miles per gallon (mpg) of gasoline. (Weighting = 25)
- **Overall Performance**—*Consumer Reports,* May 20XX. (Weighting = 15)

Comparative Evaluation

Each of the three cars was evaluated according to the four selection factors. The following paragraphs discuss these evaluations.

Price and Depreciation. The figure at right compares the purchase price and depreciation prices of all three cars over a three-year period, assuming an annual driving distance of 12,000 miles. As the figure illustrates, the Ford has the highest new price, but the lowest resale price after three years. The Mazda, although being only $896 less than the Ford initially, has a three-year resale value that exceeds that of the Ford by $4,675. The slower annual depreciation decline of the Mazda makes it a much more appealing vehicle from a financial standpoint.

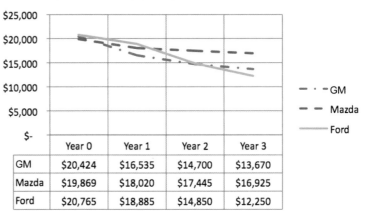

COMPARISON OF DEPRECIATION

	Year 0	Year 1	Year 2	Year 3
GM	$20,424	$16,535	$14,700	$13,670
Mazda	$19,869	$18,020	$17,445	$16,925
Ford	$20,765	$18,885	$14,850	$12,250

Figure 10.4 Sample short report. Many short reports are written in memo format.

Safety. No comparable crash statistics are available for the three vehicles, but given the safety features of each car, the highest marks go to the Mazda Model X. The Model X has antilock brakes and driver/passenger air bags. The Model Z and Model Y have antilock brakes, but they have air bags only on the driver's side.

Fuel Efficiency. The most fuel efficient car is the Mazda Model X. The Model X averages 21 mpg, one mile per gallon better than both the Model Z and the Model Y. Obviously, the fuel efficiency will vary according to the type of driving involved.

Overall Performance. As rated by *Consumer Reports,* the GM Model Z is rated highest, with Ford Model Y and Mazda Model X scoring slightly lower in overall performance. Our conclusion, however, is that any of the three vehicles would give satisfactory performance.

The following table displays the four critical factors and the ratings of all three vehicles. The total line of this table indicates a fairly wide performance spread amongst the three vehicles, with the Mazda Model X being 105 points ahead of the lowest-rated vehicle, the Model Y. High scores are marked with green icons and low scores with red.

CUMULATIVE EVALUATION OF AUTOMOBILES*

Factors	Weight	Alternatives		
		Model X	Model Z	Model Y
Price and Depreciation	30	9 = 270 👍	8 = 240	7 = 210 👎
Safety	30	7 = 210 👍	6 = 180	6 = 180
Fuel Efficiency	25	8 = 200 👍	7 = 175	7 = 175
Overall Performance	15	6 = 85 👎	6 = 100 👍	5 = 95
Total	**100**	**765** 👍	**695**	**660**

*Rating: 10–1, with 10 being high.

Conclusion and Recommendation

In light of the foregoing evaluation, I conclude that the Mazda Model X is the best alternative. The Model X equals or surpasses the other vehicles in almost all evaluation categories. Therefore, I recommend that Lakeview City purchase a new 20XX Mazda Model X for our sales fleet.

2

Figure 10.4 continued.

5. Evaluate the alternatives, using a factor-by-alternative or an alternative-by-factor sequence.

Factor-by-alternative sequence:
I. Cost
    A. Alternative A cost
    B. Alternative B cost
    C. Alternative C cost
II. Quality
    A. Alternative A quality
    B. Alternative B quality
    C. Alternative C quality
III. Ease of Implementation, etc.

Alternative-by-factor sequence:
I. Alternative A
    A. Cost of Alternative A
    B. Quality of Alternative A
    C. Ease of Implementation of Alternative A
II. Alternative B
    A. Cost of Alternative B
    B. Quality of Alternative B
    A. Ease of Implementation of Alternative B
III. Alternative C, etc.

6. Include a decision table showing the results of your evaluation. Arrange the weighting factors and the alternatives in a high-to-low sequence for easier reading.

7. Close by drawing the best conclusion and giving specific recommendations. Include any useful and appropriate appendixes, such as technical specification sheets, illustrations, or research reports.

LONG REPORTS

Long reports are required to report the findings of in-depth investigations and complex studies. Some studies may run for many months or even years. As a result, the volume of information they generate is huge, and the size of the resulting reports is also extensive. Many formal reports are bound so they can be read like a book, and some reports will run several hundred pages in length. Like a book, a long report can be organized with three sections: front matter, the report, and back matter.

Front Matter

Cover Letter: The cover letter is a short message that officially conveys the report to the reader. The letter is not a report summary, but it may tell what information the report contains, such as analyses and recommendations for action. It often closes with a statement inviting the recipient to contact the report writer for additional information or clarification.

Title Page: The title page usually contains the title, the name of the person or organization for whom the report was written, the name and position of the writer, and the date. Alphabetize multiple authors by their last name, except for the team leader, who should be listed first.

Table of Contents: A table of contents is important for longer documents for two reasons. First, it gives an overview of the report; and second, it tells the reader where the report sections begin.

Executive Summary: The executive summary is a mini-report that gives the purpose of the report (or tells why the study was conducted), the objective(s) of the report, a summary of the major findings or conclusions, and the key recommendations.

Report

The main report contains a full introduction (such as background, purpose, and methodologies used), body (including detailed findings and analysis), and conclusions and recommendations sections. For example, you might be asked to analyze the complaints being filed against a retail establishment. The following sections could be included:

- Background information and problem description
- Specific purpose of the study.
- Methods used to gather data (such as questionnaires completed in the store, a telephone survey, examination of complaints filed on the internet, or individual interviews).
- Analysis of the data, including appropriate tables and charts that reveal important findings.
- Conclusions and appropriate recommendations to solve the problems.

Figure 10.5 Some reports are the results of months or several years of work and can be several hundred pages in length.

Back Matter

References: A references or bibliography section is included in most academic reports but is not included in most management reports, because management reports usually don't include any secondary literature.

Appendix: As needed, include an appendix to supplement information given in the body. The appended pages include supplemental information, such as detailed tables and graphics. Appendixes (or *appendices*) are individually noted as Appendix A, Appendix B, and so forth.

Two reports are presented in the following sections of this chapter. The first is an analytical, problem-solving report that includes a study of state parks; the second is a report produced by the U.S. Government Accountability Office and adapted for this book. Note the pagination (page numbering) of these two reports. The front matter is numbered with lowercase Roman numerals, with page numbers omitted from the cover letter and title page. The rest of the report is numbered consecutively with Arabic numerals.

CHAPTER SUMMARY

Reports constitute an important part of business writing for most managers and professionals. A business report is a written explanation of information needed by management for decision making. Reports vary in many ways. Some are short, some are long; some are informal, some are formal. Some are written with a focus on the future; some are written to report on the past.

Many report-writing assignments will involve only short reports, often written in memo or letter format. Other reports are much longer, resulting from in-depth investigations and complex studies. Some studies may run for many months or even years. As a result, the volume of information they generate is huge, and the size of the resulting reports is also extensive. Many formal reports are bound so they can be read like a book, and some reports will run several hundred pages in length. Many long reports will include a cover letter, title page, table of contents, executive summary, body, and appendix.

CHAPTER QUESTIONS

1. List three different categories of business reports.

2. What are the three basic phases involved in the report-writing process?

3. Explain why a direct approach is best in most decision reports.

4. Describe the difference in using a factor-by-alternative and an alternative-by-factor approach. Discuss the advantages and disadvantages of each as applied in decision reports.

5. What is the difference between a factor and an alternative?

6. Why is high-to-low sequencing important in decision tables?

7. What is the function of the cover letter in business reports?

8. List the elements included on the title page of a formal report.

9. Describe the executive summary. Discuss its importance in primary reports.

10. List three major methods of data gathering for primary research reports.

11. What should be included in appendixes?

CHAPTER ACTIVITIES

1. Visit the website of the U.S. Government Accountability Office (http://www.gao.gov). Analyze two of the reports you find there, and write a half-page description of each of the reports. Explain the topic of the reports, list the total number of pages, and describe the sections included in each report. Also, describe the visuals included in the reports.

2. Using the information you obtained from Chapter Activity 3 in Chapter 9, write a formal report that shares the results of your findings. Include appropriate graphics.

3. Using the information you obtained from Chapter Activity 4 in Chapter 8, write your results in a decision report.

4. Using the information you obtained from Chapter Activity 5 in Chapter 8, write a recommendation report.

5. Using the information you obtained from Chapter Activity 6 in Chapter 8, write a report of your findings, conclusions, and recommendations.

Uharriett & Associates

1818 Riverside Drive ❧ Downtown, XX 2233X ❧ 987.483.332X ❧ uharriett@xxx.com

November 13, 20XX

Jamie Jarvis, Director
Utah Parks and Recreation Department
XXX Capitol Hill
Salt Lake City, UT 84XXX

REPORT ON VISITOR TRENDS AT UTAH STATE PARKS

Here is the report you asked us to prepare on the trends and issues in visitation throughout the Utah State Parks system. The report includes data obtained from state budget records, state park visitation records, weather records, census records, and other sources containing information related to sociological and demographic trends.

The findings of our report reveal important factors that have influenced and will continue to influence state park visitation. Public funding, weather factors, and competition are examined in detail, followed by five major recommendations that provide helpful strategies for the State of Utah.

If you have any questions about our report, or if we can be of service in any other way, please call.

Jennifer Uharriett

JENNIFER UHARRIETT, MANAGING PARTNER

Utah State Parks

Visitor Trends and Recommendations

Prepared for

Director Jamie Jarvis
Utah Parks and Recreation Department

Prepared by

Jennifer Uharriett, Managing Partner
Jason Cornwell
Roma Lee
Brennan Pierotti
November 12, 20XX

Table of Contents

Executive Summary

Problem and Purpose

Since 1996, the number of visitors to Utah State parks has decreased by 38 percent, from 7.2 million to 4.5 million visitors annually. The purpose of this report is to analyze relevant data and to provide recommendations to increase the number of state-park visitors, preferably to the original 7.2 million mark.

Conclusions

Analysis of state-park financial, weather, management, and visitation data led to the conclusion that the Utah State Parks Department is facing the following issues.

1. A lack of funding, which puts pressure on state parks to increase fees and to delay maintenance, which then has a detrimental effect on park visitation rates.

2. Recurring cycles of drought, resulting in huge decreases in the number of visitors at parks with lakes and reservoirs.

3. Ongoing competition from national parks, local museums, and personal electronic forms of entertainment.

Recommendations

After a careful evaluation of the major problems facing the State Parks Department, five specific recommendations are given to help increase attendance at Utah State parks:

1. Expand the current advertising campaign, increasing name recognition among Utah residents, and ensuring that park information is accurate and easily accessible.

2. Expand participation in educational-outreach programs.

3. Repair and renovate facilities as quickly as budgets will allow.

4. Obtain increased funding from the state legislature, and seek ways to reduce expenses.

5. Develop facilities to accommodate winter activities.

iii

Utah State Parks
Visitor Trends and Recommendations

Description of the Problem

Utah is home to 40 state parks. Over half of the parks are lakes or reservoirs that are ideal for boating, with the remaining parks including museums, sand dunes, Native American ruins, a golf course, and many geological wonders, such as Dead Horse Point and Goblin Valley. The parks are widely dispersed across the state.

Visitors to Utah's parks come from within the state, across the nation, and around the globe to enjoy these man-made and natural treasures that are managed by Utah Parks and Recreation. However, Utah's state parks have been struggling in the last few years. From 1989 to 1996, visits to Utah's state parks grew steadily from 4.3 million to 7.2 million, but they then began a downward trend which lasted through 2004 (see Figure 1).

Figure 1. Number of Visitors at Utah State Parks (1985-2005)

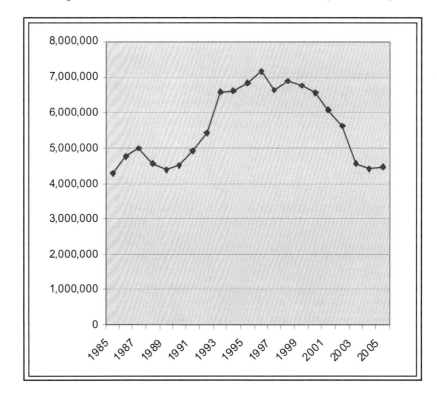

After 2004, the number of visitors began to show a slight improvement, but the Utah State Parks Department wants to find solutions to improve the attendance figures at an even faster rate. This report provides (a) an analysis of data related to the decline in visits to state parks and (b) recommendations to bring about this desired improvement.

1

Analysis of State Park Data

The following analysis examines state-park financial, weather, management, and visitation data. The analysis revealed four key factors that may have had a significant effect on the decrease in visitors.

Increase in State Park Fees
As of 2001, the upkeep of Utah's state parks has been funded by Utah's general fund, restricted general fund, federal funds, and user fees. Fees vary by park and by services used (for example, camping fees, day-passes, and green fees), while some parks are free of charge. With the slight increase in park attendance in 2005, the number of visitors last year totaled 4.5 million, less than two-thirds of the number who visited in 1996.

In 2002, the Parks and Recreation Department managers were asked to cut budget by $500,000, so they increased the green fees at the Wasatch Mountain golf course by $.50, in addition to raising the entry fees at Wasatch-area boating parks by $1. These rate hikes went into effect in January 2003, and the increases may have contributed to the lower number of total park visitors.

Transfer of Parks to Local Governments
Another factor that contributed directly to the decline in state-park visitation data is that five state parks were turned over to local-government control during 2002 and 2003: Jordan River, Mountain Meadows, Ft. Buenaventura, Veterans' Memorial Park, and Minersville. Thus, the visits to these five parks were not included after the transfers occurred.

During the three years before these parks were transferred, the five parks attracted a total average of 203,564 visitors each year. The following table shows the number of visitors to each park during the three years prior to the transfer. The regression estimate shows how many people may have visited the following year if the park status and trends had continued. If the transfer of these parks had not occurred, the state-park visitation data would have increased by nearly 300,000, suggesting that the actual state-park decline was less severe than the figures suggest.

Visitation Rate at Five Transferred State Parks

State Park	3 years Prior	2 years Prior	1 year Prior	Regression Estimate
Jordan River	71,133	65,450	71,178	69,299
Mountain Meadow	42,327	42,932	32,429	29,331
Ft. Buenaventura	44,217	47,441	24,154	18,541
Veterans Memorial	20,612	24,889	13,184	12,134
Minersville	55,148	25,798	29,799	11,566
Total	336,383	317,768	310,951	296,269

Impact of Drought and Water Levels
Utah's natural environment that brings so many visitors to our state also contributes to the fluctuations in attendance at state parks. Drought years in Utah are associated with a general

2

decrease in state park attendance because lakes and reservoirs account for a majority of Utah's state parks. Some reservoirs are affected more than others. For example, in 2002 when the water level at Quail Creek fell from 65 percent capacity to 36 percent capacity, visitors to that park decreased by 246,000. From 2002 to 2003, visits at Bear Lake fell from 310,000 to 32,000, a 90 percent decrease. Now that the drought is easing, visits are increasing at most reservoirs. However, recurring wet and dry cycles will continue to impact state-park attendance.

Increase in Competition

Two main competitors for visitors to Utah's state parks are Utah's national parks and a broad assortment of local recreational opportunities. Utah's national parks tend to be more well known than the state parks, and so they attract more visitors. However, the national parks may also contribute somewhat to state park attendance by encouraging visitors to come to out-of-the-way places where both national and state parks are located. For example, while visiting Arches and Canyonlands National Parks, many visitors also stop at Dead Horse Point State Park.

Local museums, historical landmarks, and outdoor opportunities also abound. These options are difficult to compete with because of transaction costs. For example, for Provo and Orem residents, the Provo River trail and Sundance trails are much closer to home and easier to access than the bike trails at Antelope Island or those near Rockport. For out-of-state visitors, the alternatives to Utah's state parks are even more numerous, considering the time and money that would be spent traveling to Utah for such a vacation.

Aside from direct competitors of parks services, many other activities may also be substituted in place of park activities. For instance, many people might argue that the information age has made the U.S. much less active. Instead of going outdoors or interacting in social settings, people spend more time with laptop computers, televisions, and video games. Air travel has also become more common, so while more out-of-state people are visiting Utah, more Utahns are leaving the state for a weekend in Los Angeles, Las Vegas, New York, or elsewhere.

Conclusions

In conclusion, the foregoing analysis suggests that the Utah State Parks Deparment is facing the following ongoing issues:

1. A lack of funding, which puts pressure on state parks to increase fees and to delay maintenance, which then has a detrimental effect on park visitation rates.

2. Recurring cycles of drought, resulting in huge decreases in the number of visitors at parks with lakes and reservoirs.

3. Ongoing competition from national parks, local museums, and personal electronic forms of entertainment.

Recommendations

Utah State parks comprise an important part of the state's resources, and improved creativity in managing the parks is urgently needed. The following five recommendations are presented to address the problems identified above and to produce a needed increase in state-park visitation levels.

3

1. Expand and Improve Advertising Campaigns

One roadblock to state park visits is the relative anonymity of most state parks in comparison to Utah's world-renowned national parks. Judging from interviews with a number of long-time Utah residents, few people realize that popular spots such as Deer Creek Reservoir and Antelope Island are state parks. Even fewer people have heard of Iron Mission, Edge of the Cedars, Piute Reservoir, and Red Fleet. Thus, the Utah State Parks Department needs to increase and improve state-park advertisement. Two web sites are currently being used for advertising :

- www.stateparks.utah.gov/index.php
- www.utah.com/stateparks/ (see Figure 2)

Because utah.com is accessed more frequently than stateparks.utah.gov, Utah Parks and Recreation must ensure that information on utah.com is kept accurate and up to date. Currently, stateparks.utah.gov lists three specific fees for Gunlock State Park, while utah.com states that the park has no fees. Inaccurate information may lead to frustrated visitors and may reduce the number of visitors even further.

Figure 2. Screen Shot of www.utah.com/stateparks/ Web Site

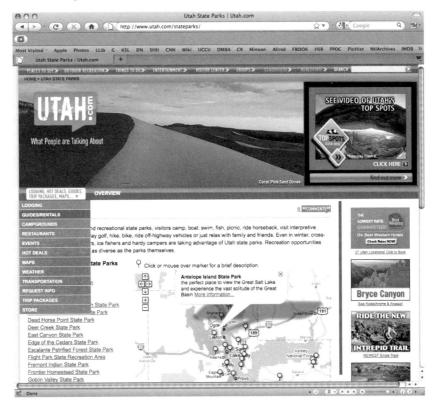

Utah Parks and Recreation also provides brochures to local travel bureaus. Interviews with travel bureau personnel revealed, however, that few potential visitors take advantage of this source of information. Thus, this form of advertisement needs reassessment.

4

Increasing advertising on college campuses in Utah and neighboring states would provide information to thousands of young adults who might be among the most likely to visit the parks. Advertising at libraries, community centers, resort areas, and youth centers would also help to reach a broader market.

Particular state parks could also be promoted among more specific audiences. For example, advertising for Wasatch Mountain may be most effective in retirement communities and resort areas, and among business executives. Utah's many lakes and reservoirs could be advertised wherever boats, jet skis, or wave runners are sold, with special attention focused on parks that are fairly close.

For all the foregoing advertising options, the initial campaign will need a special budget allocation, but the campaign should be able to fund itself in the future through increased fees.

2. Expand Participation in Educational Outreach Programs
Utah's state parks provide numerous hands-on learning opportunities in fields of history, geology, archeology, anthropology, botany, ornithology, and geography. Utah Parks and Recreation can increase the current number of park visitors by increasing their involvement in educational-outreach programs with Utah's public schools, universities, and community-education programs. This affiliation will help instill in students a love for the parks, which could lead to additional visits by those students, their families, and others (word of mouth provides some of the best advertising). School groups will not pay as much as individual guests, but school funds or grants may be able to help offset costs of these programs.

3. Repair and Renovate State Park Facilities
Given the current tight budgets, the state-park facilities are deteriorating faster than they can be repaired. Too much deterioration can be a major deterrent to increasing visitors to state parks. Therefore, state-park management must determine the repairs that are most urgently needed and place primary efforts on completing those repairs as quickly as possible.

4. Obtain increased funding and reduce expenses
State Park managers must increase their efforts in appealing to the state legislature for additional funding. Delay in making needed repairs will only make future costs more severe. Therefore, a strong case must be made for increased funding to prevent an increase in state-park deterioration.

In addition to increased funding, the financial picture could be improved by changing the ownership of one or more of the more expensive facilities. For instance, the Territorial Statehouse needs $11.3 million in renovations. From a monetary standpoint, this is not a wise investment, because operational expenses at this facility always exceed income by a large margin. The statehouse plays an important role in Utah history and has significant non-monetary value to the state; however, under current budget restrictions, Utah Parks and Recreation cannot make the needed repairs and improvements.

Transferring the Statehouse to Millard County or Fillmore City may be one solution, if either of those governments is willing and able to take on the responsibility. Either government could also appeal for help from the Daughters of Utah Pioneers, which originally renovated the building and founded the museum in 1930. Appeals could also be made to private donors who may have the most resources for preserving the building.

5

5. Develop Facilities to Accommodate Winter Activities
Some of Utah's reservoir and lake parks offer winter activities, such as ice fishing, cross-country skiing, or tubing. If these activities could be expanded at more parks, the number of visitors could increase during the off season without adding to overcrowding during the summer. However, the idea of building new facilities has been discouraged, because the state is already having difficulty caring for current facilities. If winter activities could be increased with advertising, the benefits could likely outweigh those costs, and hopefully allow for more building in the future.

To combat the downward financial pressure of the four factors identified in this report, the Utah State Parks Department needs to take immediate and decisive action. The foregoing recommendations are seen as the best ways to reverse the negative trends and return the department to a more stable financial standing.

6

Drinking Water: Experts' Views on How Federal Funding

Can Best Be Spent to Improve Security

John B. Stephenson, Director
Natural Resources and Environment
United States Government Accountability Office
GAO-04-1098T
September 30, 2004

Table of Contents

ii

Executive Summary

Why GAO Conducted This Study

After the events of September 11, 2001, Congress appropriated over $140 million to help drinking water systems assess their vulnerabilities to terrorist threats and to develop response plans. Utilities are asking for additional funding, however, not only to plan security upgrades but also to support their implementation.

This testimony is based on GAO's report, Drinking Water: Experts' Views on How Future Federal Funding Can Best Be Spent to Improve Security (GAO-04-29, October 31, 2003). Specifically, GAO sought experts' views on (1) the key security-related vulnerabilities affecting drinking water systems, (2) the criteria for determining how federal funds are allocated among drinking water systems to improve their security, and the methods by which those funds should be distributed, and (3) specific activities the federal government should support to improve drinking water security.

What GAO Found

GAO's expert panel cited distribution systems as among the most vulnerable physical components of a drinking water utility, a conclusion also reached by key research organizations. Also cited were the computer systems that manage critical utility functions; treatment chemicals stored on-site; and source water supplies. Experts further identified two key factors that constitute overarching vulnerabilities:

1. A lack of the information individual utilities need to identify their most serious threats.
2. A lack of redundancy in vital system components, which increases the likelihood an attack could render an entire utility inoperable.

What GAO Recommends

GAO recommends that EPA refine its efforts to help drinking water utilities reduce their vulnerability to terrorist attacks. According to over 90 percent of the experts, utilities serving high-density areas deserve at least a high priority for federal funding. Also warranting priority are utilities serving critical assets, such as military bases, national icons, and key academic institutions. Direct federal grants were clearly the most preferred funding mechanism, with over half the experts indicating that such grants would be "very effective" in distributing funds to recipients. Substantially fewer recommended using the Drinking Water State Revolving Fund for security upgrades.

iii

When asked to identify specific security-enhancing activities most deserving of federal support, experts' responses generally fell into three categories:

1. Physical and technological upgrades to improve security and research to develop technologies to prevent, detect, or respond to an attack (experts most strongly supported developing near real-time monitoring technologies to quickly detect contaminants in treated drinking water on its way to consumers)

2. Education and training to support, among other things, simulation exercises to provide responders with experience in carrying out emergency response plans; specialized training of utility security staff; and multidisciplinary consulting teams to independently analyze systems' security preparedness and recommend improvements.

3. Strengthening key relationships between water utilities and other agencies that may have key roles in an emergency response, such as public health agencies, law enforcement agencies, and neighboring drinking water systems; this category also includes developing protocols to encourage consistent approaches to detecting and diagnosing threats.

iv

Drinking Water: Experts' Views on How Federal Funding Can Best Be Spent To Improve Security

Purpose and Objectives of the Study

Drinking water utilities across the country have long been recognized as potentially vulnerable to terrorist attacks of various types, including physical disruption, bioterrorism, chemical contamination, and cyber attack. Damage or destruction by terrorists could disrupt not only the availability of safe drinking water, but also the delivery of vital services that depend on these water supplies, such as fire suppression. Such concerns were greatly amplified by the September 11, 2001, attacks on the World Trade Center and Pentagon and then by the discovery of training manuals in Afghanistan detailing how terrorist trainees could support attacks on drinking water systems.

Congress has since committed significant federal funding to assist drinking water utilities—with over $140 million appropriated from fiscal year 2002 through fiscal year 2004—to help systems assess their vulnerabilities to terrorist threats and develop response plans. As significant as these funds are, drinking water utilities are asking the federal government to support efforts that go beyond the planning for upgrading drinking water security to the actual implementation of security upgrades. Consequently, at the request of the Senate Committee on Environment and Public Works, we examined the following:

1. Key security-related vulnerabilities affecting the nation's drinking water systems.
2. Criteria that experts believe should be used to determine how federal funds are allocated, and the methods that should be used to distribute these funds.
3. Activities the federal government should support to improve drinking water security.

To prepare our October 2003 report on these issues, we assembled a panel of nationally recognized experts. In selecting members for the expert panel, we sought individuals who were widely recognized as possessing expertise on one or more key aspects of drinking water security. We also sought to achieve balance in representation from key federal agencies, key state or local agencies, key industry and nonprofit organizations, and water utilities of varying sizes (see Appendix A).

Background of the Study

Drinking water systems vary by size and other factors, but as illustrated in Figure 1, they most typically include a supply source, treatment facility, and distribution system. A water system's supply source may be a reservoir, aquifer, or well, or a combination of these sources. Some systems may also include a dam to help maintain a stable water level, and aqueducts and transmission pipelines to deliver the water to a distant treatment plant. The treatment process generally uses filtration, sedimentation, and other processes to remove impurities and harmful agents, and disinfection processes such as chlorination to eliminate biological contaminants. Chemicals used in these processes, most notably chlorine, are often stored on site at the treatment plant. Distri-

I

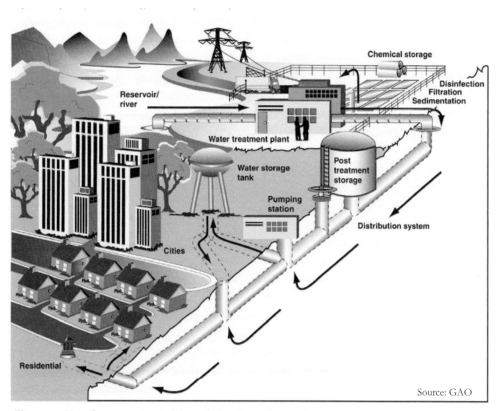

Figure 1: Key Components of a Typical Drinking Water System

bution systems comprise water towers, piping grids, pumps, and other components to deliver treated water from treatment systems to consumers. Particularly among larger utilities, distribution systems may contain thousands of miles of pipes and numerous access points.

Nationwide, there are more than 160,000 public water systems that individually serve from as few as 25 people to 1 million people or more. As Figure 2 illustrates, nearly 133,000 of these water systems serve 500 or fewer people. Only 466 systems serve more than 100,000 people each, but these systems, located primarily in urban areas, account for nearly half of the total population served.

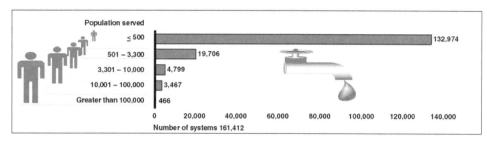

Figure 2: Number of Drinking Water Systems That Serve Various Populations

2

Until the 1990s, emergency planning at drinking water utilities generally focused on responding to natural disasters and, in some cases, domestic threats such as vandalism. In the 1990s, however, both government and industry officials broadened the process to account for terrorist threats. Among the most significant actions taken was the issuance in 1998 of Presidential Decision Directive 63 to protect the nation's critical infrastructure against criminal and terrorist attacks. The directive designated the Environmental Protection Agency (EPA) as the lead federal agency to address the water infrastructure and to work with both public and private organizations to develop emergency preparedness strategies. EPA, in turn, appointed the Association of Metropolitan Water Agencies to coordinate the water industry's role in emergency preparedness. During this time, this public-private partnership focused primarily on cyber security threats for the several hundred community water systems that each served over 100,000 persons. The partnership was broadened in 2001 to include both the drinking water and wastewater sectors, and focused on systems serving more than 3,300 people.

Efforts to better protect drinking water infrastructure were accelerated dramatically after the September 11 attacks. EPA and the drinking water industry launched efforts to share information on terrorist threats and response strategies. They also undertook initiatives to develop guidance and training programs to assist utilities in identifying their systems' vulnerabilities. As a major step in this regard, EPA supported the development, by American Water Works Association Research Foundation and Sandia National Laboratories, of a vulnerability assessment methodology for larger drinking water utilities. The push for vulnerability assessments was then augmented by the Public Health Security and Bioterrorism Preparedness and Response Act of 2002 (Bioterrorism Act). Among other things, the act required each community water system serving more than 3,300 individuals to conduct a detailed vulnerability assessment by specified dates in 2003 or 2004, depending on their size.

Since the report was issued in October, several Homeland Security Presidential Directives (HSPDs) were issued that denote new responsibilities for EPA and the water sector. HSPD 7 designates EPA as the water sector's agency specifically responsible for infrastructure protection activities, including developing a specific water sector plan for the National Infrastructure Protection Plan that the Department of Homeland Security must produce. HSPD 9 directs EPA to develop a surveillance and monitoring program to provide early warning in the event of a terrorist attack using diseases, pests, or poisonous agents. EPA is also charged, under HSPD 9, with developing a nationwide laboratory network to support the routine monitoring and response requirements of the surveillance program. HSPD 10 assigns additional responsibilities to EPA for decontamination efforts.

Research Methods Used

To obtain information for our analysis, we conducted a three-phase Web-based survey of 43 experts on drinking water security. In identifying these experts, we sought to achieve balance in terms of area of expertise (i.e., state and local emergency response, engineering, epidemiology, public policy, security and defense, drinking water treatment, risk assessment and modeling, law enforcement, water infrastructure, resource economics, bioterrorism, public health, and emergency and crisis management). In addition, we attempted to achieve participation by experts from key federal organizations, state and local agencies, industry and nonprofit organizations, and water utilities serving populations of varying sizes. To obtain information from the expert panel,

3

we employed a modified version of the Delphi method. The Delphi method is a systematic process for obtaining individuals' views and seeking consensus among them, if possible, on a question or problem of interest. Since first developed by the RAND Corporation in the 1950s, the Delphi method has generally been implemented using face-to-face group discussions. For this study, however, we administered the method over the Internet. We conducted our work in accordance with generally accepted government auditing standards between July 2002 and August 2003.

I. Key Vulnerabilities That Could Compromise Drinking Water Systems' Security

Our panel of experts identified several key physical assets of drinking water systems as the most vulnerable to intentional attack. In general, their observations were similar to those of public and private organizations that have assessed the vulnerability of these systems to terrorist attacks, including the National Academy of Sciences, Sandia National Laboratories, and key industry associations. In particular, as shown in Figure 3, nearly 75 percent of the experts (32 of 43) identified the distribution system or its components as among the top vulnerabilities of drinking water systems. Experts also identified overarching issues compromising how well these assets are protected. Chief among these issues are (1) a lack of redundancy in vital systems, which increases the likelihood that an attack could render a system inoperable; and (2) the difficulty many systems face in understanding the nature of the threats to which they are exposed.

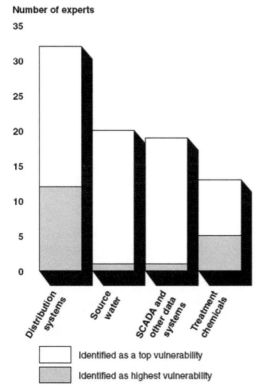

Figure 3: *Key Vulnerabilities Identified As Compromising Drinking Water*

The distribution system is discussed first, since it was cited most frequently as a key vulnerability by our panelists. The distribution system delivers drinking water primarily through a network of underground pipes to homes, businesses, and other customers. While the distribution systems of small drinking water utilities may be relatively simple, larger systems serving major metropolitan areas can be extremely complex. One such system, for example, measures water use through 670,000 metered service connections, and distributes treated water through nearly 7,100 miles of water mains that range from 2 inches to 10 feet in diameter. In addition to these pipelines and connections, other key distribution system components typically include numerous pumping stations, treated water storage tanks, and fire hydrants.

In highlighting the vulnerability of distribution systems, our panelists most often cited their accessibility at so many points. One expert, for example, cited the difficulty

4

in preventing the introduction of a contaminant into the distribution system from inside a build-ing "regardless of how much time, money, or effort we spend protecting public facilities." Ex-perts also noted that since the water in the distribution system has already been treated and is on the way to the consumer, the distribution of a chemical, biological, or radiological agent in such a manner would be virtually undetectable until too late to prevent harm. While research on the fate and transport of contaminants within water treatment plants and distribution systems is under way, one expert says limited technologies are readily available to detect a wide range of contami-nants once treated water is released through the public distribution system.

Several other components, though not considered as critical as the distribution system, were still the subject of concern. Nearly half the experts (20 of 43) identified source water as among drinking water systems' top vulnerabilities. One expert noted, for example, that "because of the vast areas covered by watersheds and reservoirs, it is difficult to maintain security and prevent intentional or accidental releases of materials that could have an adverse impact on water quali-ty." Yet some experts cited factors that mitigate the risks associated with source water, including (I) the source water typically involves a large volume of water, which in many cases could dilute the potency of contaminants; (2) the length of time (days or even weeks) that it typically takes for source water to reach consumers; and (3) the source water will go through a treatment pro-cess in which many contaminants are removed.

Also cited as vulnerabilities were the sophisticated computer systems that drinking water utilities have come to rely upon to manage key functions. These Supervisory Control and Data Acquisi-tion (SCADA) systems allow operators to monitor and control processes throughout their drink-ing water systems. Although SCADA systems have improved water utilities' efficiency and re-duced costs, almost half of the experts on our panel (19 of 43) identified them as among these utilities' top vulnerabilities.

Thirteen of the 43 experts identified treatment chemicals, particularly chlorine used for disinfec-tion, as among utilities' top vulnerabilities. Experts cited the inherent danger of storing large cylinders of a chemical on site, noting that their destruction could release toxic gases in densely populated areas. Some noted, however, that this risk has been alleviated by utilities that have chosen to use the more stable liquid form of chlorine instead of the more vulnerable compressed gas canisters that have traditionally been used.

Finally, experts identified overarching issues that compromise the integrity of multiple physical assets, or even the entire drinking water system, such as a lack of redundancy among vital sys-tems. Many drinking water systems are "linear"—they have single transmission lines leading into the treatment facility and single pumping stations along the system, and often use a single com-puter operating system. They also depend on the electric grid, transportation systems, and single sources of raw materials (e.g., treatment chemicals). Experts expressed concern that problems at any of these points could render a system inoperable unless redundant systems are in place.

Experts also cited the lack of sufficient information to understand the most significant threats confronting individual utilities. According to the American Water Works Association, assess-ments of the most credible threats facing a utility should be based on knowledge of the "threat profile" in its specific area, including information about past events that could shed light on

5

future risks. Experts noted, however, that such information has been difficult for utilities to obtain. One expert suggested that the intelligence community needs to develop better threat information and share it with the water sector.

2. Allocation and Distribution of Federal Funds

Many drinking water utilities have been financing at least some of their security upgrades by rate increases to customers. Given the cost of these upgrades, however, the utility industry is also asking that the taxpayer shoulder some of the burden through the appropriations process. Should Congress and the administration agree, they will need to address the following key issues concerning who should receive the funds and how they should be distributed:

(1)   To what extent should utilities' vulnerability and risk assessment information be considered in making allocation decisions?
(2)   What types of utilities should receive funding priority?
(3)   What are the most effective mechanisms for directing these funds to recipients?

Regarding the first of these questions, about 90 percent of our experts (39 of 43) agreed "strongly" or "somewhat" that funds should be allocated on the basis of vulnerability assessment information, with some citing the vulnerability assessments (VAs) required by the Bioterrorism Act as the best source of this information. Factors that complicate this recommendation, however, include the Bioterrorism Act's provision precluding the disclosure of any information that is "derived" from vulnerability assessments submitted to EPA. This provision protects sensitive information from individuals who might use the information to harm the utility. Hence, the law specifies that only individuals designated by the EPA Administrator may have access to the assessments and related information. Yet, according to many of the experts, even those individuals may face constraints in using the information. They may have difficulty, for example, in citing vulnerability assessments to support decisions on allocating security-related funds among utilities, as well as decisions concerning research priorities and guidance documents. Others cited an inherent dilemma affecting any effort to set priorities for funding decisions based on the greatest risk—whatever does not receive attention becomes a more likely target.

Regarding the second question concerning the types of utilities that should receive funding priority, the results in Table I were obtained:

Table I. Utilities that Should Receive Funding Priorities

Priority	High-Density Populations	Sensitive or Critical Assets	Close to Population Centers	Rural or Isolated Populations
Highest	24 (56 %)	12 (28 %)	4 (9 %)	I (2 %)
High	16 (37 %)	21 (49 %)	8 (19 %)	I (2 %)
Total	40 (93 %)	33 (77 %)	12 (28%)	2 (4 %)

6

As Table I indicates, 93 percent of the experts (40 of 43) indicated that utilities serving high-density population areas should receive a high or the highest priority in funding. Most shared the view that protecting the greatest number of people is important when setting funding priorities. Experts also assigned high priority to utilities serving critical assets (e.g., national icons representing the American image, military bases, and key government, academic, and cultural institutions.)

At the other end of the spectrum, only about 5 percent stated that utilities serving rural or isolated populations should receive a high or highest federal-funding priority. These two panelists commented that such facilities are least able to afford security enhancements and are therefore in greatest need of federal support. Importantly, the relatively small percentage of experts advocating priority for smaller systems may not fully reflect the concern among many of the experts for the safety of these utilities. For example, several cautioned that while problems at a large utility will put more people at risk, utilities serving small populations may be more vulnerable because of weaker treatment capabilities, fewer highly trained operators, and more limited resources.

Regarding the mechanisms for distributing federal funds, 86 percent of the experts (37 of 43) indicated that direct grants would be "somewhat" or "very" effective in allocating federal funds. One expert cited EPA's distribution of direct security-related grant funds in 2002 to larger systems to perform their VAs as a successful initiative. Importantly, 74 percent also supported a matching requirement for such grants as somewhat or very effective. One expert pointed out that such a requirement would effectively leverage limited federal dollars, thereby providing greater incentive to participate.

The Drinking Water State Revolving Fund (DWSRF) received somewhat less support as a mechanism for funding security enhancements. About half of the experts (22 of 43) indicated that the fund would be somewhat or very effective in distributing federal funds, but less than 10 percent indicated that it would be very effective. [Endnote 1] One expert cautioned that the DWSRF should be used only if a process were established that separated funding for security-related needs from other infrastructure needs. Others stated that as a funding mechanism, the DWSRF would not be as practical as other mechanisms for funding improvements requiring immediate attention, but would instead be better suited for longer-term improvements.

3. Activities Identified as Most Deserving of Federal Support

When experts were asked to identify specific security-enhancing activities most deserving of federal support, their responses generally fell into three categories: (1) physical and technological upgrades to improve security and research to develop technologies to prevent, detect, or respond to an attack, (2) education and training to support, among other things, simulation exercises to provide responders with experience in carrying out emergency response plans, and specialized training of utility security staff; and (3) strengthening key relationships between water utilities and other agencies that may have key roles in an emergency response, such as public health agencies, law enforcement agencies, and neighboring drinking water systems.

As illustrated in Figure 4, specific activities to enhance physical security and support technological improvements generally fell into nine subcategories. Of these, the development of "near real-time monitoring technologies," capable of providing near real-time data for a wide array of po-

7

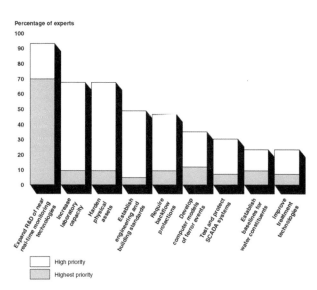

Percentage of experts

☐ High priority
▨ Highest priority

Figure 4: Activities Identified by Expert Panel to Enhance Physical Security and Support Technological Improvements

tentially harmful water constituents, received far more support for federal funding than any other subcategory—over 93 percent of the experts (40 of 43) rated this subcategory as deserving at least a high priority for federal funding. More significantly, almost 70 percent (30 of 43) rated it the highest priority—far surpassing any other category. These technologies were cited as critical in quickly detecting contamination events, minimizing their impact, and restoring systems after an event has passed. These views were consistent with those of the National Academies of Science, which in a 2002 report highlighted "improved monitoring technologies" as one of four highest-priority areas for drinking water research and development [Endnote 2]. The report noted that such technologies differ significantly from those currently used for conventional water quality monitoring, stating that sensors are needed for "better, cheaper, and faster sensing of chemical and biological contaminants."

In addition to real-time monitoring technologies, the experts voiced strong support for (1) increasing laboratories' capacity to deal with spikes in demand caused by chemical, biological, or radiological contamination of water supplies, and (2) "hardening" the physical assets of drinking water facilities through improvements such as adding or repairing fences, locks, lighting systems, cameras, and other surveillance equipment. however, some experts cited inherent limitations in attempting to comprehensively harden a drinking water facility's assets. Unlike nuclear power or chemical plants, a drinking water system's assets are spread over large geographic areas, particularly the source water and distribution systems.

Regarding efforts to improve education and training, over 90 percent of the experts (39 of 43) indicated that improved technical training for security-related personnel warrants at least a high priority for federal funding (see Table II). Over 55 percent (24 of 43) indicated that it deserved the highest priority. To a lesser extent, experts supported general training for other utility personnel to increase their awareness of security issues. The panelists also underscored the importance of conducting regional simulation exercises to test emergency response plans, with more than 88 percent (38 of 43) rating this as a high or highest priority for federal funding. Finally, about half the experts assigned at least a high priority to supporting multidisciplinary consulting teams ("Red Teams"), comprising individuals with a wide array of backgrounds, to provide independent analyses of utilities' vulnerabilities.

8

Table II. Activities Identified by Experts to Improve Education and Training

Priority	Required Training of Key Personnel	Regional Simulation Exercises	General Awareness Training	Multidisciplinary Consulting Teams
Highest	24 (56 %)	21 (49 %)	12 (28 %)	9 (21 %)
High	15 (35 %)	17 (40 %)	16 (37 %)	12 (28 %)
Total	39 (91 %)	38 (89 %)	28 (65%)	21 (49 %)

As illustrated in Figure 5, experts also cited the need to improve cooperation and coordination between drinking water utilities and certain other organizations as key to improving utilities' security. Among the organizations most often identified as critical to this effort are public health and law enforcement agencies, which have data that can help utilities better understand their vulnerabilities and respond to emergencies. In addition, the experts cited the value of utilities' developing mutual aid arrangements with neighboring utilities. Such arrangements sometimes include, for example, sharing backup power systems or other critical equipment. One expert described an arrangement in the San Francisco Bay Area—the Bay Area Security Information Collaborative (BASIC)—in which eight utilities meet regularly to address security-related topics. Finally, over 90 percent of the experts (39 of 43) rated the development of common protocols among drinking water utilities to monitor drinking water threats as warranting a high or highest priority for federal funding. Drinking water utilities vary widely in how they perceive threats and detect contamination, in large part because few common protocols exist that would help promote a more consistent approach toward these critical functions. Some experts noted, in particular, the need for protocols to guide the identification, sampling, and analysis of contaminants.

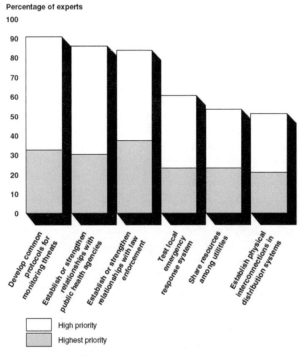

Figure 5: Activities Identified by Experts to Strengthen Relationships Among Agencies and Utilities

Conclusions

GAO's expert panel cited distribution systems as among the most vulnerable physical components of a drinking water utility. Also cited were the computer systems that manage critical utility functions; treatment chemicals stored on-site; and source water supplies. Experts further identified two key factors that constitute over-arching vulnerabilities:

1. A lack of the information individual utilities need to identify their most serious threats.
2. A lack of redundancy in vital system components, which increases the likelihood an attack could render an entire utility inoperable.

Recommendations

GAO recommends that EPA refine its efforts to help drinking water utilities reduce their vulnerability to terrorist attacks. According to the vast majority of the experts, utilities serving high-density areas deserve at least a high priority for federal funding. Also warranting priority are utilities serving critical assets, such as military bases, national icons, and key academic institutions. Direct federal grants were clearly the most preferred funding mechanism, with over half the experts indicating that such grants would be "very effective" in distributing funds to recipients. Substantially fewer recommended using the Drinking Water State Revolving Fund for security upgrades.

When asked to identify specific security-enhancing activities most deserving of federal support, experts' responses generally fell into three categories:

1. Physical and technological upgrades to improve security and research to develop technologies to prevent, detect, or respond to an attack (experts most strongly supported developing near real-time monitoring technologies to quickly detect contaminants in treated drinking water on its way to consumers).
2. Education and training to support, among other things, simulation exercises to provide responders with experience in carrying out emergency response plans; specialized training of utility security staff; and multidisciplinary consulting teams to independently analyze systems' security preparedness and recommend improvements.
3. Strengthening key relationships between water utilities and other agencies that may have key roles in an emergency response, such as public health agencies, law enforcement agencies, and neighboring drinking water systems; this category also includes developing protocols to encourage consistent approaches to detecting and diagnosing threats.

Key judgments about which recipients should get funding priority, and how those funds should be spent, will have to be made in the face of great uncertainty about the likely targets of attacks, the nature of attacks (whether physical, cyber, chemical, biological, or radiological), and the timing of attacks. The experts on our panel have had to consider these uncertainties in developing their own judgments about these issues. These judgments, while not unanimous on all matters, suggested a high degree of consensus on a number of key issues.

Such sensitive decisions must ultimately take into account political, equity, and other considerations. But we believe they should also consider the judgments of the nation's most experienced individuals regarding these matters, such as those included on our panel. It is in this context that we offer the results presented in this report as information for Congress and the administration to consider as they seek the best way to use limited financial resources to reduce threats to the nation's drinking water supply.

10

Endnotes

[1] The DWSRF program provides federal grant funds to states, which in turn allow the states to help public water systems in their efforts to protect public health and ensure their compliance with the Safe Drinking Water Act. States may use the funds to provide loans to public water systems, and may reserve a portion of their grants to finance other projects that protect sources of drinking water and enhance the technical, financial, and managerial capacity of public water systems.

[2] Making the Nation Safer: The Role of Science and Technology in Countering Terrorism, p. 250. The National Research Council of the National Academies. (Washington, D.C.: The National Academies Press, 2002).

II

Appendix A

Participating Experts on Drinking Water Security Panel

Gregory Baecher, University of Maryland
Pete Baxter, Jane's Information Group
Kevin Bennett, FBI, National Infrastructure Protection Center
Paul Bennett, New York City Department of Environmental Protection
Frank Blaha, American Water Works Association Research Foundation
Jennifer Brower, RAND
Liz Casman, Carnegie Mellon University
Jeff Danneels, Sandia National Laboratories
Rolf Deininger, University of Michigan
John Ditmars, Argonne National Laboratory
David Dobbins, Black & Veatch Company
Jane Downing, U.S. Environmental Protection Agency
Wayne Einfeld, Sandia National Laboratories
James H. Fetzer, Tennessee Valley Authority
Tim Gablehouse, Gablehouse and Eppel
Gregg Grunenfelder, Washington State Department of Health
Eugene Habiger, San Antonio Water System
Todd Humphrey, Portland Water Bureau
Gerald Iwan, Connecticut Department of Public Health
Steve Jackson, U.S. Department of the Interior, Bureau of Reclamation
Brian Jenkins, RAND
Janet Jensen, U.S. Department of Defense, U.S. Army, Aberdeen Proving Grounds
Dennis Juranek, U.S. Department of Health and Human Services, Centers for Disease Control and Prevention
Michael Keegan, National Rural Water Association
Dave Lawrence, Wisconsin Rural Water Association
Vanessa Leiby, Association of State Drinking Water Administrators
Carrie Lewis, Milwaukee Water Department
John McLaughlin, Brown and Caldwell
Christine L. Moe, Emory University
Erik Olson, National Resources Defense Council
Julian Palmore, University of Illinois
Janet Pawlukiewicz, U.S. Environmental Protection Agency
E.L. Quarantelli, University of Delaware
Brian Ramaley, Newport News Waterworks
Alan Roberson, American Water Works Association
Ken Rubin, PA Consultants
Leonard Shabman, Resources for the Future
Jim Shell, Metropolitan Washington Council of Governments
Kimberly Shoaf, University of California at Los Angeles
David Spath, California Department of Health Services
Mic Stewart, Metropolitan Water District of Southern California
Billy Turner, Columbus Water Works
Ray Yep, Santa Clara Valley Water District

12

DESIGNING VISUAL AIDS

Visual aids are used with many oral presentations, with the most common items being slide shows, paper handouts, and objects (such as a specific product model). Unfortunately, many of the slide shows and handouts reflect poor planning and design. This chapter presents guidelines to help you create professional visuals for various situations you will encounter during your business career. The chapter includes coverage of the major attributes of visuals, frequently used design treatments, and suggestions for creating slide shows and handouts.

ATTRIBUTES OF GRAPHIC ELEMENTS

Graphically oriented documents, such as brochures, flyers, slideshows, and other similar items have three types of elements on each page—text, graphics/art, and space (sometimes called empty space or white space). Text, of course, consists of the written word, and graphics/art are the drawings, illustrations, and photographs on a page. You may think of space as wasted real estate on the page that could hold content, and that the less empty space you have, the better. But that is not true. Space should be planned as carefully as text and graphics. Space provides a frame around visual and textual elements; it also adds contrast to the other two elements and makes them stand out better. Space also provides visual relief, because humans get tired of seeing page after page of solid text.

The three elements of text, graphics, and space have various attributes that can be manipulated to achieve the visual effect you desire. Some of the more important attributes are briefly discussed as follows.

Direction

Not all visual items have a distinct direction, but many do. For instance, a photo of a man walking will draw the reader's eyes in the direction he is walking, such as from left to right. Human eyes in a photo also have a very powerful directing influence—a close-up photo of a woman looking in a certain direction will draw the reader's eyes in that direction. A person pointing in a particular direction will have the same effect.

Lines also have a directing effect, such as a vertical line down the middle of a page with two columns of text. Lines can be real or they can be implied, such as a row of bullets running down the left side of a list of textual elements, or a group of books placed horizontally beside one another on a bookshelf.

As a general guideline, place directional photos so the direction of the movement is toward the middle of the page, rather than off the page. Also, place other elements so they move the reader's eyes in the desired direction. For instance, on a handout, you could use numbers, instead of just bullets, to help draw the reader's eyes down through a list of important items. Examine the photographs and other figures used throughout this book and notice how the directional effect of each one influences where your eyes move (e.g., the photographs in Figures 1.4, 9.4, and 12.6, and Figure 1 on page 157). Especially notice the line and bar charts on page 99, and notice how they move your gaze from left to right as your eyes follow the lines and bars.

Number

Elements on a page can be used alone or with others like them. For instance, you might have only one person in a photo, or you might have many. Or you might have only one line on a line chart or many (see Figure 1 on page 146). The more people you have in the photo, or the more lines in a line chart, the less each one will be noticed. For example, the photo of one person will highlight the attributes and actions of that person, whereas the photo of nine people in a meeting will tend to highlight what the group is doing, unless one person is doing something different from the rest of the group (see Figure 9.6).

People also tend to prefer odd numbers of elements, such as three or five, rather than even numbers like two or four. Obviously, you will frequently need to portray even numbers of things, such as in a portrait of a husband and wife, or a side-by-side comparison of two cell phones. Further, remember that the human brain can process fewer things more easily than it can many things. Therefore, avoid presenting too many visually related items at the same time. For instance, reorganize a long list of 18 bulleted recommendations into a shorter list of 3, each with a few subparts.

Shape

Visual elements all have a shape, which can be round, rectangular, triangular, or any of thousands of other shapes—horses are shaped like horses, violins are shaped like violins, etc. The human eye has great power to quickly recognize shapes, such as a computer screen, an office chair, or a photograph of a well-known leader. Notice how unique shapes attract your eyes in the Figures 4.8, 4.10, 4.12, and 8.2.

Even text has a shape. Each letter and each word has a unique shape, and the uniqueness of different letters enables humans to be able to read. As you work with text and typography, remember that words in lower-case type are easier to read than words with letters in all upper case, such as typography and TYPOGRAPHY. Therefore, avoid placing large amounts of text in all capitals. Further, remember that a block of text also has a shape, which is usually mostly rectangular. But when designing a creative handout on the need for low-income housing, you could shape a block of text like a house, and the audience would definitely notice the unusual shape and read the text.

Size

Pictures, text, and other elements can be small or large, as can empty space. As a general rule, large items on a page command more attention than small items and convey a message of greater importance. For example, larger text is noticed before smaller text and larger pictures are noticed before smaller pictures, such as in the screen shot on page 149. Therefore, increase the typography size for important text and for higher-order headings, as well as for more important visual elements that are placed beside those that are less important (see Figures 4.6 and 10.3).

Large items also appear to be closer when they are placed beside a smaller item. For example, if you place the image of a large basketball and a small basketball beside each other on a page, the large ball will appear to be close and the small ball farther away. Thus, shoot photographs that show the most important item as large and close, such as in Figure 10.5, with smaller, less important items smaller and in the background.

Color

Color is a powerful attribute of visual elements, whether it be the color of the paper, the color of text, or the color of a photograph or bar chart. All color comes from light, and the way different objects reflect or absorb light dictates their perceived color, or hue. For instance, a red apple reflects red but absorbs the other colors in the color spectrum. However, a red apple in a dark room will be black because there is no light reflecting from its surface.

Color on computer screens or paper comes from three primary colors. The primary colors of an electronic screen are red, blue, and green (RBG); the primary colors on a page printed on a large press are cyan (a bluish color), magenta (a reddish color), and yellow, with some black added for emphasizing important dark details (CMYK). Secondary colors are mixtures of primary colors—green, for instance, comes from mixing blue and yellow. Figure 11.1 illustrates how different colors are made from mixing different amounts (0 to 255) of red, green, and blue. Adding

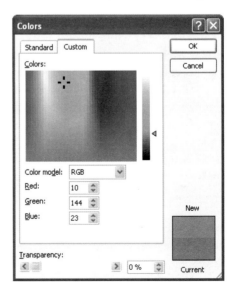

Figure 11.1 Software color palettes give precise control over color used in graphics. The color field allows hue selection while the slider bar at its right permits shading and tinting.

black to a color creates a shade; adding white to a color creates a tint.

Perhaps you learned the colors of the rainbow with the name Roy G. Biv (red, orange, yellow, green, blue, indigo, and violet). Red, orange, and yellow are considered warm colors; the others are cool colors. When different colors are used in a publication, the warm colors advance visually, while the others recede. For example, with yellow text on a dark blue background, the yellow will be more visually dominant.

You've probably seen a color wheel that has all the rainbow colors arranged in a circular fashion (see Figure 11.2). Each color's complement is the color directly across the wheel. Why is this important? If you want a color or colored object to be noticed, place it beside its complementary color. The contrast between the two colors will make them more noticeable. (Note: if you stare at a colorful object for 30 seconds and then close your eyes, you'll see the colors' complements as a "visual after-effect.")

The Color Wheel

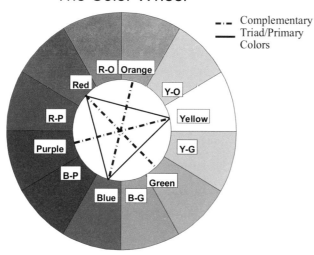

Figure 11.2 Color complements are opposite of each other on the color wheel.

The *value* of color refers to its relative darkness or lightness. For example, purple has a darker value than yellow. When deciding on the text color and background color for a slide show or a website, make sure you have highly contrasting values. You would not, for example, use black text on dark blue background, or yellow text on a white background, because of the low value contrast. White text on a dark green background, however, would be a good choice because of the high value contrast.

Which colors look good together in a printed document? Color experts have devised several basic combinations that appear harmonious to the human eye.

Monochromatic is the simplest color harmony and consists of using different values of the same color. Various tints or shades of blue would be considered monochromatic.

Analogous consists of two colors that are adjacent on the color wheel, such as blue and blue green.

Triad refers to colors that lie at the points of a triangle. Red, yellow, and blue represent a triad combination.

Complementary brings together the colors directly across from each other on the color wheel. Yellow and purple are complementary colors, as are red and green. Complementary colors are a strong combination because they represent the maximum amount of color variation.

Often, color themes are selected because of the color of a dominant element in a document. For instance, if an organization's logo is blue, the document will have a blue theme, with different typographic and visual elements being presented in the same color. Or a flyer advertising a Christmas party might use red and green as the color theme.

Gray, with all its tints and shades (including black and white), is actually an equal mix of red, green, and blue. As such, it is said to be color neutral and can be mixed successfully with all colors on the color spectrum. The more a pure color is mixed toward gray, the more that color is said to be a neutral color, and the more it harmonizes with other colors.

The mood conveyed by color is often culturally or situationally based. For example, red, white, and blue will not mean the same to a person who lives in Mexico as it does to a person who lives in the United States. But color mood is also affected by things in nature. The orange of pumpkins and leaves signifies autumn, and white snow communicates cold and wintertime.

DESIGN TREATMENTS

With an understanding of the three main elements on a page, and an awareness of the major classifications of attributes they possess, you are now ready to learn about five treatments frequently used to achieve good design. But before applying these treatments, first determine what information you need in order to achieve the goal of the document. Second, gather or create the information, including appropriate graphics to enhance the text. Finally, group the various text and graphic elements into related clusters, or chunks, and complete a general page layout—place the various chunks in the relative places you want them to appear on the page.

Because readers' eyes enter a message near the top of the page, place your main item at or near the top. This main item constitutes the focal point, or front door—it is the place where you want the reader to enter the document.

After entering at the front door, the reader should see a clear pathway through the remainder of the document, generally following a top-to-bottom, left-to-right pattern. This path might be from top to bottom for a page with only one column of text. However, it might be a path that goes from top to bottom on the left side of the page, then returns to the top right of the page, and then goes down the right side of the page. Regardless of the specific pattern on a given page, the path should be visually obvious to the reader.

With the general layout in place, proceed to apply the following five treatments, organized as an acronym (CARBS) for easy remembering (although the following section discusses them in the order they are encountered during the design process).

Balance

Once the rough layout of the information chunk is complete, balance the material either symmetrically or asymmetrically. Symmetrical balance produces a page that looks visually balanced—the left and right sides are mirror images of one another. Asymmetrical balance produces a page whose left and right sides aren't visually the same, but there should still be balance, perhaps two small items on the right counter-balancing one large item on the left. Symmetrical layout looks more formal, but less interesting. Asymmetrical layout looks less formal, but more interesting (see Figure 11.3).

Figure 11.3 Visually intensive documents should be created with either symmetrical or asymmetrical balance.

Spacing

The major spacing principle is to decrease space between items within chunks and to increase space between chunks. The space around each chunk serves as a frame or border, and it divides one chunk from the others. If you want an especially strong separator between items, you can put an actual line; but often the extra white space will suffice.

Contrast

Decide what textual or graphic element you want to draw attention to, and then make it unique. Contrast is the key to attracting attention; thus, if you want something to be noticed, make it different from everything else around it. Make sure to use great contrast with the main element, or front door.

Contrast can be achieved in countless ways, such as using a different size, color, number, or direction. At critical points in the document, use contrast to grab attention. For example, use a larger capital letter at the beginning of a paragraph that you want the audience to read, or move a photo slightly into a margin so its misalignment attracts attention. Make your headings distinctly larger than their surrounding text so they can't be missed. Don't be afraid of contrast. Feel free to experiment with headings that are 60 points tall, for example.

Repetition

Graphically rich documents should have a visual theme, and the theme is established mainly by repeating one or more elements or attributes throughout the document. You can develop a theme with a variety of textual or graphic attributes (see Table 11.1). For example, assume you are creating a flyer for a soccer team whose jerseys are red. You could choose a soccer ball and the color red as two elements of the theme, with the soccer ball being used in place of bullets in text and as a water mark on the page. Red could be used for the main heading and as the color of all horizontal or vertical lines throughout the document.

Table 11.1 Examples of repeating elements

Repeating Element	Example
Type	Arial Rounded MT Bold, 20 point, bold headings
Color	Red borders
Object	Soccer ball
Shape	Circle
Arrangement	Photograph at the top of each text column

Alignment

Generally, text in paragraphs is left aligned. That is, the left edge of every line starts at the same horizontal point on the page such as one inch from the left side of the page. For a more formal look, however, you may fully justify the text (left and right edges aligned). Headings are usually either left aligned or centered, but occasionally you might want a heading to go clear across a column of text. Thus, you would choose full justification. Columns of numbers are right aligned (or decimal aligned).

Graphic elements should also be aligned with other elements on the page. For example, align the left edge of a picture with the left edge of neighboring text, or for symmetrical layout, align the middle of a picture with the middle of a column of text. An alternate form of alignment is curvilinear. For example, you could snake the left edge of text around the curved body of a guitar in designing a flyer for a musical concert. With a finished page of text and graphics, you should be able to see that every element on the page is either left, right, center, top, or bottom aligned with something else on the page. Elements that are not aligned with anything else appear to float aimlessly on the page.

Analyze the screen shot of the "Home for Sale" flyer in Figure 11.4 and see how the techniques of balance, space, contrast, repetition, and alignment have been applied.

As you apply the various design treatments, be sure to remember the principles of simplicity and harmony. Regarding simplicity, don't over design! Know when enough is enough. A page that has too many elements, too many treatments, or too much of anything will appear cluttered and busy. Think of the main idea you want to get across with the page and then remove elements that don't add to the message or that may detract. Strive for a simple, professional, and powerful design that will get results.

Further, make sure all the elements and treatments harmonize well, both with each other and with the purpose of the message. For instance, a brightly colored, friendly type font, with photos of happy children, would complement one another and work well in a handout emphasizing the importance of establishing a neighborhood park. The same treatments, however, would not work for a handout accompanying a slide show focusing on a bank's financial problems. Rather, darker tones, conservative fonts, and business graphics revealing the major causes of the bank's problems would be more in order.

Figure 11.4 It is easy to think that if a document is colorful it will be better. While color adds visual interest and can strengthen a design, it is only one of many principles of good design that can be applied to any document. In the example below, notice how the version without color is still visually strong because it has good use of balance, spacing, contrast, repetition, and alignment.

Also, as you create visually oriented documents and apply these design treatments. remember that learning effective visual design takes time. Don't expect to become an expert overnight. Continue to examine visual design everywhere you go—look at billboards, websites, flyers, business cards, periodicals, books, magazines, and ads. For each visual design, analyze what works well and why it works. Then try to reproduce the same effect in your own designs.

SLIDE SHOWS

Computer-projected slide shows add a useful visual element to presentations and can be enhanced with graphics and other special effects (sound, video clips, transitions, and animations). Slide shows can help to clarify important points and hold the audience's attention. They can also add professionalism if they are well designed and effectively integrated into the presentation. The following guidelines for layout and design, typography, graphics, and color will help you develop effective slides.

Layout and Design

First, create a quick visual storyboard of your slides (a storyboard is a rough blueprint of what the finished product will look like). For each slide, draw a thumbnail sketch. You can work on the computer, but a white board or a pencil and paper are usually faster and simpler. Keep it simple and don't get sidetracked into focusing on the details of the content at this time. Using stick figures, shaded boxes, or squiggly lines to represent graphics and text elements can help you focus on the larger visual organization and the idea you want to get across.

Be creative, and feel free to try several ideas for a given slide before selecting the final one. For example, the Utah State Parks report in Chapter 10 draws a close relationship between the amount of rainfall and the number of visitors to state parks with water sports (such as lakes). Figure 11.5 shows two different thumbnail sketches of what this slide could look like.

After your story board is created, use your computer to create the actual slides (e.g., PowerPoint). As you launch the slideshow software, do not be tempted to use the pre-designed slide-layout templates. Stick with your storyboard sketches instead. Especially resist the tendency to create an endless parade of bullet list after bullet list.

You have many options for adding variety in the design of your slides.

Text: Enhance fonts with different color, size, and alignment.

Illustrations and photos: Flow charts, cutaways, illus-

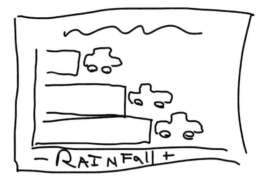

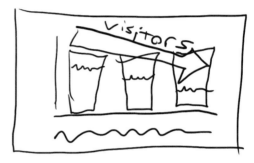

Figure 11.5 Thumbnail sketches should be simple and show the visual relationship of the basic slide elements.

trations, organization charts, photographs. Enhance with boxes, lines, arrows, shades, and clip art.

Data: Line charts, pie charts, area charts, bar charts, pictographs. Consider appropriate variety in each of these types (cluster bar, 3-D, bilateral, etc.).

Maps: Use numbers, colors, pictographs, textures, and other attributes to show quantities in different geographical areas.

Tables: Use shaded cells, typographic variations, and border variations.

Videos: Use video clips to show processes, human interactions, training instruction, news clips, dramatizations, good and bad examples, and much more. Be sure to cite the source of all photos, art, or text you have obtained from other sources. For example, for items downloaded from the internet, copy the source and then paste it beneath or beside the quoted text or borrowed graphic.

Figure 11.6 illustrates a bland slide that simply applies a software template, followed by two slides showing the same information created without a template—one as a table and the other as a graphic. Remember, the human brain can't process bullet lists well; therefore, begin with a blank slide and create the slide in the most effective way to communicate the idea you want to get across.

Show relationships visually. Avoid relying solely on text when you can illustrate a concept or idea with a visual.

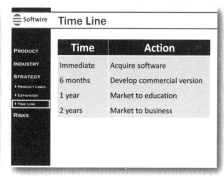
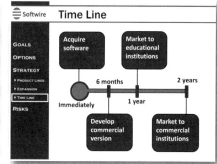

Figure 11.6 Bland slides such as the left one above can be visually enhanced with tables or graphics like those to the right of it.

Instead of showing relationships as a typical text outline, use figures and arrows or some other visual connectors to show how they relate to each other. For example, a marketing network can be better illustrated with a visual hierarchy than with just bulleted-text description, or it could be illustrated as a map (see Figure 11.7).

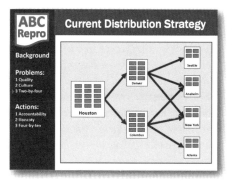

Figure 11.7 Relationships can be more easily understood with graphics than with text outlines.

Use slide transitions, animations, and builds purposefully. Transition options change the way a new slide is first brought onto the screen (e.g., moved in from left to right). Use a consistent transition throughout the slide show, rather than using a mix of different transitions, which can be distracting. Animations move individual slide objects onto, off of, or around on the screen. Avoid the temptation to use animations without a good reason. For example, making

text fly onto the slide from various directions serves no useful purpose and can be very distracting. Builds add various details of an entity one by one, eventually revealing the entire entity. For instance, showing a nationwide marketing network layer by layer may be more understandable than showing the entire network at once (Figure 11.8).

Standardize your slide design. Repeat colors, typography, and shapes so the audience will see a consistent design theme in all your slides and handouts. Consider using a four-part slide layout, with areas designated for the slide title, an agenda, working space, and, if you wish, a logo. Regarding the agenda, either down the left side, or across the bottom or top of each slide, display a running agenda so the audience will know where you are in your overall presentation.

During the presentation, highlight the agenda item that indicates your position in the presentation. As appropriate during the presentation, insert a subsection outline within the major agenda. Then remove the subsections after they are all discussed, returning to just the major agenda items. Figure 11.9 contains an example of slides using this four-part layout. For illustrative purposes, slides 3 and 4 show the agenda along the left side, slides 5 and 6 show the agenda at the bottom of the slide, and slide 7 shows the agenda at the top. However, as you design your slideshows, be consistent in the placement of the agenda.

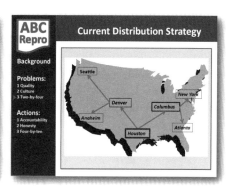

Figure 11.8 The slides above demonstrate a build as each slide (moving left to right) reveals more detail of the whole than the ones preceding it.

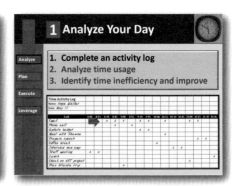
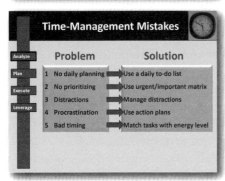

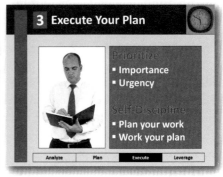

Figure 11.9 This 8-slide series illustrates several different types of slides: title, agenda, body, and Q&A. The five body slides demomonstrate possible placements for a running agenda on the left, bottom, or top. For a real presentation you would select one option and stay consistent. Also note how none of the slides follow the vendor's standard software template.

Carefully consider the beginning and ending slides of a presentation. Develop the opening slide around the opening hook, such as highlighting a problem commonly encountered by the audience. At the end of the presentation, display a similar slide and revisit the opening hook, suggesting that applying the solution given in the presentation will help solve the problem.

Finally, develop backup slides to use during the question-and-answer period. As a result of your presentation, try to anticipate questions the audience will ask, and develop slides to answer those questions. The major questions, of course, should be answered in the main presentation; but additional questions might be asked about sources of information or potential risks or areas of resistance not previously mentioned.

TYPOGRAPHY

As you prepare your slides, remember to keep the typography large enough to be seen easily anywhere in the room. As you select fonts, avoid those that are too ornate.

Use standard faces that are easy to read. Sans serif faces, such as Arial and Franklin Gothic, are usually good choices. Also, avoid excessive typographic enhancement. As a general rule, limit the number of typefaces to two that have high shape, size, or color contrast with each other.

Also, limit the amount of text you put on each slide. Some people follow the six-by-six guideline: a maximum of six words per line and six total lines. Break multi-line titles at logical places.

No: Writing and Speaking for Business

Yes: Writing and Speaking for Business

GRAPHICS

You can obtain graphics from picture or object scans (scans of actual objects, such as a hand), from digital photos, or from clip art files. Keep graphics simple. Remember the five-second principle, which means that a person should

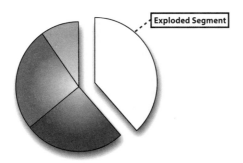

Figure 11.10 Important information should be emphasized by exploding or highlighting specific chart elements.

be able to understand the graphic in five seconds or less. Use graphics to complement the text, not compete with it.

Use line charts for showing movement or trends. As a general rule, prefer bar and line charts to pie charts.

For bar charts, use data labels to reveal exact amounts of bars. Use X and Y axis titles to clarify the elements being displayed. Arrange labels, bars, and data rows/columns in a sequence most useful to the reader (e.g., high to low). Avoid using a random sequence.

To emphasize certain elements of infographics, you can shade one or more cells in a table, explode a segment of a pie chart (pull a segment a small distance away from the rest of the segments), or use a call-out (a line going from a part of a graphic to explanatory text beside the graphic). See Figure 11.10.

In addition to slides containing text and business graphics, consider using some photographs in your presentations. Because the human mind is primarily a visually based system, it takes greater effort to process text slides and almost no effort to process pictures. Figure 11.11 illustrates the power of a good photograph in driving home one of the key recommendations of the Utah State Parks report contained in Chapter 10 (page 151).

The first slide illustrates a typical bland bullet list. The second slide is better; it introduces a photo as a side item, typical of most slides that includes photos. However, the third slide enlarges the photo to occupy the entire slide, greatly enhancing the visual and emotional power of the slide. The third slide also includes a large textual front door (effective because of its size and font, even though it is in the lower-right corner of the slide), and supporting text that is smaller but easily readable against a varied background because of a gray transparent box placed behind it. Also, all the text is right aligned, and the color of the large text repeats a dominant color in the woman's hair. By creatively combining important text and an effective photograph, along with all the contrast, alignment, repetition, balance, and spacing treatments, the third slide is much more likely to be successful than the first or second slides.

And one reminder note—with all photographs or other visual elements you obtain from outside sources, get permission to use them and give appropriate citation. Don't use text or images without acknowledging the original source.

COLOR

Use high contrast between text and its background, either with color or with value (value is the relative lightness or darkness of an object or text). Remember that warm colors visually advance (seem closer), while cool colors recede (appear farther away). Thus, if you use warm-colored text and cool-colored background, the text will seem to advance and the background will recede.

Use color consistently (e.g., all bullets in blue or all main headings in red). For emphasis, use color on just a few items. Adding more color to more items reduces the amount of emphasis each colored item gets (the *more-is-less, less-is-more* principle).

As you give your presentation, integrate your slides into your presentation effectively. For example, when showing slides during a presentation, turn toward the screen and point to a given item as you begin discussing it (see Figure 11.12). You may point with your hand or with a laser pointer. Then immediately turn again toward the audience

Figure 11.11 The slides above show not only the difference using photographs can make in your presentation, but also how the application of proper design principles can heighten the impact.

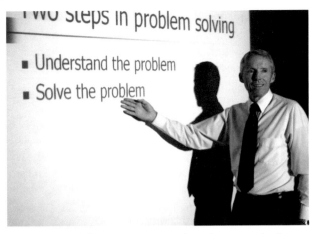

Figure 11.12 Effective presenters guide audience members' eyes by pointing to specific items on slides.

to discuss the information included on the slide, such as, "This line shows a four-fold increase in consumer demand since 20XX."

When you use technology in your presentation, go early to the presentation room and make sure it works. Also, have backups in case of equipment failure. For example, if the slide projector fails, have another projector or handouts as a backup, and take a second copy of your slideshow on a flash drive and on your computer.

HANDOUTS

For many presentations you give, you can enhance your effectiveness by providing a handout for the audience. With each handout you use, you will need to decide what content to include, how to design it, and how to integrate it in the presentation. As a general rule, use the same basic design you use in the slide show, so the two will reveal a close visual relationship. Figure 11.13 shows a handout with a creative layout that gives it good visual appeal.

1. Create the text and graphics so they are clear and easily understood. Tastefully mix serif and sans serif fonts, and use appropriate font sizes.

2. Arrange the layout so there is an obvious front door (a specific point where the audience visually enters the handout) and clear pathway through the document. Using numbers can help define the reading pathway, as does arranging the material so it follows the standard reading direction of top

to bottom and left to right. Figure 11.14 shows a poorly organized handout on the left with its clearly organized counterpart on the right.

3. Apply the CARBS treatments: contrast, alignment, repetition, balance, and space. Use contrast to draw attention to the front door and to other important elements. Arrange all elements so they align properly with other related elements. Repeat a color or graphic attribute to tie everything together visually. Use appropriate symmetrical or asymmetrical balance. Leave adequate white space between information and graphic elements.

4. Finally, during your presentation, distribute the handout at the most appropriate time. For one situation, you might distribute it during the presentation so the audience can take notes on the handout. For another situation, you might wait until the end because you don't want the audience to read the handout during the presentation.

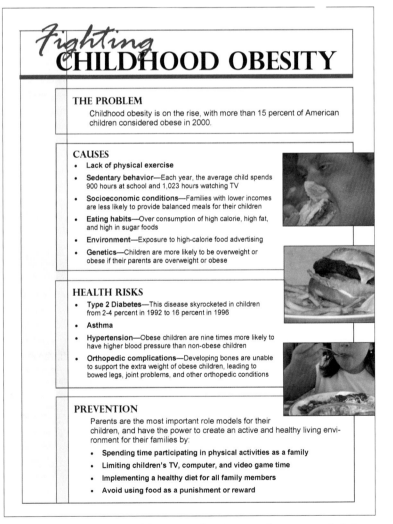

Figure 11.13 Effective visual design greatly enhances information included in handouts. (Courtesy of Marilyn Pike)

Figure 11.14 *The handout on the left is confusing and disorganized. The handout on the right has been redesigned to have a distinct front door and clear pathway.*

CHAPTER SUMMARY

Visual elements are used in many oral presentations. All visually rich pages contain three major elements—text, graphics, and space—and all three play a part in effective design. Graphic and text elements have unique attributes that can be modified for greatest effectiveness in their use: direction, number, shape, size, and color. Contrast, alignment, repetition, balance, and spacing constitute various types of treatments that can help polish visual design.

Use color effectively. Understand how color temperature affects visuals. Ensure good contrast (color and value) between text and background. Select appropriate colors to achieve good color harmony. White, black, and gray can be mixed with other colors. Use colors to portray an appropriate mood, being sensitive to the cultural influences of color. Make sure each page or slide has an obvious front door and clear pathway. Finally, remember the principles of simplicity and harmony as you develop pages that are clean, professional, and powerful.

As you develop slides, begin with a storyboard and then build the slides from the storyboard. Consider using a four-part layout, with a running agenda. Show relationships visu-

ally, and use builds and animations purposefully. Tie the opening and ending slides together thematically, and create backup slides as appropriate. Use photographs appropriately. As you develop handouts, apply the same general principles you use in creating slideshows.

CHAPTER QUESTIONS

1. Why should you not place large amounts of text in all capitals?

2. What are primary colors? What are the primary colors of computer screens?

3. What is a shade? A tint?

4. What colors are considered warm? Cool?

5. How can you determine the complement of a color? Why would you use a color and its complement in a document?

6. What is color value? Why does value matter in creating slides?

7. Describe two ways to achieve good contrast between the color of text and the background color.

8. What is the difference between symmetrical and asymmetrical balance?

9. What design treatment is the key to attracting attention?

10. What alignment option is generally preferred for body text?

11. What is a storyboard?

12. What is the five-second principle?

13. What is the more-is-less, less-is-more principle?

14. What is the "front door" of a handout?

15. Should a handout be distributed before, during, or after a presentation? Why?

CHAPTER ACTIVITIES

1. Create a flyer to sell something that belongs to you (e.g., car, computer, textbook, bicycle). Explain how to apply the attributes of contrast, alignment, repetition, balance, and spacing. Take a photo of the object with a digital camera and include the photo in the flyer.

2. Go to the website usa.gov and find information about a topic of interest to you (such as consumer safety, emergency planning, health and nutrition, or money and taxes). Create a slide show that will effectively teach others about the topic. Follow all the slide-design guidelines given in this chapter.

3. Create a basic bullet chart on a topic or chapter from one of your textbooks. Then redesign the slide, demonstrating your ability to apply the effective use of visuals and visual-design principles.

4. Create a slide that demonstrates a meaningful animation or build, such as explaining the various parts of a letter (from Chapter 6), the layout of a formal table setting (from Chapter 1), or some aspect of problem solving (from Chapter 8).

5. Find a poorly designed website, and then explain what design principles have been violated. Redesign the homepage of the website using PowerPoint or some other slideshow software. Submit your explanation, along with copies of both the "before" and the "after," to your instructor.

6. Create a one-page handout (single side) for one of the chapters in this textbook. Apply all the design principles taught in this chapter, and use color effectively.

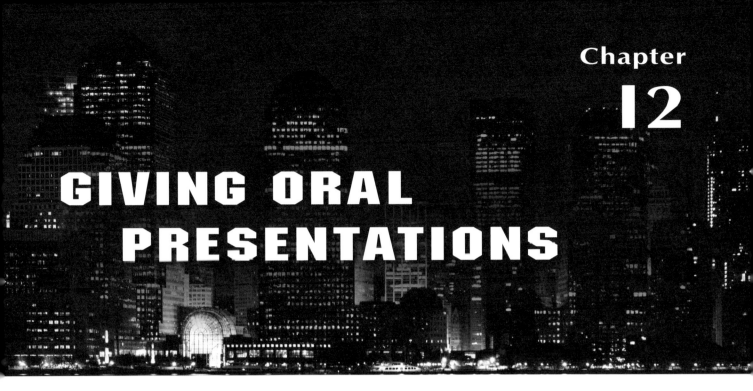

Chapter
12

GIVING ORAL PRESENTATIONS

For business professionals, a large percentage of each day involves oral communication—hallway conversations, phone calls, meetings, interviews, and so forth. Mixed in with all of the small interpersonal exchanges, you also find professionals giving oral presentations—some short and some long. Some presentations are given while seated at a table in a meeting, some are given standing up in a conference room and using a slideshow for visual support, and some are given in larger rooms at convention centers to an audience that includes people from many organizations.

Some of your informal presentations will be in response to your manager's request for an impromptu report in a meeting and you'll have very little time to prepare. Other speaking opportunities will come in a more formal way, and you'll have more time to prepare. Regardless of the setting

Figure 12.1 Business professionals have to give many presentations.

or the source of the request, you are expected to present information in a clear and effective manner—to communicate the information so the audience understands and to present in such a manner that the audience is moved to action.

To become an effective presenter, you should make the study of effective presentations a lifelong pursuit. Listen to others give presentations in every type of setting and situation, consider their overall approach to their topic, write down their overall structure, make a list of the different ways they support their key points, notice how they begin and end, and observe how they interact with the audience. After each presentation, list what went well and why it went well, and write down how to improve. Strive to develop a deep understanding of what it takes to be a good presenter.

A good online source of presentations is ted.com. On this site you can watch an almost endless supply of presentations on all kinds of topics, such as business, psychology, terrorism, brain science, animals, art, design, evolution, food, music, medicine, and poverty. Take the time to listen to a variety of the TED speakers. As they present, pay attention to the background structure of their content, notice how they begin and end, consider how they develop their theme, and observe their nonverbal communication—eyes and face, hands, and body. Seek to develop your own list of presentation tips and then constantly strive to incorporate those tips into your own informal and formal presentations.

Regardless of the many sources of help in improving presentation skills, giving a formal presentation is a frightening experience for many people. Their heart pounds, their mind races and becomes panicky, their mouth becomes dry, and they appear visibly nervous. For others, this setting is energizing—their heart pounds, but because of excitement and anticipation; their mind is alive with the excitement of being able to present their ideas to others; and their gestures and voice are animated with enthusiasm. What makes the difference? This chapter will provide the answer.

The first two sections focus on preparing the message and the messenger, followed by a section on rehearsing and evaluating the presentation, and closing with a brief section about team presentations.

PREPARE THE MESSAGE

Great presentation messages don't just happen in an instant. They usually come after multiple rounds of writing and changing and changing again. Finally, everything comes together and the audience is impressed, but they have no idea of all the behind-the-scenes work that went into the presentation. The following sections will walk you through a proven process for creating an effective message. Fortunately, this process is the same one you have already read in Chapters 2 and 3 of this book—clarify the purpose, create an outline, decide on a strategy and pattern, and strengthen the content.

Before you begin crafting the message, gather the essential 5W2H information to guide your writing.

- Who will attend (their organizations, their knowledge of the topic, their needs, etc.), who will introduce, and who else will speak (before, during, after)? If someone is speaking after you, be sure to finish on time. Few things are more annoying than speakers who go overtime and thereby reduce the amount of speaking time for the subsequent speaker.

- What is the occasion, what is the topic, what to wear, what technology will be provided (also the name and contact information of the technical-support person), and what is the room layout (size, seating arrangement, windows, etc.)? When you find out the dress standard, adjust your dress at least up to that level. Dressing below the level of the audience will damage your credibility even before you speak.

- Where is the meeting (city, building address, and room name or number), where to stay if travel is involved, where are chairs and podium located in the room, etc.? Describe your desired room layout and request that the room be arranged in that manner, if possible. Often a wider layout with fewer rows of chairs is better than a deeper layout with more rows. If possible, locate the projection screen so it is not directly behind you as you stand in the front center of the room.

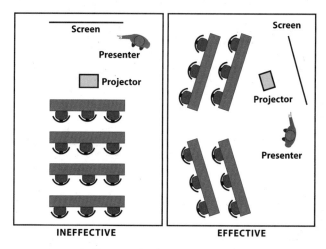

Figure 12.2 Ineffective and effective room arrangements.

- When is the meeting (date and time, beginning and end), when to arrive, etc.?

- Why is the meeting being held, why was the topic chosen, and, if desired, why were you chosen to speak?

- How to travel, how to schedule audiovisual or other presentation equipment (whiteboards, projectors, laser pointers, and so forth) how to get reimbursed for expenses, etc.?

- How many people will attend and, as appropriate, how much will you be paid as an honorarium?

Armed with the foregoing information, begin preparing your message.

Clarify Your Purpose

Write down your purpose(s), including what you want the audience to know, do, and feel as a result of your presentation. After clarifying the purpose, create a good working title. Often one of the 5W2H words works well as the opening word, such as "How to Implement the New Process of Handling Customer Complaints" or "Why We Should

Figure 12.3 Make sure to schedule needed presentation equipment such as whiteboards, markers, projectors, etc.

CHAPTER 12

Develop a Working Relationship with ABC Company." Later you might develop a more catchy title, such as "Winning Back Our Customers—How to Handle Customer Complaints."

Create an Outline

Just as outlining helps to produce well-organized written messages, it also helps to produce well-structured oral presentations. Thus, take time to prepare and use an outline. Many people don't, and as a result many presentations are poorly organized. As explained in Chapter 2, you have both top-down and bottom-up options for creating an outline.

Top-down Outline. Top-down options include traditional outlining, tree diagrams, and mind maps. Mind maps are more visual than traditional outlines, and they work very well when you know the overall structure but not the details. To create a mind map, draw a circle in the middle of a blank page and write the working title inside that circle. Then write the main presentation categories inside circles surrounding the main circle. Then draw lines outward from the main-category circles as you think of additional information that should be included (see Figure 2.3). The same basic process is involved with tree diagrams, with main branches extending out from the trunk, and smaller branches extending outward from the main branches (see Chapter 2).

Bottom-up Outline. If you don't have a clear idea of the structure of your presentation, develop your outline using a bottom-up approach. Think or read about the topic, and make an unorganized list of all the relevant information you think about or read about. Then decide on the categories into which you could place each of the items on the list. Continue to ponder and rework the categories as appropriate to come up with a final hierarchy of your presentation's main content blocks.

After you complete the general hierarchy of the mind map or tree diagram, decide on the sequence of the various parts. As Chapter 2 reveals, information typically falls into one of two sequencing categories: non-chronological or chronological. Page 21 contains various non-chronological options; page 22 contains several chronological options. Choose the option that best matches each information cluster in your outline. For example, you may you use an overall non-chronological order (such as the category order), but use a chronological order in one of the segments (such as telling a story in chronological order).

After you have selected the information, placed all the

information items into categories, and sequenced each segment of the outline, consider using the five outline tests from Chapter 2 to evaluate your outline. These tests will help reveal any inconsistencies in structure and any missing or unrelated content. When you have the complete body structure in place, just add an opening, an agenda, and a closing, and you have a complete OABC outline.

Determine the Approach and Pattern

The outline needs two additional steps to polish and perfect it. First, decide on the general presentation approach. In most cases, follow a direct approach, where you give the main point of your message at or near the beginning. In some cases where difficult persuasion is involved, consider an indirect approach that allows you to give your reasoning before giving the key point. After deciding on the overall approach, modify the outline as appropriate.

Next, decide on a specific pattern to follow. A typical OABC pattern would look like the following:

Opening: Include the hook, a statement of purpose, any needed background information, and key points or key recommendations.

Agenda: As appropriate, insert an agenda to tell about the body of the presentation. The agenda might quantify the number of sections, identify the topics of the sections, or state how the sections are organized. Or it might include a combination of these three agenda types.

Body: Include the main body sections.

Closing: Summarize, restate the key points or recommendations, transition to a Q&A session. After Q&A, give one more brief closing statement.

The basic OABC pattern can be modified in a variety of ways to meet the unique needs of each situation. For example, the body of a public hearing might use a direct approach mixed with a Question-Answer pattern or a problem-solution pattern. Figure 12.4 provides nine sample outlines for different types of presentations.

Strengthen the Content

In addition to deciding on the overall approach, think creatively about how to strengthen and enhance the message. The raw outline of the message is the *what*; the enhancement of the basic outline is the *how*. Take time to brainstorm the how, both by yourself and with others. Ask yourself, "How can I present this material in a way that will grab the audience members' attention and move them to take the action I recommend?"

PRESENTATION OUTLINES

Because each presentation situation is unique, you must tailor your approach accordingly. Presentations can vary greatly in how they are organized depending on their purpose and content. As a resource for preparing different types of presentations, rough outlines and tips for nine common presentation types are included below. Use them as a guide and starting point, but remember that no one specific way is right for all situations. Take time to analyze each situation, and develop your presentation to fit that situation.

Introducing a Speaker

Opening (direct approach): Welcome the speaker.

Point 1: Give speaker's professional credentials.

Point 2: Give any other appropriate human-interest information.

Point 3: Tell what the speaker is going to speak about.

Closing: Transition to the speaker—"We'll now be happy to hear from XXXXXX."

Tips: Make it sincere—don't give false praise or give too much praise. Keep it interesting, but keep it short—the audience came to hear the speaker, not you.

Giving a Briefing

Opening (direct approach): Explain the topic and purpose of the presentation; give an opening hook.

Agenda: Cite the main presentation parts.

Point 1: Explain the first main point, along with supporting information.

Point 2: Explain the second main point, along with supporting information.

Point 3: Explain the third main point, along with supporting information.

Closing: Revisit the opening

Q&A: Take questions for an appropriate amount of time, and then give another brief closing.

Tips: Briefings can be about various topics, from boring technical issues to highly charged societal issues. Try to keep the information informative and interesting so you don't put people to sleep. A briefing is a mostly informative presentation, so make it well organized and clear. Use clear transitions from one point to the next so the audience knows where you are in the presentation. However, sometimes audience members may have strong feelings about a topic, so maintain your composure if emotions become involved. Use effective visuals, including a slideshow and a handout.

Presenting a Project Report

Opening (usually a direct approach mixed with a chronological sequence): Quickly explain the topic and purpose of the presentation. Give the main outcome in general terms.

Agenda: List the main parts of the presentation.

Background: Tell why the project was undertaken.

Procedures: Explain the process you followed to complete the project.

Analysis and Findings: Report key points of the data analysis.

Conclusions: Cite the main conclusions drawn from the project.

Recommendations: Tell what action should be taken as a result of the project.

Q&A: Answer any questions and then give another brief closing.

Tips: Don't spend too much time on the earlier parts of the presentation. Cover them, but not in great depth. Avoid long boring stretches of data analysis. Use clear transitions from one point to the next so the audience knows where you are in the presentation Move relatively quickly to the conclusions and recommendations. Keep the recommendations clear and straightforward. This is what the audience is mainly interested in. Use effective visuals, including a slideshow and a handout.

Training

Opening (direct approach): Give an opening hook, and then explain the topic and purpose of the training

Agenda: List the main segments of the training.

Part 1: Refer to the current procedure (what they know), and then explain and demonstrate the new procedure (what they don't know).

Part 2: Have the audience practice the new procedure.

Part 3: Ask the audience to respond or give their reaction to the new procedure.

Part 4: Give appropriate feedback to the audience comments.

Figure 12.4 When preparing a presentation, review these outlines to see if one can be used as a basic framework.

Part 5: Explain implementation process and timeline (how and when the new procedure will happen).

Closing: Close with a forward-looking statement.

Tips: Take a brief moment at the beginning to establish a distinct need for the new procedure. Then move to the training. Provide clear demonstrations of the new procedures (show, don't just tell). Get everyone involved. Be somewhat flexible in time management, making sure that you achieve the purpose of the training. Allow the audience to ask questions and give input at any time throughout the meeting. Sometimes people resist change, so be prepared to address emotional and procedural concerns in a calm manner. Follow up afterward to make sure the training procedures are effectively implemented. Use effective visuals, including a slideshow and a handout.

Presenting a Proposal
(to adopt a new idea or to change a procedure)

Opening (indirect approach): Welcome and thank the audience for coming. Give a general statement about the purpose of your presentation (e.g., "to address an issue that has become an important concern").

Agenda: Probably skip the agenda, or else give just a general statement about how the presentation will proceed.

Part 1: Explain the current situation.

Part 2: Describe the problem and the negative consequences it is causing.

Part 3: Describe the solution—the new idea or procedure. Provide all appropriate five-W-two-H information.

Part 4: Highlight benefits and cover (but de-emphasize) costs.

Part 5: Provide plausible implementation timeline.

Part 6: Provide time for Q&A.

Closing: Summarize and close with a forward-looking statement.

Tips: Be enthusiastic and confident. Be prepared with all necessary content. Keep things moving along; avoid spending too much time on potentially boring sections. Be somewhat flexible in moving through the presentation, taking time to answer all relevant questions at any time and to deal with negative emotions calmly. Pay attention to the concerns of the decision makers and be sure to address those concerns. If the audience is considering other ideas or procedures, emphasize the strengths and downplay the weaknesses of your proposal; then do the opposite with the alternate proposals. Use effective visuals, including a slideshow and a handout. Don't be disappointed if you don't close the deal; situations like this sometimes take months to finalize.

Seeking Funding for a New Venture

Opening (mostly direct approach, mixed with a problem-solution sequence): Welcome and thank the audience for coming. Give a general statement about the purpose of your presentation.

Agenda: Probably skip the agenda, or give just a general statement about how the presentation will proceed.

Part 1: Quickly describe the funding opportunity.

Part 2: Describe the need (the current problem to be solved and its significance).

Part 3: Describe the solution—how how the problem will be solved.

Part 4: List all benefits and discuss costs.

Part 5: Provide an implementation timeline.

Part 6: Highlight the qualifications of you and your organization.

Q&A: Transition to a Q&A segment.

Closing: Proceed to an action ending.

Tips: Be positive and upbeat throughout the presentation. Don't go into too much detail with your analysis; stick with the few key points and keep the presentation moving along. Clearly establish a need and provide a crystal-clear description of the solution, along with your qualifications to wisely and carefully administer the funding. Focus on appropriate values, and seek to stir the audience members' emotions. Be prepared also to answer a wide variety of questions in a calm and confident manner. Use effective visuals, including a slideshow and a handout. Be prepared to follow up numerous times after the meeting, because people don't make decisions like this in a hurry.

Selling a Product or Service

Opening (mostly direct approach, mixed with a problem-solution sequence): Welcome and thank the audience for the opportunity to meet. Give a general statement about the purpose of your presentation.

Agenda: Probably skip the agenda, or give just a general statement about how the presentation will proceed.

Part 1: Quickly describe the product or service.

Part 2: Discover and discuss the customer's needs.

Part 3: Tell how the product or service will solve the customer's problem. Tell stories of others who have purchased the product or service.

Part 4: Cite benefits and emphasize why your product is superior to others.

Part 5: Discuss costs.

Figure 12.4 continued.

Part 6: Emphasize the credibility of your organization.

Closing: Proceed to an action ending, attempting to close the sale.

Tips: You must clearly establish a need so the customer will feel a need to act. Emphasize the benefits of the new product, perhaps also lightly covering the consequences of not taking action. Be a good listener and seek for input throughout the presentation. Focus on the values held by the customer, not on your desire to make a sale. Be prepared also to answer a wide variety of questions in a calm and confident manner. Use effective visuals and product models.

Defending an Unpopular Policy or Decision

Opening (mostly direct approach): Welcome and thank the audience for the opportunity to meet. Give a general statement about the purpose of the meeting.

Agenda: Explain the procedure to be followed—probably a brief statement from you, followed by questions from the audience.

Part 1: An appropriate segment by you, explaining justification for the policy or decision.

Part 2: Questions from the audience and answers by you (or others who may be accompanying you)

Closing: At an appropriate time, or when questions cease, thank the audience for their questions. Then express your hope that your answers have provided useful information to help the audience better understand the rationale behind the policy or decision.

Tips: When going before a "firing line" like this, prepare

yourself both logically and emotionally. Have a well-prepared opening statement that highlights your key talking points. Throughout the rest of the session, refer back to those talking points again and again. Know your positive points, and emphasize them. Be aware of your vulnerabilities, and address them. Focus on important values, such as fairness, honesty, integrity, and concern for people's well being. Avoid the appearance of being rigid and unbending. Tell brief stories to support your key points. Emphasize the negative consequences of taking alternative courses of action. Answer questions clearly, but concisely, and then move on. Don't get bogged down with one person or one issue, and never at any time become impatient or angry.

Giving a Keynote or Special-event Speech

Opening (depends on the content): Thank for the opportunity to speak. Acknowledge leaders and audience members. Give positive comments about the event or occasion.

Agenda: List the key topics you will cover.

Topic 1: State the topic and give supporting content.

Topic 2: State the topic and give supporting content.

Topic 3: State the topic and give supporting content.

Closing: Give a summary statement and a wish for success to the audience.

Tips: Because this type of presentation often involves a more general audience, keep the content relatively general and light. Use informative, interesting, and inspiring stories to develop the key points and to keep the audience involved. Perhaps the most important tip is—keep it short!

Figure 12.4 continued.

Content enhancement makes a huge difference in presentations. Two presenters might be given the same topic, but one might be successful and the other might fail because of how the material is packaged. For example, in a presentation intended to persuade the executives of a company to install metal-detection equipment at all building entrances, Presenter A gives a well-organized presentation, complete with a well-organized slideshow, but without anything that really grabs the audience's attention. The executives decide against the proposal.

Presenter B gives the same basic information, but at the beginning of his presentation, he reaches inside the left pocket of his jacket and pulls out a toy handgun. Then he reaches inside his right pocket and pulls out a small package representing a bomb. He then builds the presentation on the need to keep people like himself (using a bit of humor) from entering the building without detection. He connects

with the audience, gets his message across clearly and persuasively, and the executives adopt his proposal.

Remember that people learn in a variety of ways, including (a) auditory, (b) visual, and (c) kinesthetic, or experiential, learning. Auditory learning occurs by listening, visual learning occurs by watching, and kinesthetic learning occurs by doing. To appeal to all types of learning, consider incorporating a full mix of auditory, visual and kinesthetic communications in your presentations.

OPENING

At the opening of your presentation, your audience members will all be thinking about different things. Thus, you need to creatively hook their minds and pull them into your topic. Just as a fisher uses an attractive lure on the end of the line to hook a fish, you use a creative opening to hook the audience. Consider using one of the following approaches:

- A shocking statistic or trend. For instance, "Last month the number of people killed in automobile deaths in the United States was greater than the number of people killed in the World Trade Center in 2001!"

- A rhetorical question (a question used to prod the audience to think but not to actually answer aloud). For example, you might begin a presentation on highway safety with the question, "Why do we pay so much attention to the approximately 2,500 World Trade Center deaths and yet so little attention to roughly 2,500 deaths occurring every month on our highways?"

- Humor that is appropriate for the audience and the topic. The humor should be in good taste, should generate at least a smile, if not laughter, and should relate to the presentation topic.

- An attention-grabbing object or visual. For instance, training on business writing could begin with a sample of a poorly written letter, filled with writing flaws and grammatical errors.

- A short, memorable saying or quotation. An example in a presentation on creativity could be, "There's more than one way to skin a cat."

- An interesting story. Select short stories that capture attention and emotion and that clearly drive home your key point. Stories hold our attention because we want to know how the story ends.

- An example related to the topic. Examples can be either good or bad examples, whichever best drives home the point.

- A problem frequently encountered by the audience. For a group of marketing managers, talk about the challenge of getting their product message to the right people.

- A captivating video clip. Many clips are available on YouTube and can be easily downloaded for showing in a presentation.

Make sure the opening hook helps set the tone of the presentation (serious, humorous, urgent, etc.) and helps you as the presenter connect with the audience members. The hook also provides a natural transition to the key point of the presentation (unless you are following an indirect approach).

BODY

In addition to developing a creative way to launch the presentation, decide on ways to develop each of the body segments. Typical development content includes the following:

Explanations: definitions, descriptions, statistics, details and logical analyses

Illustrations: examples (both good and bad), metaphors, stories

Evaluations: qualitative comparisons and testimonials

Applications: in other organizations (past) and in this organization (future)

Illustrations: including business graphics, concept maps, and photos

For instance, if you were trying to convince management to implement a company wellness program, you could employ a number of different ways to develop your point—cite *statistics* showing an alarming rise in obesity, show a *line chart* that tracks the growth of wellness programs in the last ten years, tell the *story* of two companies that implemented a wellness program, share *testimonials* of executives from those companies, *quote* a well-known leader who talks about the moral responsibility we all have to take action, *explain* how a wellness program could work in this company, *explain* the increase in employee motivation that accompanies wellness programs, and show *pictures* of fitness center equipment that could be considered as part of a total wellness program.

In the body of your message you'll often need to persuade the audience to choose one option over other options. The most common approach is to compare and contrast the differences. Emphasize the strengths of the option you are recommending, and de-emphasize its weaknesses. Then downplay the strengths of the other options, and emphasize their weaknesses. Displaying a decision table can help with this comparative evaluation (see page 105).

CLOSING

At the conclusion of your presentation, you could revisit the opening hook to tie the beginning and ending together, and then close with an appropriate ending. For example, you might say, "At the beginning I showed you a glass only half full of water to illustrate the serious drought condition we have here in southern Texas. I encourage you to implement the water-conservation program I have described today before the water glass of our entire city literally drops to only half full."

After you strengthen and enhance the opening, the body, and the closing, complete and polish the outline.

With your presentation outline completed and polished, you are now ready to prepare appropriate media for the presentation. Chapter 11 explains how to prepare slideshows and handouts to add an extra professional touch to your presentation.

Prepare the Messenger

Up to this point, this chapter has focused on the message content. Now it is time to turn to the presentation of you, the messenger. What do other people experience when you are speaking? What is the overall ethos you are projecting? Do you come across as being confident, professional, competent, and trustworthy? Perhaps most important, what do people feel when they listen to you? To make this judgment, the audience will gather information from many sources while you are speaking:

- Verbal and voice—what you say (also what you don't say) and how you say it.
- Nonverbal—your eyes and face, your gestures, your appearance, and your movement.

They will also be watching to see how you respond to unexpected situations that arise during your presentation. The following sections provide guidance to help you improve and polish your ethos so you will give an overall impression of confidence, competence, professionalism, and integrity.

The Verbal

Choose your words carefully. Select words that are appropriate for the setting and the audience. Speak their language! When speaking to accountants, use the language of accountants; when speaking to engineers, use engineering language. Avoid language that is too technical for the audience. Also, avoid language that is either too formal or too casual.

As you deliver your message, you may choose from among four main types of delivery:

- **Memorized**—the presentation is written in full text form and is memorized word for word. This type of presentation is rarely used in management presentations.
- **Manuscript**—the presentation is also written in full text but is then read verbatim. This type of presentation is used most frequently when exact wording is critical, as in the case of a crisis-management presentation. It is also often used when addressing large audiences in formal settings.
- **Extemporaneous**—an outline is created in advance, and the presenter follows the outline while spontaneously creating the actual message. This is the most frequent type of management presentation.

Figure 12.5 Professionals are often called upon to give impromptu reports.

- **Impromptu**—the presenter has almost no time to prepare the presentation. This type of presentation occurs often in meetings, such as when the person conducting says, "Sam, could you bring us up to date on the ABC project."

Business presentations are often a combination of these four delivery types. For instance, the opening and closing might be somewhat memorized, an important statement might be read verbatim, a short section you think of during the actual delivery might be given impromptu, and the bulk of the body may be given extemporaneously.

After deciding on the appropriate types of delivery, prepare your voice and the nonverbal messages you are sending. Also, prepare to deal with unexpected situations during your presentation.

The Voice

Your voice quality is affected by the pitch (high or low frequency), rate (speed at which you speak), volume (how loudly you speak), and tone (your cumulative vocal attributes). No one pitch, rate, volume, or tone is right. Studies show, however, that a lower pitch is preferred to a high, squeaky pitch. Also, a rich tone from the throat, instead of nasal tone, is highly preferred.

Voice energy is critical in your presentations. No one likes to listen to a monotone voice for very long. Increase the volume for emphasis, slow down for articulation, and raise the pitch at the end of a question (e.g., Are you sure?). Record yourself a passage of text and then listen to your voice. Is it too slow or too fast? Is it too monotone? Make changes to ensure that your voice conveys energy, sincerity, and conviction.

In considering the use of your voice, don't forget to

think about silence—the absence of voice. Silence is one of the punctuation marks of oral communication. Just as a rise in the tone of voice can indicate a question, a pause can indicate a comma, period, dash, or parenthesis.

Closely related to voice are the factors of pronunciation, enunciation, and word choice. First, pronounce words properly. For instance, say "especially," not "eckspecially," "recur," not "reoccur," and "regardless," not "irregardless." Also, pronounce vowels properly. For example, businesses have special "sales," not "sells." Several online dictionary sources can help you with proper pronunciation, including m-w.com that provides audible pronunciation, in addition to definitions.

Enunciation refers to how distinctly you say the vowels in each word. Say "probably," not "probly," and "incidentally," not "incidently." Remember "ing" endings, and avoid the more casual runnin' and walkin' and talkin.'

The Nonverbal

To complement the verbal part of your presentation, use nonverbal communications effectively. Maintain good eye contact, gesture with energy, dress appropriately, and use the floor space effectively.

EYES AND FACE

When we as humans look at one another, we instinctively focus on the eyes and face. Thus, make sure your face projects positive expressions, such as happiness, enthusiasm, and optimism. Avoid negative expressions of frustration, impatience, or anger, unless you are telling a story where those expressions are appropriate.

Maintain good eye contact with the audience. As needed, look at your visual aid for a second or two, but quickly return to your audience. Keep your eyes alive and active. Carry on a series of three-second conversations with individual audience members located throughout the room, not just with those in front of you.

GESTURES

Your arms and hands should provide gestures to accompany your spoken message. Inexperienced speakers feel awkward in front of a group and don't know what to do with their hands. As a result, they clasp them in front of their body in fig-leaf fashion, fold their arms, put their hands in their pockets, put their fingertips together in a prayer-like fashion, or play with their rings or other jewelry. The following suggestions will help you become more comfortable with your hands:

- When they're not being used for gesturing, just drop your hands to your sides (the neutral position).

Another alternative is to return one hand to the waist area (middle of the abdomen) and drop the other hand to the side. In an informal situation, men may put one hand in a pocket.

- When you gesture, bring your hands above your waistline so they convey more energy and can be seen.
- Make the gestures match the content. Improvement in sales could be accompanied by an upward sweep of the hand; a series of three items would be accompanied by one, two, and three fingers, reference to a personal experience might be accompanied by a brief touch to the upper chest. Minimize meaningless, empty gestures. During your practice sessions, perhaps overdo the gestures just to get yourself to relax and to be more animated. Your gestures might seem awkward and forced at first, but continuous practice will make them more spontaneous and natural.

Figure 12.6 Effective presenters use gestures to accompany their spoken message.

APPEARANCE

Pay careful attention to your appearance—what the audience sees. Check your personal hygiene and grooming. Select appropriate clothing for the occasion (business formal vs. business casual). Avoid faddish clothing, jewelry, and hair styles that would draw attention to themselves. The way you appear should never distract or detract from your message or damage your ethos. Always strive to look the part, as well as be the part.

FLOOR SPACE

Use your floor space effectively. Unless you are speaking from a podium, move out toward the audience so you don't appear too distant. Reducing the space between you and the audience will help make your presentation feel more conversational and comfortable. During your presentation, move purposefully. For example, at a major transition point you might move a few feet to the left or right as you say, "Now, let's move on to the third reason for recommending this change." However, don't wander aimlessly back and forth in front of the group. Also, don't rock back and forth from one foot to the other.

The Unexpected

Many presentations require adaptation during the presentation. This can involve modifying the content, the presentation style, the length, or other aspects of the presentation. Even the most seasoned presenters have to adapt and modify as they encounter technology problems, unexpected time limitations, or audience problems. While you're talking, you also have to listen and watch, noting signs of misunderstanding, boredom, and fatigue. What do you do when you encounter such problems? A few suggestions are given in Table 12.1.

Following the delivery of your presentation, you will often need to provide some time for the audience to ask questions. Taking questions during the presentation can be risky, because questions can easily get you off track. They can also take excessive time and prevent you from finishing your presentation on schedule. So in most cases, hold off questions until the end.

To introduce the Q&A session, end your presentation and then say, "I'd now be happy to answer any questions you may have." Prepare a special slide to show at this point in your presentation (Figure 12.7). During the Q&A session, follow five major guidelines.

1. Make sure everyone has heard the question. If they haven't, repeat it. Also, make sure you understand the question. If you're unsure, paraphrase for clarification. For example, "You're asking about the human aspect of this new program, is that it?"

2. Involve everyone in your answer. Look at the person who asked the question for the first few seconds of your response, and then speak to the rest of the audience for the remainder of your response (remember three-second conversations). You can also invite other mem-

Table 12.1 Adaptation Ideas for Oral Presentations

Problem	Possible Solution
Boredom	• Get more energy and variety in your voice and gestures. • Ask a thought-provoking question, or ask the audience to share a personal experience related to the subject. • Tell an engaging story, joke, or humorous incident related to the subject. • Switch to more interesting, engaging, and important information. • Involve the audience in a small-group activity. • Display a visual aid or artifact.
Disruptive behavior (whispering, etc.)	• Move closer to the offending person. • Look at the person for a few seconds while you continue talking. • Stop momentarily until the person stops talking. • Ask the person a question about the topic being discussed.
Fatigue	• Take a brief break and have the audience stand up and stretch. • Have the group participate in a small-group activity. • Cut the presentation short. • Move closer to the audience.
Misunderstanding	• Give an example, or use a metaphor. • Define misunderstood points or terms. • Create a visual.
Equipment breakdown	• Have a backup plan (e.g., paper handouts). • Take a moment to fix the problem (if it's a simple problem). • Move on without the equipment, adapting the best way you can.
Time reduction	• Hit the high points, but eliminate supporting information. • Give information in more general terms, omitting some details.

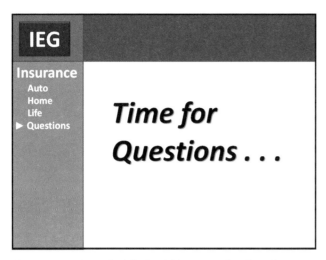

Figure 12.7 A specific slide should be prepared to show during the Q&A session.

bers of the audience to respond to the question, as appropriate. This conveys an attitude of openness on your part, and it gives others a chance to share their insights.

3. Answer each question clearly and concisely. Avoid overly long answers. Give the answer and then move on. At the conclusion of an answer to a difficult question, you might ask the questioner, "Did that answer your question?" or "Is that the information you were asking about?"

4. If you don't know the answer, admit it and tell the questioner you will find the information and call him or her with the answer. Then be sure to follow through.

5. As appropriate, use visuals to support your answers. These may be visuals you've already used or new ones held in reserve for the Q&A session.

When your allotted time has expired or when no more questions are asked, give another strong closing to reiterate your main message: "Thank you for your questions. In closing, let me again emphasize the importance of taking immediate action on . . ."

REHEARSE AND IMPROVE

Just as polished writing requires good reviewing and revising (as discussed in Chapter 5), good presentations require rehearsing and improving. Rehearsing helps polish a presentation better than anything else. Even question-and-answer sessions can be rehearsed. Rehearsing will also reduce the level of stage fright better than anything else. Rehearsing is not merely talking through a presentation while sitting at your desk; it is literally giving the presentation, complete with gestures and visuals, as though you were

giving it to the real audience. Rehearsing a minimum of three times is recommended for most presentations.

Rehearsing also serves as the editing phase of your presentation. Initially, you can perform your own critique and make needed changes. Later, however, get a few other people to give you feedback. One approach is to present a basic walk-through to two or three reviewers, simply telling them step by step what you plan to cover. Then ask them for feedback. Beyond the basic walk-through approach, you can rehearse your presentation in front of others and request their feedback. Presenters in some organizations use in-house pink teams and red teams. Pink teams act as friendly audiences, and they give feedback in a supportive sort of way. Red teams, however, are intentionally more critical in their feedback.

Figure 12.8 In a basic walk-through, explain to a few reviewers what you plan to cover step by step.

An even better approach is to video record yourself, using real-time coaching technology that enables you to see and hear yourself and that allows others to give detailed feedback during your rehearsal or presentation. For example, with technology by SpeakWorks (see speakworks.com), the audience gives you a continuous rating line and time-stamped feedback, which you can then use as a basis for improvement (see Figure 12.9).

Presentation evaluations should include audience reactions to the three "M" areas discussed in Chapters 11 and 12: message, messenger, and media. (A rubric for conducting a good review is included at the end of this chapter.) Use the following three sections to guide your review of presentations.

Message

☐ Is the content clear and coherent? If your message isn't clear, nothing else matters much. Generally avoid having more than three or four key points. Remember the

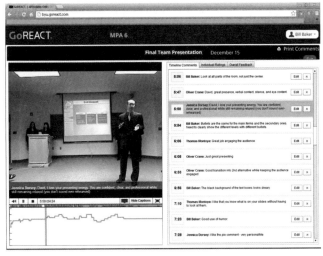

Figure 12.9 A screenshot of software enabling audience members to record time-stamped feedback that presenters can review afterwards.

more-is-less and less-is more principle—more complexity generates less comprehension. Make sure everything in the presentation helps to drive home those key points. Use words that are appropriate for the audience. Use examples, stories, and metaphors to help achieve clarity of message.

☐ Is the content correct? Is it free from error?

☐ Is it complete and well developed? Does the presentation provide appropriate support and development for all the major points?

☐ Is it creative and compelling? Do the audience members find the presentation to be engaging and persuasive? Are stories, unexpected twists, provocative rhetorical questions, visuals, and human emotions appropriately included in the presentation to make it memorable and mentally sticky? Do the audience members feel inclined to take the desired action after the presentation is complete?

☐ Does the presentation stay within the required time limits? Does any content need to be cut back to make the presentation more concise?

☐ Is the organization clear, with a distinct opening, agenda, body, and closing?

☐ Is the question-and-answer segment preceded and followed by good closing segments?

Messenger

☐ Does the messenger portray an ethos of confidence, professionalism, and integrity?

☐ Is the messenger knowledgeable and well prepared?

☐ Is the presenter's voice enthusiastic and energetic? Is the volume appropriate? Does the presenter pronounce words accurately and enunciate clearly?

☐ Does the presenter maintain good eye contact with people in all parts of the presentation room?

☐ Does the presenter use gestures adequately and effectively? Does the presenter have any distracting nonverbal mannerisms that should be eliminated?

☐ Is the presenter's dress and appearance appropriate?

☐ Does the presenter use floor space well?

Media

☐ Do the slides and handouts portray an image of professionalism in layout and design? Do any elements look amateurish and unprofessional?

☐ Are the slides and handouts clear and easy to read and understand? Do any slides contain too much text?

☐ Are borrowed graphics appropriately documented?

☐ Is the typography large enough to be easily read? Are appropriate fonts used?

☐ Is there adequate contrast between the typography and the background?

☐ Do the slides and handouts portray effective use of design treatments—contrast, alignment, repetition, balance, and spacing?

☐ Does the presenter point to individual slides and slide elements as they are introduced to the audience?

☐ Do the slides complement the presentation, rather than distract or detract?

With a well-crafted message, carefully designed slides and handouts, and thorough personal preparation, you will be well prepared for your presentation. As you stand to present, you will believe in your message and be excited to share it, and this excitement will energize your voice, illuminate your eyes and face, and animate your gestures. Everything will come together to make a truly superb presentation.

TEAM PRESENTATIONS

In some situations you will participate in giving a team presentation. Remember a few guidelines unique to team presentations.

Appearance

Coordinate messenger appearance so everyone is dressed at the same level of formality (see Figure 12.10). Coordinate media appearance for consistency in typography, graphics, color, and layout.

Figure 10.10 All team presenters should dress at the same level of formality.

Introductions

At the beginning of the presentation, introduce group members, their positions, and the part they'll play in the presentation. You might include their names, and perhaps even their photos, with the agenda on a PowerPoint slide.

Transitions Between Presenters

Most presentation teams include frequent transition statements to inform the audience where they are in the presentation. For example, you might have all presenters (1) give an agenda of their segment, (2) present their segment, (3) and then introduce the next speaker: "Marilyn will now discuss such and such."

Another technique is to give the presentation as a planned dialogue among the speakers, with each presenter entering and exiting without a formal introduction. This approach offers greater speaker variety, but it must be well rehearsed to work effectively. Regardless of the transition method, you can include a running agenda on the screen to help the audience keep track of where you are in the presentation.

Attentiveness

Make sure all group members remain attentive throughout the presentation. Non-presenters should continuously watch the speaker attentively and avoid any actions that might distract the audience.

Q&A

Determine in advance how to handle the question-and-answer session. Decide what types of questions each person will answer, and determine who will moderate the

Q&A session. The session should be well organized but not overly structured. Team members should feel free to contribute whenever they think they can provide additional useful information.

REHEARSAL

Nothing takes the place of effective rehearsal! Make sure everyone knows what everyone else is going to do and how they're going to do it. Rehearse three or more times—precisely as the presentation will be delivered in the actual setting.

Group presentations will be unsuccessful if poorly planned or executed. Wise, thorough preparation and effective practice are the keys to success.

CHAPTER SUMMARY

Professionals depend on effective oral presentations to be successful in their work. When you are asked to give an effective presentation, prepare the message carefully. Clarify your purpose and create an outline. Analyze the audience and determine the most effective way to approach the topic. To begin your presentation, use a good opening hook. Then give an agenda and move into the body of the presentation, developing each section effectively. Close the presentation by revisiting the opening hook and giving appropriate wrap-up comments. Provide sufficient opportunity for questions.

As the messenger who delivers the message, you should maintain good voice energy. Also, make sure your eyes and face reflect enthusiasm for your topic. Use effective gestures, and make good use of floor space. Be sure your appearance is appropriate. Anticipate and prepare for unexpected situations. Finally, rehearse your presentation several times, evaluating the message, messenger, and media aspects of the presentation.

Team presentations present several challenges not faced by solo speakers. Team members' appearance, transitions, and Q&A participation should all be well coordinated. Further, all members should remain attentive while other members of the team are presenting. As with solo presentations, good rehearsal is critical for teams.

CHAPTER QUESTIONS

1. List two guidelines for effective room arrangement.
2. Explain the difference between top-down and bottom-up outlines.
3. What are the two main sequencing options?
4. What is the purpose of an opening hook?

5. What is a rhetorical question and why it is used?

6. List five different types of support you could use to develop an important point in a presentation.

7. What tactic can you take when you are persuading the audience to choose one option over others?

8. List three major ways that people learn.

9. List the four major types of presentation delivery.

10. What is the difference between pronunciation and enunciation?

11. What should you do with your hands when you are not gesturing?

12. List two different ways to deal with boredom in one of your presentations.

13. List two guidelines for conducting an effective Q&A session.

14. List the three M's of presentation evaluation.

Chapter Activities

1. Attend, analyze, and evaluate a public presentation. Take notes regarding the content of the presentation as you listen to it. Prepare a written analysis and evaluation of the content, organization, and delivery. Give suggestions for improvement.

2. Prepare and deliver a 3–5 minute training presentation on a topic from this textbook. Use the chalkboard or whiteboard to provide appropriate visual support.

3. With a classmate as your audience, give a stand-up presentation in which you tell about a personal experience. Use effective gestures and voice animation. Have your classmate critique your gestures and voice.

4. Give a short informal persuasive presentation to a classmate. Convince your classmate to purchase something, such as such as a car or electronic device. Apply an appropriate persuasive strategy, including a discussion of features and benefits. Have your classmate critique your presentation.

5. Prepare and deliver a 3–5 minute oral presentation on a topic approved by your instructor. Organize the presentation using the OABC pattern. Use no note cards or visuals. Demonstrate your very best nonverbal communication skills to compensate for the lack of media.

6. Prepare and give a 5–7 minute individual presentation with visuals. Design an effective handout to use in conjunction with the presentation. If possible, video your presentation and then watch yourself afterward. Write a short memo on what you did well and what you need to improve. Evaluate the message, messenger, and media aspects.

7. With a team of your peers, give a 15–20 minute presentation with PowerPoint slides. Leave time for a question-and-answer session. If possible, video your presentation and then watch yourself afterward. Write a short memo on what you did well and what you need to improve. Evaluate the message, messenger, and media aspects.

Rubric for Evaluating Oral Presentations

Presenter_____   Topic_____

Rating (10-1)	Evaluation Factors Circle (strengths), underline weaknesses, add +/- comments
Message	—***Content:*** clear and coherent, correct, creative and compelling, complete and well developed, concise (within time limits) —***Organization:*** clear and distinct opening, agenda, body, closing, and Q&A *Comments:*
Messenger	—***Ethos:*** confidence, competence/preparedness, professionalism, integrity —***Voice:*** volume, energy, pronunciation, enunciation —***Nonverbal:*** eye contact, gestures, energy, dress/appearance, use of floor space *Comments:*
Media	—***Slides, handouts, etc.:*** professional layout, design, graphics, typography, animations —***Clear, relevant information:*** easy-to-comprehend, effective in achieving objectives —***Integrated into presentation*** *Comments:*
_____ /30 **Total**	

APPENDIX:
BUSINESS WRITING BASICS

CONTENTS

This appendix provides instruction on the fundamentals of composing effective sentences. Although it is not a comprehensive grammar guide, it will provide a solid foundation of the grammar and style basics you will most frequently encounter in business writing. For easy remembering, the appendix is organized under five headings whose initials form the word SPELL—Structure, Punctuation, Errors, Language, and Length.

STRUCTURE OF SENTENCES

Sentences are groups of words organized together to express meaningful ideas. The word syntax refers to the structure of different words and elements in a sentence. This section discusses (a) word classifications, (b) subjects, verbs, and complements, (c) phrases and clauses, (d) sentence expansions, (e) sentence types, and (f) sentence guidelines.

Word Classifications

Words are the basic building blocks of language. They are classified into one of eight categories, called *parts of speech*. The classification depends on how the word is used in a sentence. Thus, the same word may be classified differently, depending on how it is used.

Example: Mary was *running* along the path by the river. [Running is a *verb*.]

Example: *Running* is my least favorite activity. [Running is a *noun*.]

Example: The *running* water is interrupting my concentration. [Running is an *adjective*.]

The eight parts of speech are described as follows.

Noun: A word that names a person, place, or thing.

Examples: Jill, dog, Salt Lake City, vaccination

Example: *Jill* took her *dog* to *Salt Lake City* for a *vaccination*. [These nouns are persons, places, or things.]

Example: *Patience* is a *virtue*. [These two nouns describe human attributes.]

Pronoun: A word used in place of a noun.

Examples: I, you, she, it, they, who, him

Example: *She* gave the report to *him*. [*She* and *him* are pronouns that replace nouns, such as *Tiffany* and *Andrew*.]

Verb: A word or word group that describes the action or state of being of the sentence subject.

Examples: Ran, tried, thought, felt, was, is, are

Example: Chris *saved* the file on his hard disk [*action* verb].

Example: Sharon *is* the new manager [*being* verb].

Adjective: A word that modifies or describes a noun or pronoun.

Examples: Red, new, poor, warm, tall

Example: Rick fixed the *leaky* pipe. [*Leaky* modifies, or describes, the noun *pipe*.]

Example: She is *qualified* for the job. [*Qualified* modifies or describes the pronoun *she*.]

Adverb: A word that modifies or describes a verb, adjective, or other adverb.

Examples: Really, very, extremely

Example: Rachel walked *slowly* back to the car. [*Slowly* modifies the verb *walked*.]

Example: Jeannie is a *very* beautiful woman. [*Very* modifies the adjective *beautiful*.]

Example: Lon sang *exceptionally* well today. [*Exceptionally* modifies the adverb *well*.]

Preposition: A word that relates a noun or pronoun to some other word in the sentence. The preposition plus its following related words constitute a prepositional phrase.

Examples: In, on, into, for, to, beside, at

Example: The worm *in* the apple will soon become a moth. [*In* relates *the worm* to *the apple*.]

Example: The book is *on the desk*. [*On* is the preposition; *on the desk* is a prepositional phrase.]

Conjunction: A word used to join or connect words, phrases, or clauses.

Examples: And, or, but

Example: Joshua *and* Ryan swim often. [*And* joins two words—*Joshua* and *Ryan*.]

Example: We'll have our meeting *and* then we'll break for lunch. [*And* joins two clauses.]

Interjection: A word used to express emotion or surprise.

Examples: Oh, ouch, yikes

Example: *Oh,* I hadn't thought of it that way before. [*Oh* expresses surprise.]

Subjects, Verbs, and Complements

A sentence is a group of words expressing an *idea*. Most sentences have three main *elements*:

- Subject—the thing that is *doing* something or *being* something
- Verb—what the subject is *doing* or *being*.
- Complement—the *completion* of the idea started by the subject and verb

Consider the following sentence: **Roger** <u>drove</u> *to St. George.*

Subject:	Roger (the thing that did something)
<u>Verb:</u>	drove (the action)
Complement:	to St. George (the rest of the idea started by the subject and verb)

Phrases and Clauses

Words in sentences are organized into word groupings called phrases and clauses.

Phrase—a group of *related* words *without* a subject *and* verb.

Clause—a group of *related* words *with* a subject *and* a verb.

Let's add a phrase to the basic sentence just discussed:

[After passing Cedar City,] **Roger** <u>drove</u> to St. - George.

"After passing Cedar City" is a prepositional phrase. It is a phrase because it does not have a subject; it is a prepositional phrase because it begins with the preposition "after." "To St. George," the complement identified earlier, is a prepositional phrase. It is a phrase because it contains no verb; it is a prepositional phrase because it begins with the preposition "to." "Roger drove to St. George" is a clause. It is a clause because it contains a subject (**Roger**) and a verb (<u>drove</u>).

Clauses are of three types: independent, dependent, and embedded.

Independent clause—a clause that conveys a complete idea and that can stand alone.

Dependent clause—an idea that cannot stand alone; it *depends* on an independent clause to complete its meaning.

Embedded clause—a minor clause used within an independent or dependent clause.

Let's add a dependent clause to our earlier sentence:

[After **he** <u>made</u> *the final decision,*] [**Roger** <u>drove</u> to St. George.]

This sentence has two clauses, the first being a dependent clause and the second being an independent clause. You can see that each clause has a subject, a verb, and a complement. If you encountered "After he made the final decision" as a sentence by itself, you probably would ask, "What happened after he made the final decision?" This is a dependent clause because it depends on the second clause (the independent clause) to answer that question.

Independent clauses are called *main* clauses, and dependent clauses are called *subordinate* clauses. A sentence may have more than one main clause and more than one subordinate clause.

After **he** <u>made</u> *the final decision,* | **Roger** <u>drove</u> to St. George.

Subordinate clause   **Main clause**

An embedded clause is a clause within a clause. It is a minor clause attached to either an independent or a dependent clause, such as, "I noticed that you were at the meeting," or, "Although I noticed you were at the meeting, I decided to stay." In both cases, "you were at the meeting" is the embedded clause because it is the complement of the clause "I noticed".

Let's add an embedded clause to our sample sentence:

[After **he** <u>made</u> *the final decision,*] [**Roger** <u>drove</u> to St. George, **which** <u>is</u> *south of Cedar City.*]

Notice how the embedded clause in this example is part of the independent clause, describing the complement "St. George." Although embedded clauses are important in sentence construction, they are *not* important in determining basic sentence type, as we will see later on.

CONJUNCTIONS

Independent and dependent clauses are often connected by a conjunction. These conjunctions can be classified as (a) coordinating conjunctions or (b) subordinating conjunctions.

Coordinating conjunctions (for, and, nor, but, or, yet, so) connect clauses of equal strength.

Subordinating conjunctions (e.g., if, as, unless, although, when, after, because) connect clauses of unequal strength—they place the main emphasis on one clause and secondary emphasis on the other.

Subordinating conjunctions generally fall into one of five categories:

Category	Example
Cause	because
Concession	although, even though
Condition	if, unless
Place	wherever
Time	after, before, since, when, while, until

The following sentences give examples of main and subordinate clauses separated by conjunctions:

- I will work for you on Saturday, *and* then you can work for me next Tuesday. [Two main clauses joined by the coordinating conjunction *and*.]

- I will invite Kristy to the game, *or* you can invite Ashley. [Two main clauses joined by the coordinating conjunction *or*.]

- I attended his game *because* I hadn't seen him play before. [One main clause joined by the subordinating conjunction *because*.]

- I am majoring in accounting, *although* I don't plan to be an accountant for the rest of my life. [One main clause joined by the subordinating conjunction *although*.]

- She will be able to go on the trip *if* she meets all the academic requirements. [One main clause joined by the subordinating conjunction *if*.]

- We will be happy to talk with you *wherever* you'd like to meet. [One main clause joined by the subordinating conjunction *wherever*.]

- He will call to arrange an appointment *after* you submit your forms. [One main clause joined by the subordinating conjunction *after*.]

The sequence of two clauses in a sentence can be reversed. If a coordinating conjunction is involved, it remains between the clauses as follows:

- I will work for you on Saturday, *and* you can work for me next Tuesday.

- You can work for me next Tuesday, *and* I will work for you on Saturday.

If a subordinating conjunction is involved, however, the conjunction is moved with the subordinate clause.

- I am majoring in accounting, *although* I don't plan to be an accountant for the rest of my life.

- *Although* I don't plan to be an accountant for the rest of my life, I am majoring in accounting.

- He will call to arrange an appointment *after* you submit your forms.

- *After* you submit your forms, he will call to arrange an appointment.

Sentence Expansions

Sentences can be expanded in many ways. In addition to adding clauses, the following sentences show a number of other ways to expand sentences by adding words or phrases. These sample sentences all build on the basic two-word main clause, "*Gary reads.*"

Subject Variations

This intelligent, hard-working Gary reads computer manuals. [Adjectives describing the subject]

Gary and *Brian* read computer manuals. [Two or more subjects are called a compound subject]

Verb Variations

Gary reads *slowly* and *carefully*. [Compound adverbs describing the verb]

Gary *reads numerous books* and *watches televised sports events.* [Compound verb phrases]

Complement Variations

Gary reads *novels.* [Simple noun complement]

Gary reads *recent historical* novels. [Noun complement with two modifiers]

Gary reads *manuals at work* and *historical novels at home.* [Compound complement phrases]

Introductory Phrases [phrase occurs before the subject]

Almost daily, Gary reads computer manuals.

To understand the new software, Gary reads computer manuals.

Interrupting Phrases [phrase occurs between the subject and verb]

Gary, *before installing new software,* reads computer manuals.

Gary, *to understand the new software,* reads computer manuals.

Concluding Phrases [phrase occurs after the complement]

Gary reads computer manuals *before installing new software.*

Gary reads computer manuals *to understand the new software.*

Sentence Types

Most sentences can be classified as one of four types. This classification is based on the number and types of *clauses* in a sentence, not on the *phrases.* The number or location of phrases in a sentence does not influence the sentence classification, nor does the presence of embedded clauses.

Simple—Contains one independent clause and no dependent clauses:

Example: After last week's events, [**nothing** <u>surprises</u> me].

Example: [**I** <u>will take</u> her to the airport this morning.]

Compound—Contains two independent clauses and no dependent clauses:

Example: [**I** will compose the text] and [**you** create the graphics].

Example: [**I** will take her to the airport this morning,] and [**I** will pick her up on Friday.]

Complex—Contains one independent clause and one or more dependent clauses:

Example: [When the **copier** arrives,] [**you** complete the warranty paperwork].

Example: [If **you** will take her to the airport this morning,] [**I** will pick her up next Friday.]

Compound-complex—Contains a minimum of two independent clauses and one dependent clause.

Example: [After the **meeting** starts,] [**I** will present the report] and [**you** answer the questions].

Example: [**You** take her to the airport this morning;] [when **she** returns,] [**I** will pick her up.]

As you read each sentence, see if the main subject(s), main verb(s), and associated complement(s) are obvious. Where you find problems, reconstruct the sentence for improved wording and structure. For example, you might (a) put secondary information in an introductory phrase or subordinate clause and (b) place the primary information in a main clause, as follows.

No: Over 60 percent of the 1,086 respondents in this nationwide study agree to the fact that the implementation of Regulation 605 in their organizations has improved controls in two big areas of mine safety and health protection. [This 38-word sentence is cluttered and disorganized, making the main message and sentence structure difficult to discover.]

Yes: Of the 1,086 respondents in this nationwide study, over 60 percent agree that Regulation 605 has improved their miners' safety and health. [In this 22-word sentence, the introductory segment serves as a gathering place for background information, which is then followed by the main clause containing the key message.]

Readers tire of multiple sentences of the same type. Therefore, incorporate appropriate sentence variety.

No: Starting a business requires you to develop a business plan. A business plan includes a description of the business. The description covers marketing, competition, operating procedures, and personnel. A business plan also includes financial data. The financial data section includes a balance sheet, sources of funding, pro-forma income projections, and cash flows. A business plan must also include any other relevant supporting documents. [All six sentences are structured as single clauses with a similar length.]

Yes: If you decide to start your own company, a business plan can be of great assistance to you. Most business plans start with a description of the business, with subsections on marketing, competition, operating procedures, and personnel. Following the description of the business, business plans need a financial data section, usually consisting of a balance sheet, sources of funding, pro-forma income projections, and cash flows. Finally, business plans may include any other sections or supporting documents that the writer considers relevant.

[These four sentences vary in length and structure. The first is an 18-word complex sentence (one dependent and one independent clause). The next is a 19-word simple sentence (one independent clause), with a concluding segment containing four items in a series. Sentence 3 contains 28 words, starting with an introductory phrase, followed by a main clause, and concluding with a four-part series. Finally, sentence 4 consists of 16 words in a simple-sentence construction (independent clause).]

Sentence Guidelines

To make your sentences structurally sound, as well as clear and effective, remember the letters S, V, and C (representing subject, verb, complement). The following mnemonic will help you remember the most important sentence-structure guidelines:

S for Subject—Use Strong Subjects.

V for Verb—Place verbs in the Vicinity of subjects, and use active Voice.

C for Complement—Keep sentence complements Clear and unCluttered.

The following guidelines elaborate more on sentence-construction guidelines that will help you write sentences that are clear and easy to follow. The first two sections focus on subjects and verbs. The other two sections cover parallelism and modifier guidelines to help with writing sentence complements.

SUBJECTS

Subjects are the actors of sentences. Subjects may be nouns (e.g., athlete), pronouns (e.g., they), or even verbs forms (e.g., thinking) or other parts of speech acting as nouns. For example, the word "and" is usually a conjunction, but here it can be used as a noun subject as follows: "*And* is an interesting word."

1. Use strong, clear subjects in preference to vague "*It is*" and "*There are*" structures. Also, avoid complex nominalizations as subjects (*nominalizations* are nouns made from verbs).

   No: *There* will be no classes held on Friday.

   Yes: No classes will be held on Friday.

   No: *It* is imperative that we reduce our taxes.

   Yes: We must reduce our taxes.

   Yes: The new computer has arrived. It will be installed tomorrow. [*It* is acceptable because it has a clear antecedent: computer.]

   No: Consideration of the new hiring policy was the committee's first subject of discussion. [*Consideration* is a nominalization.]

   Yes: The committee first considered the new hiring policy.

VERBS

Verbs indicate two things about subjects. First, verbs can indicate *action* being taken by the subject, such as, "The applicant *described* her experience." Second, verbs can indicate the *state* or *condition* of the subject, such as, "The applicant *is* ill today."

2. Place verbs in the vicinity of their subjects. Sentences with subjects and verbs placed far apart can be hard to follow.

   No: The *purpose* of this report on the causes and effects of global warming *is* to educate the public.

   Yes: The *purpose* of this report *is* to educate the public about the causes and effects of global warming.

3. In most cases, prefer the use of active-voice verbs.

   Active voice—a clause in which the actor is the subject of the sentence. Example: Julie drove the car.

   Passive voice—a clause in which the object of the action is the subject of the sentence. Example: The car was driven by Julie. (Note: Passive voice always requires an extra verb: e.g., was driven.)

   Only clauses with transitive verbs can be written in passive voice—clauses with state-of-being verbs or with intransitive verbs cannot. A transitive verb (noted as *vt* in the dictionary) requires a direct object that receives the action of the verb. An intransitive verb (noted as *vi* in the dictionary) does not require a direct object.

   Transitive verb: The supervisor *fired* the disobedient clerk. [*Fired* is a transitive verb; *clerk* is the object of that firing. This sentence can be rewritten as "The disobedient clerk was fired by the supervisor."]

   Intransitive verb: Today I've been *running* around in circles. [Running is an intransitive verb; it requires no object. The sentence cannot be written in passive voice.]

   Use active voice in most situations, especially when you want to emphasize the actor or de-emphasize the action. Use passive voice in situations when you want to de-emphasize the actor or emphasize the action.

   Active: My secretary *purchased* an airline ticket. [The secretary is the actor and is the subject of the clause.]

   Passive: An airline ticket *was purchased* by my secretary. [The airline ticket is the object of the action but is the subject of the clause.]

   Passive: An airline ticket *was purchased*. [This passive clause omits the actor.]

   Neither: Whitney *is* my secretary. [No action is involved with this state-of-being verb.]

   No: A new proposal was submitted by ABC Corporation. [Writer wants to emphasize ABC Corporation.]

   Yes: ABC Corporation submitted a new proposal.

   No: Michael overlooked several important details. [Writer wants to emphasize the overlooked details.]

   Yes: Several important details were overlooked by Michael.

Yes: Several important details were overlooked. [This option completely omits mention of the guilty person.]

No: The neighbor called the police about the child-abuse problem. [Writer wants to emphasize the police.]

Yes: The police were notified about the child-abuse problem. [Properly emphasizes the police.]

No: I have decided to put you on disciplinary probation because of your behavior last week.

Yes: You are being put on disciplinary probation because of your behavior last week. [Hides the person who made the decision.]

COMPLEMENTS

After the subject and verb of a sentence, you write the complement, or the completion of the sentence. As you do so, remember parallelism and modification guidelines.

Parallelism

The principle of *parallelism* requires that structurally parallel sentence parts be grammatically parallel.

4. Use words of the same part of speech after parallel connectives. (Connectives link sentence branches to the main trunk of the sentence.) Four examples of parallel connectives (connective *twins*) are as follows:

- Not only/but also
- Both/and
- Either/or
- Neither/nor

No: Liz is going *not only to* Chicago *but also New York.* ["To" is a preposition; "New York" is a noun. They aren't parallel.]

Yes: Liz is going *not only to* Chicago *but also to* New York.

For long parallel elements, repeat the connecting word as necessary to ensure clarity. Sometimes a better option is to identify long parallel items with letters, numbers, or bullets.

No: Effective systems analysis requires that we study and identify the major problems to be solved and describe our solutions in an understandable manner. [Confusing!]

Yes: Effective systems analysis requires *that we* study and identify the major problems to be solved and *that we* describe our solutions in an understandable manner. [Better.]

Yes: Effective systems analysis requires that we (a) study and identify the major problems to be solved and (b) describe our solutions in an understandable manner. [Much clearer.]

Yes: Effective systems analysis requires two major steps:

1. Study and identify the major problems to be solved.

2. Describe our solutions in an understandable manner. [Clearest of all!]

5. Use parallel parts of speech for words in a series.

No: Before you leave town, make sure to fill the car with gas, check the oil, and I recommend checking the tire pressure as well. [Two of the three ideas in the series begin with verbs (*fill* and *check*); the last one begins with a pronoun (*I*). Thus, the three parallel ideas do not use parallel grammar.]

Yes: Before you leave town, make sure to *fill* the car with gas, *check* the oil, and *check* the tire pressure. [The three parallel ideas in the series all begin with a verb—*fill, check,* and *check.* Thus, they now have parallel grammatical construction.]

Modification

Adjectives and adverbs are known as modifiers; they help to give clear descriptions of other words. The two major classes of modifiers are adjectives and adverbs:

Adjectives limit, describe, qualify, or make more exact the meaning of any noun, pronoun, or subject of a clause.

Examples: *The real* winners are *the* children. [*Winners* is described by *The real; children* is described by *the.*]

Her red hair is *beautiful.* [*Hair* is described by *Her red* and *beautiful.*]

This business report needs *some careful* proofreading. [*Report* is described by *This business; proofreading* is described by *some careful.*]

Adverbs limit, describe, qualify, or make more exact the meaning of any verb, adjective, or other adverb.

Examples: He walked *very slowly* back to his office. [*Walked* is modified by *very slowly.*]

I am *really* happy you came. [*Happy* is modified by *really*.]

He doesn't feel *very well*. [*Feel* is modified by *very well*.]

6. Use adjectives and adverbs correctly.

No: I did good in my basketball game today.

Yes: I did well in my basketball game today.

No: You're doing a real good job.

Yes: You're doing a really good job. [Remember the necessary *ly* ending for certain adverbs.]

No: I'm sure happy you're on our team.

Yes: I'm surely happy you're on our team.

7. Place modifying words and phrases close to the words they modify.

No: I'm giving the clock to the older woman with a broken face.

Yes: I'm giving the clock with a broken face to the older woman.

No: I'll *only* ask for $10,000. [Only ask?]

Yes: I'll ask for *only* $10,000. [Only $10,000.]

No: Daniel asked her to dance sheepishly.

Yes: Daniel sheepishly asked her to dance.

8. Avoid *dangling* (ambiguous) *modifiers.* The most common type of dangling modifier consists of (a) an introductory verbal phrase that tells of an action, followed by (b) a main clause whose subject does not tell who performed the action. Introductory verbal phrases can be gerunds (an "ing" form of a verb used as a noun) or infinitives (a "to xxxx" form of a verb used as a noun).

No: Screaming uncontrollably, the babysitter tried to feed the baby a bottle of formula. ["Screaming" is a gerund. The introductory phrase does not tell who was screaming, so the reader assumes the subject of the subsequent clause (babysitter) to be the one who was screaming.]

Yes: Screaming uncontrollably, the baby refused the bottle of formula. [The *baby* was screaming uncontrollably.]

No: As an authority on sea life, I am sure you will be a very interesting speaker. [*I* am not the authority.]

Yes: As an authority on sea life, you will be a very interesting speaker.

Yes: Because you are an authority on sea life, I am sure you will be a very interesting speaker. [Introductory *phrase* is changed to an introductory *clause,* clearly showing who is the sea-life authority.]

No: To succeed professionally, I suggest that you get a college education. [I am not the one who is concerned about succeeding professionally.]

Yes: To succeed professionally, you should get a college education. [You are the one who is wanting to succeed professionally.]

Sentence Structure Quiz

For questions 1–10, mark A for simple sentences, B for compound sentences, C for complex sentences, and D for compound-complex sentences.

1. A B C D After selling one of the smaller presses, the company acquired two new ones.

2. A B C D Even though she arrived before the doors opened, she still was unable to get a ticket.

3. A B C D We moved from St. Louis to Chicago, feeling the need to be closer to my wife's parents.

4. A B C D After a brief introduction, we watched an interesting video and then we walked through the flower gardens.

5. A B C D The new policy manual, developed last year, is much clearer than the old one.

6. A B C D After I purchased my new bike in Miami, I shipped it to Atlanta and then rode it in the 25-mile race.

7. A B C D Although I couldn't attend this year's conference, I enjoyed reading the proceedings and I plan to attend next year's meetings.

8. A B C D I have some good news for you—you have been cleared to receive the loan.

9. A B C D The conference rooms on the first and second floors are occupied, but the third-floor conference room is available.

10. A B C D I'd like to play racquetball with you, although I don't have a good racquet.

For questions 11–15, mark A for phrases, B for dependent clauses, and C for independent clauses.

11. A B C Although the group voted in favor of this proposal

12. A B C In spite of his excellent score on the ACT test

13. A B C To find your way to the library
14. A B C A new freeway entrance is being constructed
15. A B C Think about it

16. Which of the following sentences includes a coordinating conjunction?
    a. Sale items may not be returned under any circumstances.
    b. If we want to prevent a decline in employee morale, we must implement a pay increase.
    c. After the nurse completes the training, she will be given a completion certificate.
    d. Our temporary employees feel undervalued, and their motivation suffers as a result.

17. Which of the following is a subordinating conjunction?
    a. but
    b. nor
    c. if
    d. yet

18. Which of the following sentences includes the best subject?
    a. There will be a special orientation meeting for new employees every Thursday at 10 a.m.
    b. Financial specialists will be available to answer questions after the meeting.
    c. Anticipation of the weekend sale caused great excitement among the high-school students.
    d. It is important for you to gain two years of business experience before you apply for the MBA program.

19. "A formal cross-training program for the compensation and benefits employees is proposed." The foregoing sentence suffers from all but which one of the following?
    a. The subject and verb are too far apart.
    b. Passive voice is used.
    c. A prepositional phrase is in the wrong place, given the voice used in the sentence.
    d. A transitive verb is misplaced.

20. Which of the following is written in active voice?
    a. The charges were filed last November.
    b. The charges were filed by the attorney last November.
    c. The new music will be performed during next week's symphony.
    d. Matthew McCallister will direct the music and will expect everyone to attend the daily practices.

21. Which of the following is an adverb?
    a. carefully
    b. slow
    c. high-pitched
    d. diligent

22. Which of the following is a transitive verb?
    a. think
    b. sit
    c. throw
    d. run

23. Which of the following is an adjective?
    a. extremely
    b. slow
    c. very
    d. beauty

24. Which of the following does not contain a parallelism error?
    a. Once everything is set up, we can train the employees and then the customers can be notified.
    b. The strengths she offers are that (a) she has related work experience, (b) a strong educational background, and (c) a great personality.
    c. I suggest that we stay an extra day (unless you object) and visit the home office of American Family Insurance.
    d. Fifty-two of the participants said their accommodations were comfortable and would recommend the hotel to others.

25. Which item is correct?
    a. I'm going to have only fish and chips for dinner.
    b. To do well in this class, lots of homework must be completed.
    c. Go borrow that boat from the old man with only one oar in the water.
    d. I'm sure excited that their band is going to be playing on Friday night.

26. Which of the following sentences does not contain a modifier error?
    a. The on-line system enables all employees to make investment changes at their convenience.
    b. Please bring me a cold glass of water.
    c. Taking the earliest flight that morning, his noon-time arrival surprised Katie who expected him at 3:30.
    d. She said she thought I did real well in my presentation last week.

PUNCTUATION OF SENTENCES

The English language contains over a dozen punctuation marks. Punctuation marks help us break sentences into meaningful units so readers can more clearly understand the intended message. The following section covers the punctuation marks most frequently encountered in management writing.

Rules

Comma [,]

The comma is a mark used for two basic functions: (1) to divide and (2) to replace.

To divide: Before I came to college, I worked at a fast-food restaurant. [The comma *divides* the dependent clause from the main clause.]

To replace: I flew to Boston; Brian, to Miami. [The comma in the second clause *replaces* the word "flew."]

Few problems occur with the replacement function. Therefore, the following comma rules will highlight the most frequent problems encountered with the dividing function.

1.   Use a comma to divide main clauses joined by a coordinating conjunction (for, and, nor, but, or, yet, so).

  Yes: I will send you my report next week, and you can give me feedback when we meet next month. [The comma divides two independent clauses joined by *and*.]

  Note: If the first clause in a compound sentence is very short (five or fewer words), you may omit the comma. However, use commas whenever you want to *force* a pause in the reading.

  Yes: I'll turn off the lights and you lock the door.

  Yes: Marianne called 9-1-1 and I administered the Heimlich maneuver to dislodge the candy.

  Yes: He heard my message, but he didn't respond.

  Note: A clause with two verb phrases generally does not require commas to divide the verb phrases.

  No: We'll launch the new marketing plan on January 1, and expect to see improved sales within two weeks. [This sentence includes one independent clause with two verb phrases beginning with *launch* and *expect*.]

  Yes: We'll launch the new marketing plan on January 1 and expect to see improved sales within two weeks. [No comma is required between the two verb phrases.]

  Yes: We'll launch the new marketing plan on January 1, and we'll expect to see improved sales within two weeks. [Here the sentence is changed from one independent clause with two verb phrases to two independent clauses, thus requiring a dividing comma before the word and.]

2.   Place a comma after many *introductory* elements, such as dependent clauses, introductory phrases, and transitional words, and wherever confusion might occur without a comma.

  Yes: Before you attempt to fix the switch, be sure to turn the computer off. [A dependent clause.]

  Yes: After working with that group for more than a year, I think I understand where they're headed. [A long introductory phrase.]

  Yes: Nevertheless, I think she is the best person for the management position. [An introductory transition word.]

  Yes: Before shooting, the hunter looked beyond his target to make sure no people would be injured. [Confusion would occur without the comma.]

3.   Use a comma to divide *all* items in a series.

  No: I asked for markers, erasers and flip charts.

  Yes: I asked for markers, erasers, and flip charts. [DO use a comma before the conjunction preceding the last item in a series.]

  No: For this class you'll need a textbook, a computer and printer and pencils and notepads. [Confusing!]

  Yes: For this class you'll need a textbook, a computer and printer, and pencils and notepads. [Much better.]

4.   Use a comma to divide adjacent adjectives that could be divided with the word *and* or that could be reversed without changing the meaning.

No: The lengthy detailed report was finished last night.

Yes: The lengthy, detailed report was finished last night. ["The lengthy *and* detailed report" or "the detailed, lengthy report . . ."]

5. Use a comma to divide nonessential, or interrupting, sentence elements from essential sentence elements.

Yes: He was, however, flawless in the way he presented the material. [*However* interrupts the main sentence flow.]

Yes: He was flawless in the way he presented the material, however.

Yes: Pick up the annual report, assuming it is completed, and take it to the printer. [*Assuming it is completed* interrupts the main sentence flow.]

Yes: Let's use red for the company logo, not blue. [*Not blue* gives additional, or nonessential, information.]

Yes: I'd like you to meet Gary, my second-oldest son, who will be traveling with us. [My second-oldest son is not essential to the meaning of the sentence.]

Yes: My son Gary is the person you'll meet this morning. [*Gary* is an essential appositive. Without the word *Gary,* the sentence would not be clear.]

6. Insert commas before and after the year when the month, day, and year are given. Don't use a comma with a partial date or a date written in day, month, year format.

Yes: The meeting on July 23, 20XX, will be held in Dallas.

Yes: The September 20XX deadline cannot be adjusted.

Yes: The report was first issued on 16 September 20XX.

7. Use commas to divide elements of an address. Place commas before and after the last element, except when a ZIP code is the last element.

Yes: We'll be moving our corporate office to Chicago, Illinois, next year.

Yes: He lives at 460 North Oakcrest Lane, Springville, UT 84663, but he'll be moving soon.

8. Use commas where they are needed for clarification.

Yes: Tess, we must take action now. [Use a comma in a direct address.]

Yes: He remarked, "I have lived here for less than a year." [Insert a comma before a full-sentence direct quotation.]

Yes: She said the article reported "hundreds of lay-offs during the economic downturn." [A comma is not needed for partial-sentence quotations.]

Semicolon [;]

Think of a semicolon as a *super-comma,* a divider more powerful than the lowly comma.

1. Use a semicolon to divide two independent clauses not joined by a coordinating conjunction.

No: Last year was our worst since 1989, next year will be much better. [This is an example of a *comma splice.*]

Yes: Last year was our worst since 1989; next year will be much better. [No conjunction is used; therefore, a semicolon is required.]

Yes: Last year was our worst since 1989, but next year will be much better. [A comma is acceptable because a conjunction is used.]

Yes: Last year was our worst since 1989. Next year will be much better.

2. Use a semicolon before a conjunctive adverb that joins two independent clauses. Examples of conjunctive adverbs are however, nevertheless, thus, and hence.

Yes: The shipment arrived on schedule; however, the chemicals were not included. [*However* is a conjunctive adverb joining the two independent clauses.]

Yes: The shipment did, however, arrive on schedule. [Here the word *however* is not used between two independent clauses; therefore, it is not preceded by a semicolon.]

3. If necessary to prevent confusion, a semicolon may be inserted to divide parallel sentence elements that have commas.

Yes: I can't attend the executive meeting this month; but I'll send Steve, the assistant store manager, who will present our status report.

[The second clause has internal commas. Therefore, the two clauses are divided by the more powerful semicolon, showing that the main sentence division occurs where the semicolon occurs, not where the commas occur.]

Yes: Attending this meeting will be Steve, Assistant Store Manager; Avery, Director of Purchasing; and Natalie, Director of Advertising. [Semicolons are used *between* items in this series; commas are used *within* each item in the series.]

4. Use a semicolon before *e.g.* (meaning *for example*) and *i.e.* (meaning *that is*) when no other punctuation is used to set off the e.g. or i.e.

Yes: Let's also involve several other media; e.g., brochure, website, and billboard.

Yes: Let's also involve several other media (e.g., brochure, website, and billboard).

Yes: This year, let's work hard on the most pressing problem in our department; i.e., lack of proper training.

Yes: This year, let's work hard on the most pressing problem in our department (i.e., lack of proper training).

Colon [:]

Use the colon to introduce. Leave only one space after a colon, and do not begin the following word with a capital letter unless it is a proper noun or begins a direct quotation or complete sentence.

1. Make sure the colon is preceded by a full independent clause that introduces.

No: I bought presents for: Bridget and Kyle. ["I bought presents for" is not a full independent clause.]

Yes: I bought presents for Bridget and Kyle.

No: Make hotel reservations for: (a) March 10, (b) April 13, and (c) May 11.

Yes: Make hotel reservations for the following dates: (a) March 10, (b) April 13, and (c) May 11.

Note: When items in a series follow a colon, they may be arranged in one of several ways, depending on how much emphasis is desired.

Yes: The following three shipments arrived on schedule: January 15, March 1, and May 30. [Low emphasis]

Yes: I'll be responsible for three of the tasks: (a) scheduling the building, (b) sending out fliers, and (c) welcoming the guests. [Moderate emphasis]

Yes: I'll bring the following items:

1. Hamburgers
2. Soft drinks
3. Dessert

[Heavy emphasis. Notice that no comma is required after *"Hamburgers"* or *"Soft drinks,"* and no period is required after *"Dessert."*]

2. Use a colon after the salutation in formal business letters.

No: Dear Mr. Gentry, [A comma may be used in very informal letters, such as "Dear Mom,"]

Yes: Dear Mr. Gentry:

Dash [—]

A dash may be used to set off sentence interrupters, to emphasize, or to introduce.

1. Use a dash to set off interrupters or to emphasize.

Yes: He implied—although he didn't exactly say it—that our plant might be the next one to shut down.

Yes: Plan to attend Friday's training session—it will be very worthwhile.

Yes: We're holding a party Friday evening to socialize—and to highlight our record-setting sales.

2. Use a dash to introduce (in place of a colon).

Yes: He had only one message for her—find a new job!

Note: A dash is longer than a hyphen. If you don't use a real dash (the one in your word processor's special character set), use two hyphens. As a general rule, do not leave any space before or after the dash.

Hyphen [-]

A hyphen is used to connect prefixes and word pairs.

1. Use a hyphen in the following situations:

- The prefix ends with the same letter that begins the main word; e.g., anti-inflammatory.
- The word might be mistaken for another word; e.g., reform vs. re-form.

- The prefix is *self;* e.g., self-assured (but not selfless or selfish).
- The word is likely to be mispronounced; e.g., coworker vs. co-worker.
- The base word is capitalized; e.g., non-American.
- The base is a number; e.g., pre-1990.

2. Hyphenate compound adjectives when they *precede* a noun or pronoun. A compound adjective is two or more modifiers that act *jointly* as one modifier.

No: Send me an up to date report. [Not an *up* report, a *to* report, or a *date* report, but an *up-to-date* report.]

Yes: Send me an up-to-date report.

No: Is this report up-to-date?

Yes: Is this report up to date? [The modifier *follows* the noun; therefore, no hyphens are needed.]

No: The small business managers will meet next month in St. Louis. [Small managers?]

Yes: The small-business managers will meet next month in St. Louis. [The businesses are small, not their managers.]

No: We used the six and eight-foot ladders last year.

Yes: We used the six- and eight-foot ladders last year. [A *floating* hyphen is needed to show the connection between *six* and *foot.*]

Note: Hyphens aren't needed after adverbs with *ly* endings. The *ly* ending adequately indicates that the adverb modifies the subsequent word.

No: That was a carefully-calculated strategy.

Yes: That was a carefully calculated strategy.

3. Usually do not use hyphens with the following prefixes: re, pre, sub, mis, or semi.

No: You will be required to take a pre-test before the course begins.

Yes: You will be required to take a pretest before the course begins.

Note: To enhance the readability of text, try to avoid hyphenating words at the end of a line or page.

No: Riverside School has introduced a program that enables parents to participate as volunteers. Although this program has been success-

ful, it has not been without an accompanying set of problems.

Yes: Riverside School has introduced a program that enables parents to participate as volunteers. Although this program has been successful, it has not been without an accompanying set of problems.

Parentheses [( )]

1. Use parentheses to set off incidental comments, to introduce abbreviations that will be used later in the document, or to enclose enumerations.

Yes: Use red and green (Christmas colors) for the December ads.

Yes: I attended Oklahoma State University (OSU) for two years.

No: I have attended three schools: 1) Utah State University, 2) University of Arizona, and 3) Oklahoma State University. [Both left and right parentheses are preferred.]

Yes: I have attended three schools: (1) Utah State University, (2) University of Arizona, and (3) Oklahoma State University.

Apostrophe [']—see "Possessive Case" p. 213.

Quotation Marks [" "]

Quotation marks indicate just what their name implies: They surround *verbatim* statements spoken or written by someone else. They may also be used to surround some titles or words used in a special way.

1. Use quotation marks for direct quotations but not for paraphrases.

Yes: Christine said, "I'll accept your proposal." [Direct quotation.]

No: Christine said she "would accept his proposal." [A paraphrase—not a direct quotation.]

Yes: Christine said she would accept his proposal.

2. Use quotation marks properly with other forms of punctuation.

No: Christine said, "I'll accept your proposal".

Yes: Christine said, "I'll accept your proposal." [Commas and periods at the end of a quotation always go inside the quotation marks.]

Yes: He has a good understanding of the "underground movement"; therefore, he should be a member of the special-investigation team. [Colons and semicolons at the end of a quotation nearly always go outside the quotation marks.]

Yes: Jesse asked, "What have we here?" [Place the question mark and exclamation point inside the quotation marks when they apply only to the quoted material.]

Yes: Jacob said, "I'd like to quote my father: 'Never underestimate the power of determination.'" [A quotation within a quotation requires single quotation marks.]

Ellipsis [. . .]

An ellipsis is a series of three periods, with a space before and after each period, usually used to indicate an omission in a quotation. (In informal writing the ellipsis may be used to indicate an omission or a pause.)

1. Leave a space before and after an ellipsis.

   No: "Our goal is to be the best. . .in the industry."

   Yes: "Our goal is to be the best . . . in the industry." [Ellipsis replaces "Arizona-based firm."]

2. Use the ellipsis to indicate omitted text, retaining the same punctuation marks (e.g., commas or periods) that would occur with full text.

   Yes: "Before we build . . . , we will have to increase sales by 200 percent." [Omitted from the first clause is "a new building."]

   Yes: "Before we build, . . . we will have to increase sales by 200 percent." [Omitted from the second clause is "the budget director says."]

   Yes: "This policy will produce a major snowball effect. . . ." [In an unfinished but grammatically complete sentence, the first dot is the period; the last three dots are the ellipsis.]

   Yes: "This policy will produce . . ." [In an unfinished and incomplete sentence, there is no terminal punctuation.]

Period [.]

1. Use periods with the following abbreviations. Do not use periods with acronyms (initials pronounced as a word).

Yes:

Dr.	Jr.	Mr.	Ms.	C. W. Smith
Ave.	Corp.	Inc.	Ltd.	a.m. (or AM)
et al.	etc.	e.g.	i.e.	No.
				(Nos. = plural)

No: The rocket was launched this morning by N.A.S.A. [An acronym pronounced as "nasa."]

Yes: The rocket was launched this morning by NASA.

2. Avoid commas or semicolons at the end of items in a bulleted list. Generally, use periods only at the end of complete sentences. Use consistent punctuation for all items in a list.

   No:
   - 20 reams of paper.
   - 8 boxes of pencils.
   - 3 staplers.

   Yes:
   - 20 reams of paper
   - 8 boxes of pencils
   - 3 staplers

   Yes:
   - Close the Dallas office.
   - Combine the two Canadian offices.
   - Hire a new manager for the Portland office.

3. Use a period with a polite request that asks for an action rather than for a yes or no response.

   No: Will you please send me your email address?

   Yes: Will you please send me your email address. [Requests action.]

Punctuation Quiz

For each of the following quiz questions, select the best option (a, b, c, or d).

1. Which of the following is punctuated correctly?
   a. Andrew learned about bears, which are mammals, sharks, which are fish, and alligators, which are reptiles.
   b. This job requires long, tiring hours of work, but you will have great people to work with.
   c. I'm going to plant: broccoli, spinach (a cool weather variety), and lettuce.
   d. We rode our mountain bikes to the top of the trail, we then turned around and came back.

2. Which of the following is punctuated correctly?

   a. You call Sam and I'll call Ryan—then we can relax.

   b. Eilley said her experience with this low budget airline company has been great, so she said she is going to "recommend it without hesitation . . ."

   c. Coming down the home stretch the lead horse fell, and threw the rider.

   d. Jess Lamb, my new boss said he is planning some major changes but he declined to say what they will be.

3. Which of the following is punctuated correctly?

   a. I didn't really like the main course, however, the dessert was wonderful.

   b. Frank's birthday party, which will be at noon on Friday; will be held at Roberto's Restaurant.

   c. His stubborn minded attitude about the change made life difficult for everyone on the sixth-floor.

   d. Be sure to bring your (a) pencil, (b) notebook, and (c) water bottle.

4. Which of the following is punctuated correctly?

   a. She said the terrorism threat: "would continue to pose a threat throughout the summer."

   b. We'll have lunch at El Rio Cafe, and then go shopping at several hardware stores, e.g., Home Start, Long's, and Anderson Home Center.

   c. Matt asked Linden, "When can you meet on Friday"?

   d. We have several seven- and ten-passenger vans in our motor pool.

5. Which of the following is punctuated correctly?

   a. His pace was slow and erratic, nevertheless, he finished the marathon ahead of 47 other runners.

   b. He's a plodder but he always does top-notch work.

   c. You'll find; however, that you get ahead only when you speak up.

   d. I'm taking my son, Matt, on the Boston trip. [I have three sons.]

6. Which of the following is punctuated correctly?

   a. We'll return on February 27, 200X and will be available to meet within a few days after that.

   b. Jacob said he could meet on 3 March 200X or on 17 March 200X.

   c. He says he'll accept nothing but cold-hard cash!

   d. Erin said, "Karen, I think you should be in charge of that activity".

7. Which of the following is punctuated correctly?

   a. The first is obvious, provide more healthy lunches to school children.

   b. On August 13, 2002 their group filed a class action lawsuit against the company.

   c. She lives on 178 Elkhorn Drive, Alpine, UT 84004.

   d. He lacks self control but should not be given any anti-depressants.

ERRORS OF SENTENCES

Grammatical errors in your writing can severely undermine your credibility and present an image of ignorance or laziness, rather than that of a competent professional. The best way to avoid making errors in sentences is to understand and apply proper rules of case, agreement and reference, tense, numbers, and capitalization.

CASE

Case encompasses the three different types of nouns and pronouns: (1) subjective (or nominative), (2) objective, and (3) possessive. Deciding which of the three "cases" is appropriate depends on how nouns and pronouns are used in each sentence.

- Subjective case (as the *subject* in a clause)
- Objective case (as the *object* of some action)
- Possessive case (as the *owner* of something)

She	gave *me*	a copy of *her* book.
Subjective case (she)	**Objective case** (me)	**Possessive case** (her)

The charts that follow show the different case types for first-, second-, and third-person situations, and how the different cases can be used in a simple sentence.

Case Chart

Case	1st Person Singular Pronoun	1st Person Plural Pronouns	2nd Person Singular and Plural Pronouns	3rd Person Singular Pronouns	3rd Person Plural Pronouns	Relative Pronouns
Subjective	I	we	you	he, she, it	they	who, which, that, what, whatever, whoever
Objective	me	us	you	him, her, it	them	whom, whomever, which, whichever
Possessive	my, mine	our, ours	your, yours	his, her, hers, its	their, theirs	whose

Using Cases in a Simple Sentence

Subjective Case		Objective Case		Possessive Case	
I	gave	me	a copy of	my	book.
We		us		our	
You		you		your	
He		him		his	
Who		whom		whose	
She		her		her	
It		it		its	
They		them		their	

Rules

Most case situations are easy to understand, but the following rules sometimes cause confusion.

Subjective Case

1. Always use the subjective case for the subject of a clause.

   No: Me and him have been there many times.

   Yes: He and I have been there many times. [With two subjects or two objects, one of which is you, always put yourself last. Do not say, "I and he have been there many times."]

   Note: Use the subjective case for the subject of a clause, even when the subject is also the object of a previous clause.

   No: Assign the task to whomever is there.

   Yes: Assign the task to whoever is there. [*Whoever* is the subject of *is there,* but *whoever* is also the object of *Assign the task to.* In this situation, the subjective case takes precedence over the objective case.]

2. Use the subjective case for a noun or pronoun that completes the meaning of a being verb (am, is, are, was, were, will be, has been, etc.).

   No: It was her who answered the phone.

   Yes: It was she who answered the phone. [Think of a *being verb* (e.g., is, are, was) as an *equal* sign: "*It is she*" is the same as "*It = she.*"]

Objective Case

1. Use the objective case for all objects.

   No: Send your replies to Richard or myself.

   Yes: Send your replies to Richard or me.

   Note: The word *myself* may be used for intensive or reflexive situations.

   Intensive: I myself will be there.

   Reflexive: I hit myself with the racquet.

   No: Julia asked she and I to give the report.

   No: Julia asked her and I to give the report.

Yes: Julia asked her and me to give the report. [To decide which case is appropriate with compound pronouns, think of each pronoun alone; e.g., "Julia asked *her* to give the report" and "Julia asked *me* to give the report."]

No: The technical support representative showed we sales representatives how to use the new program.

Yes: The technical support representative showed us sales representatives how to use the new program.

No: You gave the message to who?

Yes: You gave the message to whom? [In who/whom situations, think of *who* as being *he* and of *whom* as being *him*. For example, think of "You gave the message to *whom?*" as "You gave the message to *him?*"]

Possessive Case

The possessive case enables nouns and pronouns to show ownership. Instead of saying "the home of the man," we can say, "the man's home." Many possessive-case applications require using the apostrophe ['']. The apostrophe is used to indicate possession, to mark omissions in contractions, and to prevent confusion in certain unusual situations.

1. For a singular noun or pronoun, show possession by adding an apostrophe and an *s*.

   Yes: Give the gift to Jennifer's sister Carol.

   Yes: The company's stock price has fallen dramatically during the past eight months.

2. To show possession by more than one person, place the apostrophe after the plural form of the word. First form the plural and then apply the apostrophe.

Singular Form	Plural Form	Plural Possessive Form
manager	managers	managers' handbook
Mr. and Mrs. Jackson	the Jacksons	Jacksons' new house
man	men	men's clothing store
child	children	children's toys
boy	boys	boys' bikes

No: The boys bike got stolen. [One boy's bike.]

Yes: The boy's bike got stolen. [One boy's bike.]

No: The boy's bikes got stolen. [Two or more boys' bikes.]

Yes: The boys' bikes got stolen. [Two or more boys' bikes.]

No: The childrens' mother was selected to represent the school. [More than one child.]

Yes: The children's mother was selected to represent the school. [More than one child.]

Note: Usually you should apply Rules 1 and 2 for possessive words ending in an s or z sound; but be aware that it is also common to add the apostrophe without an extra *s*, especially if the word sounds better without the extra *s*.

No: General Motors's first-quarter earnings were up by 3 percent.

Yes: General Motors' first-quarter earnings were up by 3 percent.

No: Bill Gates's influence has been immense.

Yes: Bill Gates' influence has been immense.

Yes: Jose Gonzalez' house is on fire! [Acceptable.]

Yes: Jose Gonzalez's house is on fire!

Yes: The Gonzalez' house is on fire! [Acceptable.]

Yes: The Gonzalezes' house is on fire!

3. Do not add an apostrophe for personal possessive pronouns, such as hers, his, its, ours, theirs, or yours. Add an apostrophe with indefinite possessive pronouns, such as everyone's, no one's, and anybody's. Also, add an apostrophe for inanimate objects.

No: Look at the poor dog; it's left ear has been bitten. [Because "it's" is a contraction for "it is," this sentence is saying: "Look at the poor dog; it is left ear has been bitten."]

Yes: Look at the poor dog; its left ear has been bitten.

No: Wednesdays meeting will be short.

Yes: Wednesday's meeting will be short.

No: The new products entry into the marketplace had an immediate impact on everyones bottom line.

Yes: The new product's entry into the marketplace had an immediate impact on everyone's bottom line.

4. For multiple owners of an item, place an apostrophe only with the last owner. For individual ownership, place an apostrophe with each owner.

   No: Joan's and Brent's cars were sold a month ago. [Joan and Brent jointly owned the cars.]

   Yes: Joan and Brent's cars were sold a month ago.

   No: Joan and Brent's cars were sold a month ago. [Joan and Brent own cars individually.]

   Yes: Joan's and Brent's cars were sold a month ago.

5. Use the apostrophe for clarification in unusual constructions.

   Yes: Two Ph.D.'s attended the event.

   Yes: Last semester she earned all A's on her report card.

6. Whenever a noun or pronoun occurs before a gerund (the "ing" form of a verb), use the possessive case if the emphasis is on the gerund (the action). Use the objective case if the emphasis is on the performer of the action. (Note: The possessive case is appropriate in most situations with this type of sentence construction.)

   No: Maria questioning every decision is annoying.

   Yes: Maria's questioning every decision is annoying. [Emphasis is on the gerund *questioning,* not on Maria.]

   No: I can't imagine his being late.

   Yes: I can't imagine him being late. [Emphasis is on *him,* not on the gerund *being.*]

Case Quiz

For each of the following quiz questions, select the best option (a, b, c, or d).

1. In the sentence, "I am sorry you missed yesterday's meeting," what case is represented with "I"?
   a. Subjective
   b. Possessive
   c. Objective
   d. Declarative

2. Which of the following represents "third-person singular objective" case?
   a. Mine
   b. Him
   c. They
   d. Who

3. Which item is correct?
   a. I sent the laser pointer to Dan and Jake; I assume it is their's.
   b. Dan and me will be in charge of the activities.
   c. Dan and I will be in charge of Friday's activities.
   d. Dan and myself will take charge of the activities.

4. Which item is correct?
   a. Katherine and myself are going to sponsor next months racquetball tournament.
   b. Katherine asked if you and me would help with the publicity.
   c. Call Jennifer Larkin and see if it is she who wants to work with the children's program.
   d. If Jennifer isn't home, talk with whomever answers the phone.

5. Which item is correct?
   a. She and I visited the school to recruit any volunteers whom would like to participate.
   b. After our work on the December project, he gave the new design assignment to Heather and I.
   c. When you're finished, give the completed document to the receptionist or myself.
   d. They encouraged us sales representatives to revisit all our old accounts.

6. Which item is correct?
   a. Tyler's wife's friend came to spend the weekend.
   b. Tylers wife's friend came to spend the weekend.
   c. Tylers' wife's friend came for the weekend.
   d. Tyler's wifes' friend came for the weekend.

7. Which item is correct?
   a. Lets drive to Kaysville and see the Hansen's new house.
   b. Let's drive to Kaysville and see the Hansens' new house.
   c. Let's drive to Kaysville and see the Hansen's new house.
   d. Lets drive to Kaysville and see the Hansens' new house.

8. Which item is correct?
   a. Terry and Ben's immunization records have not been updated.
   b. Terry's and Ben's immunization records have not been updated.
   c. Terry's and Ben's pet fish is four inches long.
   d. Terry and Ben let their fish finish it's meal before changing the water in the fish bowl.

9. Which item is correct?

   a. The Rodriguez's reputation was tarnished by their son's bad behavior. [One son]

   b. Jesus' teachings include many memorable parables.

   c. The mens' department is upstairs.

   d. My childrens' teacher said she will be retiring in two more years. [Two children]

10. Which item is correct?

   a. I get tired of him jumping to conclusions before we have a chance to present our whole story. [Emphasis is on the person, not on the action "jumping."]

   b. I get tired of his jumping to conclusions before we have a chance to present our whole story. [Emphasis is on the person.]

   c. Whom do you think will win the competition?

   d. I told the counselor that we would work with whomever needed the most help.

AGREEMENT AND REFERENCE

Agreement refers to consistency among the various parts of a sentence. Sentence elements must agree in three major ways: (1) number—singular or plural, (2) person—first, second, or third, and (3) gender—masculine, feminine, or neuter (neither). In each of your messages, be sure to maintain a consistent point of view within each of these three writing aspects.

Number:

Singular—one person or thing; e.g., "*Ken is* my brother."

Plural—more than one person or thing; e.g., "*We are* competing on Saturday."

Person:

First—the writer or speaker; e.g., "*I am* the speaker."

Second—the person to whom the message is being written or spoken; e.g., "*You are* going to like this movie."

Third—someone or something else; e.g., "*She is* going to call me back."

Note: When writing business messages, maintain a consistent point of view with regard to *person*. Writing in first person is usually preferable, except in very formal situations where third person is appropriate.

First person: *We* recommend that you sell this property. [Less formal]

Third person: *The analysts* recommend that the property be sold. [More formal]

Gender:

Masculine—male; e.g., "*He* cannot keep *his* appointment."

Feminine—female; e.g., "*She* hurt *her* ankle."

Neuter—neither/either male or female; e.g., "The *dollar* found *its* way back into my wallet."

To help achieve sentence agreement, follow a two-step process:

1. Find the true subject(s) of the clause.

2. Make the rest of the clause agree with the subject(s).

Follow a similar two-step formula to make pronouns and their antecedents (the words to which they have reference) agree:

1. Find the true antecedent of the pronoun.

2. Make the pronoun agree with the antecedent.

RULES

1. When a subject and verb are separated by a prepositional phrase ending with a plural word, make the verb agree with the subject, not with the plural word in the prepositional phrase.

    No: One of our owners are planning to retire next year.

    Yes: One of our owners is planning to retire next year. [*One* is the subject, not *owners*.]

    No: One of the women who is running for mayor is dropping out.

    Yes: One of the women who are running for mayor is dropping out. [This sentence actually has a minor clause nested within the main clause. It could be rewritten as, "Of the women **who** are running for mayor, **one** is dropping out."]

    Note: Treat company names as singular.

    No: Robert Jensen & Associates were omitted from our list.

    Yes: Robert Jensen & Associates was omitted from our list.

2. Use plural verbs with all compound subjects (two or more subjects) joined by *and*.

No: The computer and printer is on sale.

Yes: The computer and printer are on sale.

No: Having an idea and implementing it is two different things.

Yes: Having an idea and implementing it are two different things.

No: Planning the conference and the party are very taxing.

Yes: Planning the conference and the party is very taxing. [This clause has only one subject: *Planning.*]

3. If two subjects are joined by *either-or, neither-nor,* or *not only-but also* conjunctions, the latter subject governs the verb form. If a singular and a plural subject are used, place the plural subject nearer the verb to avoid awkward-sounding construction.

No: Either Dale or Wally are up for promotion.

Yes: Either Dale or Wally is up for promotion.

Yes: Either is capable of being a good manager.

No: Neither Dale nor Wally are up for promotion.

Yes: Neither Dale nor Wally is up for promotion.

Yes: Neither is up for promotion.

No: Roger Anderson or the Smiths is going to host the meeting.

No: The Smiths or Roger Anderson are going to host the meeting.

Yes: The Smiths or Roger Anderson is going to host the meeting. [Grammatically correct, but awkward sounding.]

Yes: Roger Anderson or the Smiths are going to host the meeting. [Best.]

4. Treat collective words as singular or plural, depending on how they're used in the sentence; e.g., all, any, more, most, none, some, who, that, and which.

Yes: Some of the soup is left.

Yes: Some of the flowers are dying.

Yes: All of the fans are leaving the stadium.

Yes: All of the morning is left for free time.

Note: The following words are always singular—anybody, each, everybody, everyone, much, no one, nobody, and one.

5. Be consistent in using singular or plural forms.

No: Each member told of their experiences with Michael.

Yes: Each member told of his or her experiences with Michael. [Better.]

Yes: All members told of their experiences with Michael. [Best.]

6. Use relative pronouns (who, that, and which) properly.

Who Refers to people.
Introduces essential and nonessential clauses.

That Refers to things or to groups.
Generally introduces essential clauses.

Which Refers to things or to groups.
Generally introduces nonessential clauses.

No: He's the one that will be hired.

Yes: He's the one who will be hired. [*That* refers to things. *Who* refers to people.]

Yes: Give a notebook to all the programmers who attend.

No: The team who wins will be honored next week.

Yes: The team that wins will be honored next week. [The team is a group.]

No: The memo which is in my mailbox came from Spencer.

Yes: The memo that is in my mailbox came from Spencer. [*That is in my mailbox* is essential to the meaning of the sentence.]

No: This car, that I dearly love, has over 200,000 miles on it and must be sold.

Yes: This car, which I dearly love, has over 200,000 miles on it and must be sold. [*Which I dearly love* is not essential to the meaning of the sentence.]

7. Avoid inappropriate gender references.

No: Each manager should make sure he stays within budget guidelines. [Not all managers are male.]

Yes: Each manager should make sure he or she stays within budget guidelines. [Better than the first, but wordy.]

Yes: Managers should make sure they stay within budget guidelines. [Best.]

8. Avoid ambiguous antecedents and references.

No: If the food is too hot for the baby, put it in the refrigerator for a few minutes. [Who is *it,* the baby or the food?]

Yes: If the food is too hot for the baby, put the food in the refrigerator for a few minutes.

No: Fifteen employees will be laid off next Friday. This will trim our payroll expenses to a more manageable level. [This what?]

Yes: Fifteen employees will be laid off next Friday. This *layoff* will trim our payroll expenses to a more manageable level.

No: When Kristen talked with Amy, she said her mother was feeling better. [Unclear *she!*]

Yes: When Amy talked with Kristen, Amy said, "My mother is feeling better."

Agreement and Reference Quiz

For each of the following quiz questions, select the best option (a, b, c, or d).

1. Which item is correct?
   a. The road to three of the most famous canyons are not passable after heavy rainstorms.
   b. The person that you have to talk with won't be available until next Tuesday.
   c. One of the candidates who are being evaluated is my nephew.
   d. Two of the candidates, which I believe are the strongest, are cousins.

2. Which item is correct?
   a. Each college athlete tries to surpass his personal best.
   b. Every fireman will participate in the nationwide food drive next Thursday.
   c. Each flight attendant must be thoroughly trained in first aid before she can fly.
   d. One of my grandparents is coming for a visit this weekend.

3. Which item is preferable?
   a. Either Alisha or her roommates are responsible for cleaning the apartment.
   b. Either her roommates or Alisha is/are responsible for cleaning the apartment.
   c. Either Alisha or her roommates is responsible for cleaning the apartment.
   d. Either her roommates or Alisha are responsible for cleaning the apartment.

4. Which item is correct?
   a. Each of the workers are planning to attend the Christmas party next Friday night.
   b. I think she is the one that should be put in charge of the San Francisco office.
   c. The legislation which governs PM10 standards has been particularly important in this valley.
   d. The researchers discovered that their hard drive had crashed and that all their data had been destroyed.

5. Which item is correct?
   a. This old sweater, which I've had for over ten years, is ready for retirement.
   b. Neither bad weather nor armies is enough to stop our progress.
   c. Kaleb's father said he needs to eat more healthful food and lose about 20 pounds.
   d. One of the athletes who is competing in the international track meet is being held hostage.

6. Which item is correct?
   a. If the parents haven't picked up their children by 5:30 p.m., have them go to Room 266.
   b. Fred Jepson & Sons is a reliable plumbing company.
   c. Fred Jepson & Sons are a reliable plumbing company.
   d. The players and the coach is to attend the orientation meeting on Saturday.

7. Which item is correct?
   a. Either Andrew or Benson are being considered for a promotion.
   b. One of the ads we placed in Sunday's newspapers is printed upside down.
   c. If the children are too noisy for the teachers, remind them of our discipline policy.
   d. The young students will visit our campus on Project Youth day; this will be a positive influence in their lives.

TENSE

Tense refers to *when* some action occurred or *when* some condition existed, whether in the past, present, or future. As a writer, you are responsible for placing your words in accurate time sequences. The key is to decide the precise time from which you are writing. Then write everything that occurred prior to that time in past tense, everything that is happening at that time in present tense, and everything that will happen after that time in future tense.

For example, if I were sitting in a meeting on January 13 at 1:30 p.m., I might write the following: "I didn't feel well [past] before I came to the meeting; therefore, I think [present] I will leave [future] early." There you have all three tenses in one sentence, and they are correct because they are consistent with your particular "time" point of view. The chart at the top of the next page will help you understand different conjugations of verb tenses.

Using proper tense is quite intuitive, and most writers have little difficulty with tense in their writing. However, five rules will help where problems seem to occur most frequently.

RULES

1. Maintain a consistent point of time. Decide the exact time point on which your document's tense will be based, and then adjust the tense of all verbs accordingly. (This rule is most frequently violated in spoken communication.)

   No: I was running down the hall when I see the doctor coming out of the delivery room.

   Yes: I was running down the hall when I saw the doctor coming out of the delivery room. [All happened in the past.]

2. Use the present tense to describe a relatively permanent truth or condition.

   No: I was always taught that the Bible was true.

   Yes: I was always taught that the Bible is true. [The Bible is still true.]

   No: In her *Wall Street Journal* article, Gabriella described the problems of a multicultural neighborhood.

   Yes: In her *Wall Street Journal* article, Gabriella describes the problems of a multicultural neighborhood. [The article still exists.]

   No: He remembered that I liked chocolate-covered nuts.

   Yes: He remembered that I like chocolate-covered nuts. [I still do.]

   Note: You may also use the present tense for text that you want the reader to assume is happening in the present.

   Yes: In the year 20XX, I see us expanding into more international markets.

   Yes: "President of XYZ Corporation Dies in Tragic Plane Crash" [Newspaper headline.]

3. When an infinitive (the word *to* followed by a verb) follows a verb in the past or past-perfect tense, shift the infinitive verb to the present tense.

Tense Chart*

Verb Form	Past Tense	Past-Perfect Tense	Present Tense	Present-Perfect Tense	Future Tense	Future-Perfect Tense
Being verb	I was	I had been	I am	I have been	I will be	I will have been
Irregular action verb	I wrote	I had written	I write	I have written	I will write	I will have written
Regular action verb	We hired	We had hired	We hire	We have hired	We will hire	We will have hired
Progressive form	I was writing	I had been writing	I am writing	I have been writing	I will be writing	I will have been writing

*Remember, *regular* verbs form their past tense by adding the "ed" sound to the end of the word as in taste/tast*ed* or consider/consid*ered*. *Irregular* verbs form their past tense by changing the verb itself, such as run/*ran* and drive/*drove*. Check the dictionary when in doubt (if the dictionary gives no additional forms, the verb is regular).

No: I wanted to have attended your wedding reception, but I couldn't.

Yes: I wanted to attend your wedding reception, but I couldn't. [*To have attended* is shifted to the present tense *to attend*.]

No: We would have liked to have spent more time in Germany, but we had to get back home.

Yes: We would have liked to spend more time in Germany, but we had to get back home.

4. For irregular verbs, use the correct form for all "perfect" tenses, as shown in the chart on the next page.)

No: Grace hadn't went to get the supplies when I last talked with her.

Yes: Grace hadn't gone to get the supplies when I last talked with her.

5. Use the appropriate verb for subjunctive mood. Sentences can be constructed in one of three moods: indicative, imperative, and subjunctive.

Indicative mood is used to make a statement of fact. Most management writing is in indicative mood.

Example: More parents should be involved in education.

Example: We will likely receive three benefits.

Imperative mood is used to give a command or make a direct request. It always involves the implied second-person subject "you." Imperative mood is concise and direct and is useful in giving commands or explaining procedures. If it seems too strong, add softening words before the main verb; e.g., "*Please* get more parents involved . . ."

Example: Get Annabelle to cover for you in today's meeting. [Understood as "*You* get Annabelle . . ."]

Example: Turn the power switch to the "on" position. [Understood as "*You* turn . . ."]

Subjunctive mood is used to express a supposition, an indirect command or request, or a condition that is not true or not likely to be true.

Example: Suppose parents were to help the teacher. [A supposition.]

Example: I suggest that parents be more involved. [An indirect command.]

Example: If more parents were involved in education, our students would not be having these behavior problems. [A condition that is not true.]

No: If I was you, I'd accept the offer.

Yes: If I were you, I'd accept the offer. [Present tense, subjunctive mood.]

No: If that statement was true, I'd take a different action.

Yes: If that statement were true, I'd take a different action. [Present tense, subjunctive mood.]

No: I wish Tara was here to conduct this meeting.

Yes: I wish Tara were here to conduct this meeting. [Present tense, subjunctive mood.]

Irregular Verb Tense Examples

Base Form	Past	Past Perfect	Base Form	Past	Past Perfect
begin	began	had begun	lie (recline)	lay	had lain
buy	bought	had bought	prove	proved	had proved/en
cling	clung	had clung	see	saw	had seen
come	came	had come	shrink	shrank/shrunk	had shrunk/en
do	did	had done	sing	sang	had sung
go	went	had gone	sit	sat	had sat
hang (suspend)	hung	had hung	swim	swam	had swum
hang (execute)	hanged	had hanged	swing	swung	had swung
lay (put)	laid	had laid	take	took	had taken
lead	led	had led	write	wrote	had written

Yes: I wish Tara had been at the meeting. [Past tense, subjunctive mood.]

Yes: I wish Tara were going to be at the meeting. [Future tense, subjunctive mood.]

Tense Quiz

For each of the following quiz questions, select the best option (a, b, c, or d).

1. Which item is not correct?
   a. He was reading a mystery novel when he heard a loud clap of thunder.
   b. He was slow during the first part of the race, but he is catching up and will likely finish in the top three.
   c. Are you sure he was the one who called you for a date last Saturday?
   d. In five years, I see him starting his own business.

2. Which item is correct?
   a. We would have liked to have stayed for all nine innings, but I had to leave for a meeting.
   b. Mom usually bakes our bread at home, but yesterday she decides to buy several loaves from the bakery.
   c. After I asked her what her maiden name was, I realized that we were cousins.
   d. Jill told me that she doesn't see any point in our continuing negotiations with Robert.

3. Which of the following is a regular verb?
   a. try
   b. go
   c. write
   d. tell

4. Which of the following is written in past-perfect tense?
   a. By the time the Olympics came, he had run over 10,000 miles.
   b. I thought about running for the legislature.
   c. Have you considered working for private industry instead of for a CPA firm?
   d. I have eaten at all the Wendy's restaurants in Utah Valley.

5. Which of the following statements is written in imperative mood?
   a. I wish we were able to purchase the home on Maple Street.
   b. They were all just having fun until the accident happened.
   c. Just to be sure, take her to the emergency room.

   d. The paramedic says he thinks she will need stitches in her forehead.

6. Which of the following statements is not correct?
   a. I want to major in accounting or management information systems.
   b. If I were interested in plants, I would major in horticulture.
   c. After graduation, I plan to work for a major CPA firm.
   d. I suggest that you should attend the important kickoff meeting this Friday.

7. Which of the following statements is correct?
   a. I was driving down 100 South when I suddenly see two vehicles obviously involved in a road-rage incident.
   b. I think what the Bible was trying to say is that we shouldn't condemn, not that we shouldn't judge.
   c. When I heard of his minor theft, I tried to convince him that honesty was the best policy to follow.
   d. I would have liked to attend your reception, but I was out of town attending my uncle's funeral.

8. Which of the following statements is correct?
   a. First, his wife filed for divorce; then his mother dies suddenly.
   b. If today's weather was better, I would be happy to take you to the airport.
   c. If he had went to class like he should have, the accident wouldn't have happened.
   d. Even though I couldn't attend yesterday, I'll be there for sure tomorrow.

9. Which of the following is written in indicative mood?
   a. It is not my responsibility to follow up; you need to have more self-discipline.
   b. Before the weather turns colder, turn the water off in the sprinkler system.
   c. I suggest that she be nominated as next year's co-chair.
   d. Please take the garbage out before you go to school.

10. Which of the following is an example of past-perfect tense?
    a. I was
    b. I had written
    c. We have hired
    d. I will be writing

NUMBERS

The major concern about numbers is whether to write them as numerals (1, 2, 3) or as text (one, two, three). The following number rules will cover most situations you'll encounter. But because number rules have so many exceptions, you'll occasionally have to consult a major style guide for additional answers.

RULES

1. In general, spell out single-digit numbers (one through nine); write as numerals everything larger than nine. All other rules are exceptions to this basic rule. (Some standards vary from this basic rule.)

   No: She is 3 years old.
   Yes: She is three years old.

   No: Bring me fifteen widgets.
   Yes: Bring me 15 widgets.

2. Always spell out numbers that begin sentences.

   No: 11 violations of this policy have occurred since February.
   Yes: Eleven violations of this policy have occurred since February.

3. Use numerals in dates, addresses, percentages, and page references.

   No: I'll call you on March 3rd.
   Yes: I'll call you on the 3rd of March. [Use the "rd" ending only when the day precedes the month.]
   Yes: I'll call you on March 3. [You would normally read this aloud as "March *third*."]
   Yes: I live at 135 North Maple Drive.
   Yes: This year's net income represents a 3.5 percent increase. [Spell out *percent,* rather than using *%*.]
   Yes: Turn to page 5.

4. Use numerals to express time when a.m. or p.m. is used (use a colon to separate the hour figure from the minute figure). Don't use the colon and zeros with full hours unless the full hour is in the same text with a partial hour. Spell the hour in full when *o'clock* is used (e.g., eight o'clock).

   No: Joe will come at eight; Eliza will come at 8:30; and London will come at 9.

   Yes: Joe will come at 8:00 p.m., Eliza will come at 8:30 p.m., and London will come at 9:00 p.m.

   No: Joe will come at 8:00 p.m., and London will come at 9:00 p.m.
   Yes: Joe will come at 8 p.m., and London will come at 9 p.m.

5. Use numbers consistently for mixed numbers in the same category. If the largest number is more than 10, express all numbers in the group as numerals. Spell out the smaller number when numbers of two categories occur side by side.

   No: The group consisted of one major, three lieutenants, and 26 enlisted personnel.
   Yes: The group consisted of 1 major, 3 lieutenants, and 26 enlisted personnel. [All are military offices.]
   Yes: The 11-person delegation visited six European countries. [People and countries are not in the same category.]

   No: I printed 100 30-page booklets.
   Yes: I printed 100 thirty-page booklets.

6. Except in legal documents, write money amounts as numerals. Express even sums of money without the decimal and zeroes, unless the sums are in a group of money amounts that includes both even and uneven figures.

   No: Send the eighty-three dollars you owe me.
   Yes: Send the $83 you owe me.

   No: I received checks for $28, $36.42, and $73.50.
   Yes: I received checks for $28.00, $36.42, and $73.50.

7. For large numbers, use a combination of words and numerals.

   No: Their net profit for last year was seven point two million dollars.
   Yes: Their net profit for last year was $7.2 million. [Read this out loud as "seven point two million dollars."]

8. Use numerals to express decimals and whole numbers with fractions; spell out and hyphenate fractions that stand alone.

Yes: That time period shows a jump of 1.89 points.

Yes: Increase the material by 8 2/3 inches.

No: I took 1/2 of the year for a sabbatical leave.

Yes: I took one-half of the year for a sabbatical leave.

No: I give 1/10 of my income to my church.

Yes: I give one-tenth of my income to my church.

Numbers Quiz

For each of the following quiz questions, select the best option (a, b, c, or d).

1. Which item is correct?
   a. On August 18ᵗʰ, I'll call to confirm my reservation.
   b. I called at 7:00 a.m. and again at 7:30 p.m., but he must have slept through both of my calls.
   c. Only six percent of the voters turned out for this election.
   d. Our company showed a profit of $1,200,000 for the fourth quarter of 2000.

2. Which item is correct?
   a. 10 percent of our clients are enrolled in all three programs.
   b. Although he owed me $56.60, I accepted $50 to settle the debt.
   c. In the months since December, our complaint calls have dropped from 16 to 10 to 6.
   d. I pay 1/10 of my income to my church.

3. Which item is correct?
   a. Our branch office is about twenty miles west of our home office.
   b. 11 of our accountants will be transferred next month.
   c. Our customer research disclosed that 9 percent of our customers are generating over half of our revenue.
   d. We'll leave for Europe on May 15ᵗʰ and return home on June 3ʳᵈ.

4. Which item is correct?
   a. The remainder of the discussion is on page eight.
   b. The meeting will run from 8:00 p.m. until 10:00 p.m., but we'll take a 5-minute break at 9 p.m.
   c. Please send $150 for next month's payment, and then send the remaining $150.58 the following month.
   d. Our firm's assets are over $6.5 billion.

5. Which item is correct?
   a. When the merger is completed, we'll have to lay off about 1/3 of our Atlanta employees.
   b. I'm happy to report that the company made a $3,800,000 after-tax profit.
   c. Five of the 12 passengers were killed in the crash.
   d. I covered only three of the six guidelines in my training session last Friday.

6. Which item is correct?
   a. She is 11 years old and lives at 13990 South 1850 East.
   b. The class consisted of eight boys and 13 girls.
   c. I sold 5 six-volume sets of the author's personal history.
   d. We received checks for $56, $21.88, and $28.75.

CAPITALIZATION

Alphabetic characters should be capitalized according to standard conventions. Using capital letters helps guide readers by calling attention to certain words. Capital letters indicate proper nouns and mark the beginning of sentences. Capital letters can also affect the meaning of words, such as march or March and china or China.

Nonstandard and inconsistent use of capital letters slows reading and inhibits understanding. Equally inappropriate is the practice of writing in all lowercase or all capital letters. For example, writing an email message in all caps suggests that you are shouting at the reader.

The following capitalization rules will cover most situations you'll encounter. But because capitalization rules have so many exceptions, you'll occasionally have to consult a major style guide for additional answers.

Rules

1. Capitalize the first word of every sentence, question, command, or expression that has terminal punctuation (period, question mark, or exclamation point).

   No: What would most people change in their lives if they could? their physical appearance? their job? their income?

   Yes: What would most people change in their lives if they could? Their physical appearance? Their job? Their income?

2. Capitalize the first word of a quoted complete sentence.

   No: The international office has stated that the company will hire only translators who are "Native speakers of the language."

Yes: The international office has stated that the company will hire only translators who are "native speakers of the language."

Yes: According to the international office, "We will hire only translators who are native speakers of the language."

Yes: "Integrity," says my supervisor, "is essential for someone in that position."

3. Capitalize proper nouns (nouns naming a specific person, place, or thing) and adjectives created from proper nouns. Do not capitalize seasons (spring, summer, fall, winter).

Yes: When did you go to *England?* [Proper noun]

Yes: I enjoy *English* literature. [Proper adjective]

No: I'm taking math, german, and physics.

Yes: I'm taking math, German, and physics.

No: My findings are presented in exhibit a.

Yes: My findings are presented in Exhibit A.

No: I bought a new xerox copier.

Yes: I bought a new Xerox copier. [Xerox is the name of a company; copier is a generic term.]

4. Capitalize business and professional titles when they immediately precede names and when they appear in addresses.

No: He briefly introduced president James Martin.

Yes: He briefly introduced President James Martin.

Yes: The president of our company will attend the celebration.

Yes: Mr. James Martin, President
1500 North Maple
Anywhere, US 842XX
[Address in a business letter]

5. Capitalize the beginning and ending words and all the principal words in titles of organizations, reports, books, magazines, journals, newspapers, etc.; but do not capitalize prepositions of four or fewer letters unless they begin or end the title. Also, do not capitalize articles, such as the, a, or an, unless they begin a title or are officially part of the proper noun.

No: An Analysis Of Central California's Fight With Water Pollution

Yes: An Analysis of Central California's Fight with Water Pollution

Yes: The Church of Jesus Christ of Latter-day Saints

6. Capitalize directions only when they refer to a specific area.

No: In the south, you'll find people to be very friendly.

Yes: In the South, you'll find people to be very friendly.

No: Drive South until you come to Highway 6.

Yes: Drive south until you come to Highway 6.

No: You'll find that westerners resist government intrusion.

Yes: You'll find that Westerners resist government intrusion.

7. Capitalize the first letter of items in a vertical list:

Yes: The shipment delay was caused by the following factors:
- Bad weather
- Poor scheduling
- Equipment failure

8. Capitalize specific academic degrees.

Yes: I'll be getting my Bachelor of Science degree next April. [Not *Bachelor's* of Science.]

Yes: I'll be getting my bachelor's degree next April. [Does not identify the specific degree.]

Capitalization Quiz

For each of the following quiz questions, select the best option (a, b, c, or d).

1. Which item is correct?
   a. Mr. Green said he is "Being tried without any solid evidence to convict."
   b. The coroner's report is included in appendix G.
   c. The Samsons moved to the west where Justin got a job with Boeing.
   d. Because I'm on Susy Slim's low-cholesterol diet, I avoid French pastries.

2. Which item is correct?

   a. When he was in the Middle East, he learned much about Jewish culture.

   b. The Bookkeeper was blamed for the error.

   c. I plan to get my Master's degree at the University of Texas.

   d. A Study Of Water-Pollution Causes In The State of Texas [Report Title]

3. Which item is not correct?

   a. Brin told us to bring our "Detailed goals for the new year."

   b. We're going to move to the East when I graduate from college.

   c. I'll be receiving my bachelor's degree next April.

   d. I think I'll take classes in physics, astronomy, and German literature.

4. Which item is correct?

   a. My talk included general christian doctrine but avoided specific church doctrines.

   b. Congratulations on receiving your mba degree.

   c. I'm going to be visiting his father this weekend, so I'll ask about Robby then.

   d. Wesley asked, "will you be going to the service project this Saturday?"

5. Which item is correct?

   a. I like English people, but I don't like english literature.

   b. The senior mechanic told me my Mazda was fixed and ready to go.

   c. I just bought a new panasonic digital camera at the bookstore.

   d. Sample documents are included in appendix A.

6. Assuming the following is a title, which item is correct?

   a. Working With Teens And Young Single Adults—A Discussion About Drug Intervention Programs

   b. Working With Teens and Young Single Adults—A Discussion About Drug Intervention Programs

   c. Working with Teens and Young Single Adults—A Discussion about Drug Intervention Programs

   d. Working with Teens and Young Single Adults—A Discussion About Drug Intervention Programs

LANGUAGE OF SENTENCES

The choice of words (diction) for a writer is as critical as the choice of paint colors for an artist. For every purpose and every setting, you must select your words carefully or run the risk of conveying the wrong message. The following text provides guidelines for choosing the right words to convey the desired message—words that are clear, complete, correct, and compelling.

Clear—Words that Are Understood

Some writers will use uncommon or esoteric words in an attempt to impress. However, most people will be much more impressed by your ability to communicate clearly than by your use of fancy language. Choose words that will be understood by your audience. The following list gives examples of uncommon words that should be used with caution, as well as more widely understood words that may be used in their place.

Fancy Word	Preferred Word
ascertain	find or determine
eschew	avoid
exacerbate	worsen or make worse
exasperate	annoy
remuneration	payment

In business be careful using words considered to be jargon. Jargon pertains to technical terms used in a unique situation or context. For instance, insurance personnel use specific terms unique to insurance, marketing specialists use specific terms unique to marketing, and computer technicians use their own unique terms. Using such terminology is appropriate when the audience understands, but not otherwise.

No: The font should be Futura 11 bold, set solid on an 18-pica line. [Unacceptable if the reader does not understand the typography jargon.]

Yes: The font should be Futura 11 bold, set solid on an 18-pica line. [Acceptable if the reader understands the technical words.]

Complete—Words that Are Appropriately Precise

Different words have different levels of precision in meaning. Some are general, and others are very specific. Choose words that have the appropriate level of precision to provide complete information. For example, the table below shows a spectrum of words from general to specific.

More general	vehicle
	⇓
	truck
	⇩
	pickup
	⇩
More specific	blue 20XX 4WD Dodge Ram

For a report on traffic patterns you may want to use the term *vehicle,* because the word covers different types that are all involved in traffic. However, when you advertise your vehicle for sale, you will want to use more specific terms like make, model, year, or trim line. In each instance, the selected words are appropriately precise because they convey the level of information needed.

No: We need to hire a new employee.

Yes: We need to hire a new data analyst.

No: In a few days, we'll meet again.

Yes: On Friday at 3 p.m., we'll meet again.

No: I'd like to present a few ideas.

Yes: I'd like to present three ideas.

No: I won't be in because I'm vomiting.

Yes: I won't be in because I'm ill.

Correct—Words that Are Correct in Meaning and Spelling

Today's software will catch most spelling errors; therefore, it is expected that documents will be free of spelling mistakes. Make sure the words you choose are spelled correctly, and don't let tight deadlines pressure you to skip your duty to proofread for spelling. Also, watch for correct spelling when you review the work of others. Be particularly mindful of words with troublesome spelling such as *accommodate, dependent, judgment, questionnaire, receive,* and *separate.*

Unfortunately, a word may be spelled correctly and yet have the wrong meaning. For instance, a person might write "then" for "than" and "past" for "passed." Such words are prone to be missed by spellchecking software. To catch errors in word meaning, watch for homonyms (a word with the same pronunciation as another but with a different meaning, such as *compliment* and *complement*) and with other related word pairs that have different meanings. The following words are frequently misused.

Appraise is a verb meaning to determine the value, quantity, or amount of something.

Apprise is a verb meaning to inform.

Yes: I'll appraise the Albertson property and then keep you apprised on the progress of our project.

Affect as a verb means to influence.

Effect as a noun is the consequence or result of something; *effect* as a verb means to cause or implement.

Yes: Next month our company will effect a modified retirement policy for new employees; however, the policy will not affect current employees, nor will it have any effect on people who have already retired.

Allow gives permission.

Enable empowers.

Yes: Karen will allow us to visit her company Friday morning, enabling us to gather the data we need.

Compliment is a nice comment.

Complement means to complete.

Yes: I gave her a nice compliment on how her experience complements her education.

Counsel refers to advice itself or to the process of giving advice.

Council refers to a group of people.

Yes: The student council will counsel the president. The president requested the counsel.

e.g. means "for example."

i.e. means "that is."

Yes: We will be studying many of our favorite American sports; e.g., soccer, basketball, and football.

Yes: I think his announcement is a decoy; i.e., they are covering up their product-defect problems.

Ensure means to guarantee.

Insure refers to insurance.

> **Yes:** Because you are properly insured, your spouse's financial welfare is ensured.

Farther refers to distance.

Further indicates degree.

> **Yes:** Let's discuss this matter further as we walk farther along this jogging trail.

Fewer refers to individual items.

Less refers to uncountable bulk or quality.

> **Yes:** We can order less pancake flour since fewer people visit our restaurant this time of year.

Its is the possessive form of *it*.

It's is the contraction of *it is*.

> **Yes:** It's up to the committee to determine its mission.

Lay means to put or place.

Lie means to rest.

> **Yes:** I'm going to lay this book down while I go lie down for a nap.

Principal refers to money, the CEO of a school, and the main element.

Principle refers to a belief or concept.

> **Yes:** The principal reason for our meeting is to discuss the principal's delinquent payment on the principal and interest of the loan. He has apparently forgotten the principle of honesty.

Stationary means not moving.

Stationery refers to paper.

> **Yes:** The stationary box of stationery is collecting dust.

Your refers to something you possess.

You're means "you are."

> **Yes:** You're invited to a birthday party at your sister's house.

In addition, make sure you *pronounce* the following words correctly:

> Asterisk (not *asterix*)
>
> Especially (not *exspecially*)

Etcetera (not *ecksetera*)

Pronunciation (not *pronounciation*)

Sales (not *sells*)

Jewelry (not *julery*)

Realtor (not *relitor*)

Compelling—Words with Desired Emotional Impact

A word that is clear, complete, and correct must also be compelling. That is, it must have the necessary level of formality and the appropriate tone needed to achieve the desired effect.

FORMALITY

Formality varies according to the social closeness of people in a communication relationship. It also is dictated by the social setting. For example, you would not address your supervisor in the same way you would address your golfing partner. In addition, if your golfing partner is also your supervisor, you would probably address him differently while in a board meeting than on the golf course.

Highly formal style employs respectful words and language. For instance, you might use the word "father" in a more formal setting, but use the word "dad" for informal situations. Formal writing avoids the use of casual speech and sometimes uses more passive voice.

Informal style employs more conversational wording and a more casual writing style. The situation and the people involved in the situation dictate the level of formality to be reflected in the writing. The following examples illustrate when to use formal and informal language.

Use more formal language for . . .

- An invitation to an awards banquet
- A request for an interview with the CEO
- A written proposal to a client
- An office policy regarding dress standards

Use less formal language for . . .

- An email announcing an upcoming department meeting
- A flyer announcing an office party
- An email to a long-time friend
- A thank-you note to a fellow worker

Slang is very casual language used in some settings but considered to be substandard and undignified in most. It often substitutes novel meanings for existing words, such as using "cool" to mean "very good." It may also use initials, such as LOL, for texting between people who know each other well. Using slang in your writing can have a powerful negative effect on the formality of the document, so avoid its use in nearly all communications. The following list shows slang words on the left and the preferred words on the right.

Slang Word	Preferred Word
grouse	complain
nab	catch
smooth	clever
snow job	deception
wrinkle	clever idea

TONE

Many words carry an emotional element in addition to their meaning. The dictionary definition of a word is referred to as its *denotation*. Ideas or feelings associated with a word in addtion to its definition are called its *connotation*. The connotations of the words you choose will create the tone of your communication. Therefore, select terms and expressions that would be appropriate for your intended audience. In general, prefer words and expressions with positive connotations rather than negative connotations.

Compare the tone of the following two examples that deliver bad news:

Positive:

Thank you for your request to return the shipment of books you purchased from us. After receiving your request, we checked the shipment date and found that the books were purchased four months ago—one month past our three-month return deadline. If the books had been returned one month earlier, we would have been happy to give a full refund.

Negative:

We received your request to return the shipment of books you purchased from us. Unfortunately, you didn't return the books by the three-month deadline. Therefore, your request is denied. Next time you have books to return, remember the deadline.

Be aware that the connotations of words may change over time. For example, words that tie gender to job titles (*mailman*) have become less appropriate than gender-neutral terms (*mail carrier*). Euphemisms that replace socially unacceptable words or expressions (*pass away* vs. *die*) may also change. Use appropriate terms and euphemisms, and when in doubt, always err on the side of more formal language.

No: She had a kid last month. [Socially insensitive—goats have *kids;* people have *babies.*]

Yes: She had a baby last month. [Socially acceptable.]

No: We are cognizant of the magnitude of your current engagements. [This sentence sounds stuffy and pompous.]

Yes: We are aware of your current project commitments.

For all of your writing, check the wording of sentences to ensure that the tone is appropriate. Generally, use words that are positive, cordial, conversational (yet professional), and reader oriented—customized to the reader's vocabulary and circumstances.

No: We can't ship your parts until March 1. [Wording is negative; focuses on what you can't do.]

Yes: We will ship your parts on March 1. [Words focus on the positive—states what you can or will do.]

No: Your order was received today. It will be shipped within the next two working days. [Words are mechanical and uncaring.]

Yes: We appreciate your order and will ship it to you within the next 48 hours. [Words are warm and friendly.]

No: Per your request that we scrutinize the various purported illegalities suggested in the management audit report, we hereby submit the attached. [Words are too pompous and arrogant—not conversational.]

Yes: Here is our analysis of the three illegal actions described in the management audit report. [Words reflect "conversational language."]

Language Quiz

For each of the following quiz questions, select the best option (a, b, c, or d).

1. Which of the following is most socially acceptable?
   a. firefighter
   b. stewardess
   c. fireman
   d. woman attorney

2. Which of the following words is misspelled?
   a. accommodate
   b. judgment
   c. principle (referring to *money*)
   d. receive

3. Which of the following words is used correctly?

    a. complement (a nice comment)

    b. council (advise)

    c. i.e. (for example)

    d. ensure (to make sure)

4. Which of the following sentences has no words that are misused?

    a. After driving further down the road, he finally found the stationery store.

    b. He gave me counsel not to let her bad attitude effect my performance.

    c. After laying down for a nap, I noticed that the magazine had its cover torn off in the mail.

    d. The new insurance coverage will ensure that we are protected against that type of loss.

5. Which of the following are homonyms?

    a. near and close

    b. compliment and complement

    c. hot and cold

    d. farther and further

LENGTH OF SENTENCES

Sentences may be structurally sound, with proper punctuation and language, and free from any grammatical errors, yet still be too long and therefore difficult to read. This problem can be overcome with concise writing. Concise writing is not short, choppy writing that has had its conversational style or relevant content removed. Rather, concise writing reflects carefully crafted sentences with no unnecessary words. As you review sentences for conciseness, constantly ask yourself, "How can I convey the needed information with appropriate style in as few words as possible." Keep in mind, however, that clarity, not conciseness, is the ultimate goal.

Read the following sentence:

Much of the writing currently done in business today contains an excessive number of words, and this excessive wordiness makes it necessary for each and every reader of a message to spend much more time reading it than he or she would have to do if the message were more concise."

The foregoing sentence contains 51 words and is difficult to read. What is the problem? First, it contains seven prepositional phrases: of the writing, in business, of words, for each, of a message, to spend, and to do.

Second, it contains redundant wording. Redundancies include two or more words that mean the same thing:

each and every (use each or every, but not both)

currently and *today* (use currently or today, but not both)

Third, the sentence contains several wordy passages that could be shortened with more careful wording, such as the following:

Much of the writing currently done in business today (could be stated as, "Much of today's business writing...")

contains an excessive number of words (could be stated as, "... is wordy.")

You could rewrite the 51-word sentence as follows:

Much of today's business writing is wordy, unnecessarily increasing the time required for reading.

The sentence is now 14 words long, reflecting a 37-word reduction. Yet it still conveys the essential information and maintains a clear, readable style.

Long, wordy sentences can be shortened by completing two simple steps:

1 Omit useless words

    No: Today's current technology has made your life and my life much easier.

    Yes: Today's technology has made life much easier.

2. Replace more words with fewer words

    No: It is my intention to make contact with our current state senators.

    Yes: I plan to contact our state senators.

The prevalence of mobile technology has created a level of conciseness that has even sacrificed traditional style for brevity. For instance, an email might contain the following: "Angie, can you join Alisha, Katie, Tesla, and me for lunch today at noon? We're meeting at Ivy's Place on Pine Ridge Road. Please RSVP by 11 a.m. so I can make appropriate reservations." However, a text message may be shortened to something like the following: "Lunch today at noon? Ivy's Place; Pine Ridge Rd. RSVP by 11."

While this condensed style may be appropriate for texting or for informal, close relationships, it may not be appropriate for other relationships or forms of communication. Always make sure that your style is appropriately formal for

HOW READABLE IS YOUR WRITING?

Two factors play the most central roles in determining the readability of a document: word difficulty and sentence length. The more difficult words and long sentence you have, the more difficult your writing will be to read. Conversely, fewer difficult words and fewer long sentences will make writing easier to read.

To analyze the readability of your writing, choose a 100–200 word text sample, calculate the average sentence length and the percentage of difficult words. Then see where your writing falls in Readability Standards Chart.

Count every occurrence of a difficult word (for this procedure, difficult words those that are three syllables or more). For instance, if the word "analyze" occurs three times, count it three times. However, do not classify words as difficult if they are two-syllable words made into three-syllable words by adding *ed* (e.g., reported), *es* (e.g., oranges), *l* or *ing* (assuming). Also, do not consider proper nouns to be difficult words, such as "Chicago."

Readability Standards Chart

Rating	Average Sentence Length	Percentage of Difficult Words
Very Easy	<10	<10
Average	11–20	11–20
Difficult	21–30	21–30
Very Difficult	31+	31+

the situation. If you are not sure how formal you should be, choose to be more formal. When in doubt, leave the informality out.

Length Quiz

1. Which of the following does not contain a redundancy?
   a. If you sign today, you'll get an added bonus.
   b. Just bring the basic necessities on our hike today.
   c. The large room contained nothing but empty space.
   d. It's your turn to write the monthly newsletter column.

2. Which of the following is most concise?
   a. It is my intention to hire him by July 1.
   b. The book that was on my desk is missing.
   c. I would like to introduce you to my friend Ashley.
   d. The red spot on the left side of my car was caused by a paint ball.

3. Which sentence best employs concise writing?
   a. His main argument is that the manager should have included the group in the decision.
   b. You should be sure to plan in advance for the emergency drill.
   c. A great many writers fail to adequately and appropriately proofread their written emails.
   d. The three triplets will keep their two parents very busy.

4. Which sentence best employs concise writing?
   a. I believe his overall approach to fixing the troublesome problem is appropriate, but I think he has overlooked some small details.
   b. In order to implement the new training, we must first get prior approval from Brian's manager.
   c. To succeed in business, you must write and speak well.
   d. The key to the car is hanging on the key rack.

5. Which sentence best employs concise writing?
   a. In the event that Jill does not attend the committee meeting, we will not discuss the proposed change in benefits.
   b. The reason for his failure was due to the fact that he couldn't get all of his employees to support his plan.
   c. After Marianne edits the manuscript, Liam will complete the layout and design work.
   d. The fact that he is the only prospective candidate to follow up after the employment interview improves his chance of being hired.

ANSWERS TO QUIZ QUESTIONS

STRUCTURE	PUNCTUATION	ERRORS	LANGUAGE	LENGTH
(page 168)	(page 174)	Case (page 177)	(page 162)	(page 162)

STRUCTURE (page 168)

1. A
2. C
3. A
4. B
5. A
6. C
7. D
8. B
9. B
10. C
11. B
12. A
13. A
14. C
15. C
16. D
17. C
18. B
19. D
20. D
21. A
22. C
23. B
24. A
25. C
26. A

PUNCTUATION (page 174)

1. B
2. A
3. D
4. D
5. B
6. B
7. C

ERRORS

Case (page 177)

1. A
2. B
3. C
4. C
5. D
6. A
7. B
8. B
9. B
10. A

Agreement/ Reference (page 180)

1. C
2. D
3. A
4. D
5. A
6. B
7. B

Tense (page 183)

1. C
2. D
3. A
4. A
5. C
6. D
7. D
8. D
9. A
10. B

Numbers (page 185)

1. B
2. C
3. C
4. D
5. D
6. A

Capitals (page 187)

1. D
2. A
3. A
4. C
5. B
6. D

LANGUAGE (page 162)

1. A
2. C
3. D
4. D
5. B

LENGTH (page 162)

1. D
2. B
3. A
4. C
5. C

INDEX

SPELL QUICK REFERENCE

Structure

1. Use clear, specific subjects.
2. Keep verbs close to their subjects.
3. Use active and passive voice appropriately.
4. Use words of the same part of speech after parallel connectives.
5. Use parallel parts of speech for words in a series.
6. Use adjectives and adverbs correctly.
7. Place modifying words and phrases close to the words they modify.
8. Avoid dangling (ambiguous) modifiers.

Punctuation

Commas

1. Use a comma to divide main clauses joined by a coordinating conjunction.
2. Place a comma after many types of introductory elements.
3. Use a comma to divide all items in a series.
4. Use a comma to divide adjacent adjectives that could be separated with *and* or that could be reversed without changing the meaning.
5. Use a comma to divide nonessential sentence elements from essential sentence elements.
6. Use commas in dates written in month/day/year format.
7. Use commas to divide elements of a mailing address.
8. Use commas where needed for clarification.

Semicolons (super-commas)

1. Use a semicolon to divide two independent clauses not joined by a coordinating conjunction.
2. Use a semicolon before a conjunctive adverb that joins two independent clauses.
3. May use a semicolon to divide parallel sentence elements that have internal commas.
4. Use a semicolon before e.g. and i.e. when no other punctuation is used to set them off.

Colons

1. Use the colon after a complete independent clause that introduces.
2. Use a colon after the salutation in business letters.

Dash

1. Use a dash to set off sentence interrupters or to emphasize.
2. Use a dash to introduce (in place of a colon).

Hyphen

1. Use a hyphen in the following situations:
   - Prefix ends with the same letter beginning the main word (anti-inflammatory)
   - Word might be mistaken for another word (re-form)
   - Prefix is "self" (self-assured)
   - Word is likely to be mispronounced (co-worker)
   - Base word is capitalized (non-American)
   - Base is a number (pre-1990)
2. Hyphenate compound adjectives preceding a noun or pronoun, but not with adverbs ending in "ly."
3. Usually don not use hyphens with the following prefixes: re, pre, sub, or semi.

Parentheses

1. Use parentheses to set off incidental comments, to introduce abbreviations, or to enclose enumerations.

Quotation Marks

1. Use quotation marks for direct quotations, but not for paraphrases.
2. Put commas and periods inside quotation marks; semicolons and colons outside quotation marks; question marks and exclamation marks either inside or outside quotation marks, depending on their usage; and single quotation marks within double quotation marks, such as a quotation within a quotation.

Ellipsis

1. Leave a space before and after an ellipsis.
2. Use ellipses to indicate omitted text, retaining the same punctuation marks that would occur with the full text.

Period

1. Use periods with most abbreviations, but not with acronyms.
2. At the end of items in a bulleted list, avoid commas and semicolons. Use periods when the items are complete sentences. Use consistent punctuation for all items in a bulleted list.
3. Use a period with a polite request that asks for an action.

Errors

Case

Subjective Case

1. Use subjective case for the subject of a clause.
2. Use subjective case for a noun or pronoun that completes the meaning of a being verb.

Objective Case

1. Put all objects in the objective case.

Possessive Case

1. If a noun or pronoun doesn't end with an s or z sound, show possession by adding an apostrophe and an s.
2. Place the apostrophe after the plural form of the word to show possession by more than one person.